GERMINAL AND ZOLA'S
PHILOSOPHICAL AND RELIGIOUS THOUGHT

29

PURDUE UNIVERSITY MONOGRAPHS
IN ROMANCE LANGUAGES

William M. Whitby, General Editor
Allan H. Pasco, Editor for French
Enrique Caracciolo-Trejo, Editor for Spanish

Associate Editors

I.French

II.Spanish

Volume 14

Philip Walker

"Germinal" and Zola's
Philosophical and Religious Thought

PHILIP WALKER

GERMINAL AND ZOLA'S
PHILOSOPHICAL AND RELIGIOUS THOUGHT

JOHN BENJAMINS PUBLISHING COMPANY
Amsterdam/Philadelphia

1984

Library of Congress Cataloging in Publication Data

Walker, Philip D.
  Germinal and Zola's philosophical and religious thought.

(Purdue University monographs in Romance languages, ISSN 0165-8743; v. 14)
Bibliography: p. 133
Includes index.
1. Zola, Emile, 1840-1902. Germinal. 2. Zola, Emile, 1840-1902 -- Philosophy. 3. Zola, Emile, 1840-1902 -- Religion and ethics. 4. Philosophy in literature. 5. Religious thought -- France -- 19th century. I. Title. II. Series.
PQ2504.W3   1984   843'.8   84-9285
ISBN 90-272-1724-6

The old world is disintegrating, the old doctrines are flickering out; but in the midst of a confused travail, an apparent disorder, we can see new doctrines dawning, a new world taking shape . . .

F. Lamennais
Esquisse d'une philosophie

We have entered a period of crisis, of religious transformation or renewal.

E. Poitou
Les Philosophes français contemporains et leurs systèmes religieux

A god is creating himself out of our tears.

Ernest Renan
Le Prêtre de Némi

The development of modern art with its seemingly nihilistic trend toward disintegration must be understood as the symptom and symbol of a mood of world destruction and world renewal that has set its mark on our age. . . . We are living in what the Greeks called the "right time" for a metamorphosis of the gods— that is, of the fundamental principles and symbols.

Carl G. Jung
"God, the Devil, and the Human Soul"

Contents

Contents

Preface

In preparing this book, I was primarily motivated by the following two questions—questions that had haunted me ever since I had begun exploring Zola at Yale in the early fifties: what was Zola really like as a philosophical and religious thinker, and what reflections or possible reflections of his philosophical and religious thought can be found in *Germinal,* his masterpiece and one of the most moving and at the same time intellectually and spiritually stimulating and influential novels ever written?

Not only were these questions of interest to me in themselves; I suspected—with good reason, as it turned out—that it was impossible fully to understand and appreciate *Germinal* without the answers.

In my efforts to discover them, I was led, first of all, to make a survey of all the philosophical and religious ideas that I could perceive in the immense corpus of Zola's writings (novels, work notes, correspondence, essays, poems, short stories, etc.)—forgetting for the moment everything previously done on the subject, so as not to be misled by other critics' possible distortions. After this, it was necessary to note which of these ideas tended to recur, the period and extent of their recurrence, the nature of their hold on Zola, their interrelationships, the patterns, logical or otherwise, into which they fell, the systems or movements to which they could be related, the over-all tendencies that they seemed to manifest. I was then obliged, needless to say, to contemplate *Germinal* in the light of what I had found, identifying all its various reflections or possible reflections.

Much of what I found simply confirmed, of course, what was already known or assumed. Yet I came to see some of the elements of Zola's philosophical and religious thought, including such well-known ones as his positivism, pessimism, and pantheism, more fully and in sharper focus than they had been seen before. I also discovered more than one aspect that, insofar as I could tell, had gone uncommented upon by other critics, for example, the strong connection between Zola's positivism and cult of fact, on the one hand, and the longing for certainty born of his metaphysical and religious doubt, on the other hand; the persistence in his mature writings of the central elements of his youthful "new faith" based on geology; or the remarkable multiplicity of his definitions of God or of the whole new "creeds" and secular "religions" or religion-substitutes that he identified himself with in the course of his life-time. I realized how much more complex, unstable, and incoherent Zola's philosophical and religious thought was than previous descriptions had led me to suspect. At the same time, I saw to what a great extent Zola kept drawing throughout the whole of his career on essentially the same stock of hetero-geneous, largely incompatible philosophical and religious ideas. I discovered much evidence of a more or less conscious struggle to weld them together into some kind of logical unity. Moreover, as I searched for their expressions in *Germinal*, I was impressed by the considerable degree to which its themes, characters, actions, setting, imagery, symbolism, and structure were—or at least could have been—determined by Zola's philosophical and religious thought. I perceived how much closer *Germinal* comes—or would seem to come—than most of Zola's other novels to expressing all its principal recurrent elements. Thanks to what I had learned, I arrived at a clearer, more comprehensive defini-tion of the imaginary world, the realism, the message, and even the social role, or function, of *Germinal* than any I had so far encountered. I was also impressed by the way Zola would seem to have managed in *Germinal* to cope artistically with the contradictions in the philosophical and religious ideas that he was—or so we may infer—struggling to express. I was struck in this connection by his mastery, still largely ignored by other critics, of the art of ambiguity. I was struck by how he had achieved in this novel, despite the chaotic vision of reality I have perceived at its heart, an illusion of reality quite as powerful as that which characterizes any of his more philosophically consistent writings. I was also struck by how well the novel compensates through its wonderful unity, stability, and order on the aesthetic level for its extreme ambiguity on the philosophical and religious levels.

Needless to say, I have not tried to report in the following pages all the observations that I made in the course of my preparatory studies. This would have resulted in much too long a work. I have limited myself to those which seemed to me most important and essential.

Those readers who are interested in learning about the philosophical and religious dimensions of *Germinal* or in acquainting themselves with Zola's philosophical and religious thought in general will, I would like to think, find in this book (including the supplementary information provided in the footnotes) the most complete and definitive introduction that presently exists. Although I have written it with the needs of the nonspecialist particularly in mind, I would also hope that even my fellow specialists who are more or less familiar with much of what I say will nevertheless find what I have done here of some utility and worth. They might want to compare their own conceptions of, for example, Zola's positivism, pessimism, or pantheism and its expression in *Germinal* with mine—noting not only those points on which we agree, but also the points of divergence, which may give rise to further fruitful discussion.

They may be intrigued by the spectacle of my struggle to be comprehensive, to grasp my various subjects holistically. Even in Chapters 1 and 2, where I treat sides of the novel about which one would think all that could be said had been said, I have, I believe, made several new observations which my fellow specialists may find worthy of consideration. (It should be noted, moreover, that a distinction must be made between what has traditionally passed as Zola's "positivism" and what I am largely concerned with in Chapter 1: evidence in *Germinal* of Zola's *philosophical positivism*, in the sense defined by D. G. Charlton.) As for Chapter 3, no one, I believe, has as yet attempted, as I do here, to break down what has up to now been generally referred to rather vaguely as Zola's "pantheism" (which is really several kinds of pantheism) into its different components—much less to point out the possible reflections of each of them in *Germinal*. Chapter 4 treats an important aspect of the novel which has so far gone completely unremarked—the reflections or possible reflections that it contains of Zola's youthful new religion based on geology, itself an element of Zola's thought that has never received the attention it deserves. Chapter 5 includes a distinction between the "geological" view of man, nature, and history that I have to do with in Chapter 4 and the one implicit in Zola's romantic humanitarianism, which, as I have tried to show more completely than anyone else has so far, is, it would seem, also reflected in the novel. Chapter 6, largely inspired by a study of Zola's thought and its expression in *Germinal* in the light of Mircea Eliade's *Le Mythe de l'éternel retour: Archétypes et répétitions* and *Mythes, rêves et mystères,* will perhaps be of some interest to those concerned with the central problem of time-in-Zola. In the final chapter, I make the first attempt that I know of to suggest the full range of Zola's philosophical and religious incoherences and contradictions and to point out how typical the major ones are of his age. In the same chapter, I rapidly enumerate among other things the principal devices that he uses in *Germinal* and elsewhere to achieve ambiguity, and I suggest what seem to me to be the major specific ambiguities of the novel, including those inherent in its title and basic structure.

I am deeply grateful to my friend Henri Mitterand for having read the manuscript of this book and for his comments, which have resulted in more than one improvement. I am also very much indebted to Professor D. G. Charlton, whose books and other writings on the philosophical and secular religious thought of nineteenth-century France I found indispensable in my attempts to analyse Zola's thought and relate it to that of his contemporaries and who very generously helped me with important details of the last chapter. Although, as I have already intimated, I have done my best to base my conclusions as completely as possible on a direct examination of the texts, I could hardly have progressed as far as I have toward my goals without the precious insights that I have gained from a host of other critics—contemporaries of Zola's like Jules Lemaitre, Gustave Geffroy, or Maurice Le Blond, not to mention such recent commentators as Pierre Cogny, Marcel Girard, Henri Guillemin, F. W. J. Hemmings, J. H. Matthews, Henri Mitterand, Robert J. Niess, Guy Robert, René Ternois, David Baguley, B. H. Bakker, Chantal Bertrand-Jennings, Jean Borie, Patrick Brady, A. A. Greaves, Lewis Kamm, Alain de Lattre, Allan H. Pasco, Sandy Petrey, Roger Ripoll, James Sanders, Naomi Schor, Michel Serres, Richard Zakarian, and many others whose names I have mentioned in my notes and bibliography. I wish to thank the following for permission to quote from copyrighted works: The New American Library: *Germinal*, translated by Stanley and Eleanor Hochman, copyright 1970. The Oxford University Press: *Positivist Thought in France During the Second Empire, 1852-1870* (1959) and *Secular Religions in France: 1815-1870* (1963), both by D. G. Charlton. I am also grateful to the John Simon Guggenheim Memorial Foundation for having enabled me to spend many uninterrupted hours both at home and in Paris laying the foundations of this book. Last but not least, I should like to thank my beloved wife for her always valuable criticism and unfailing moral support.

May 1983

1

The Factualistic, Positivistic Basis

> *... this life of suffering, of doubt, which makes you
> deeply love naked, living reality.*
>
> Zola
> "Gustave Doret," *Mes haines*

Everywhere we turn in *Germinal,* Zola's masterpiece, we find, of course, reflections or possible reflections of that factualism and philosophical positivism[1] which have always been among his best-known traits and which, I am convinced, were primarily rooted in his intense philosophical and religious doubts, confusions, and anxieties.[2]

His factualism may be seen in the very great extent to which *Germinal*—even when compared with *Au Bonheur des Dames, La Débâcle,* or *Lourdes*—approximates his ideal of a fiction consisting exclusively of true details.[3] Not only are most of its major details absolutely authentic (for example, the destruction of Le Voreux, a direct transposition into fiction of both the mining disaster of Poder-Nuovo near Volterra, Italy, in 1864, and the complete flooding and annihilation of the Marles Mines in Pas-de-Calais on April 28, 1864);[4] so also are an enormous number of its multitudinous small details. Indeed, *Germinal* could serve, I believe, as an excellent illustration of that *"fait-alisme,"* or enthusiasm for little firm facts, which Nietzsche, writing during the same decade in which Zola composed *Germinal,* regarded as the most striking symptom of the extraordinary intellectual and spiritual uncertainty then reigning in Western thought—the same uncertainty as that from which Zola himself acutely suffered.[5] The beet fields through which Etienne strides on his way to Montsou in the first chapter, the thick palings separating the road and the railway tracks, settlement names like Bas-de-soi and Paie-tes-dettes, are lifted directly from reality. The candle that Catherine lights in the predawn darkness, the square two-windowed room she shares with Zacharie, Jeanlin, Lénore, Henri, and Alzire, her coarse cloth jacket, her blue cap, her piled-up reddish hair, her boyish look in her work clothes, the harsh black soap that has ruined her complexion—all these are things that Zola had actually seen and noted down in Anzin. So also are the apple-green walls of the Maheus' combined kitchen, living, and dining room, the cast-iron stove, the varnished pine cupboard, the cuckoo clock, the garishly colored portraits of Napoleon III and Eugénie, the soldiers and saints spattered with gold. Zola's descriptions of the pithead, machine, lamproom, and almost all the other elements of the vast, navelike landing room of Le Voreux are made up of details taken directly from his notes on actual mines he visited in Anzin, especially the Thiers and Renard pits.[6] The contorted positions taken by the miners, their Davie lamps, the temperatures they work in—there is hardly anything in Zola's accounts of life in the depths of the mines in *Germinal* which he had not seen with his own eyes or at least read about in his documentary sources. The descent of a new mine horse, Trompette, in Part I, Chapter v, for example, is based on a paragraph in Simonin's *La Vie souterraine* and a photograph by Larcher reproduced in the same text.[7] Everywhere else in the novel we find further evidence of Zola's determination to make his fiction insofar as possible into a compilation of facts—not fictional "facts" of the sort that abound in such authors as Sterne or Rabelais, but real, observed facts. For instance, the finch contest recounted in Part III, Chapter ii, is true in almost every detail to real finch contests held in the Anzin region.[8] Or when Zola shows us, in Part VI, Chapter v, Maheu opening his shirt, baring his chest, and pushing up against the steel points of the soldiers' bayonettes, so maddened with rage that when one of them pricks his breast he tries to force it in even more deeply, here again the novelist is not imagining anything, but basing his fiction on actual events.[9]

Zola's cult of fact may be seen in *Germinal,* furthermore, in the way he strains here as elsewhere in his fiction to give us all the facts, to be encyclopedic. Goaded by his insatiable appetite for that infallibility which he despaired of finding in anything but observable facts and scientific truths, he was never satisfied with merely introducing into the fictional reality of his novels fragments of factual reality. Like a shark (one of his favorite metaphors for himself), he tried to devour whole everything that came his way. Instead of simply showing us part of Le Voreux, as Stendhal or Flaubert might have done, he treats us in Part I to a veritable Cook's Tour of this vast mine. He includes in the novel all the different kinds of coal mining jobs: director, engineer, foreman, inspector, cutter, carman, fireman, tilterman, checker, engine man, hauler, stableman, trammer, etc. He recounts for us the whole day of a typical coal miner, the whole day of a typical coal miner's wife. He shows us in comprehensive detail his miners at play as well as at work. Like a bridge player dealing out cards, he distributes among them all the main occupational maladies from which coal miners suffer: black lung disease, anemia, ephemeral fevers, scrofula, asphyxia.[10] He depicts all ages and conditions of miners, supplying us in the process with a remarkably thorough cross section of proletarian society. He represents through Etienne, Pluchart, Rasseneur, Souvarine, and others all the important left-wing political movements of his day. Always interested in the sociology of religion, he treats of the part played by the Church in the life of the proletariat and economic class conflict and describes the religious beliefs and mores of his miners; and here again his approach is inclusive, as if, having once broached the subject, he had to treat it as completely as the framework of his fiction would allow, showing us along with what remains of the Christian tradition among his workers the essentially religious nature of the revolutionary new social gospels which they have embraced.[11]

At the same time, we may be struck by his predilection in *Germinal* as frequently elsewhere for precise numerical facts. His cult of hard, firm fact leads him to reach for mathematical certainty. Everywhere he goes, he counts, measures, weighs. There can be no doubt that he surpasses in this respect all of the great French realists who came before him. Compare, for example, Balzac's description of a printing plant at the beginning of *Illusions perdues* or Flaubert's description of Arnoux's faience factory in Montaire in Part II, Chapter iii, of *L'Education sentimentale* with Zola's account of what Etienne sees when he enters the landing room of Le Voreux in Part I, Chapter iii, of *Germinal.* The pit headframe has four lanterns. The engine, placed about twenty-five meters back from the shaft, is four-hundred horsepower. The wheels on which the cable is wound have a radius of five meters and can lift up to twelve thousand kilograms at a speed of ten meters a second. The machine is served by three workers. The whole passage teems with additional statistics—the precise number of men loaded into each cage, the precise depth of the shaft, etc. Throughout the book we can find many other examples of this same obsession with exact numbers, an integral part of what, in a letter to Henry Céard discussing *Germinal,* Zola himself, with no little insight, referred to as "my hypertrophy for true detail" (XIV, 1440).

Certain major stylistic traits that *Germinal* has in common with most of Zola's other novels—and not only Zola's, of course, but those of many of his contemporaries—must also doubtlessly be regarded as expressive, or symptomatic, of the same cult of fact: the third-person narrative; the impassive, impersonal tone; the nearly total elimination of the more obtrusive types of authorial commentary; the tendency to stick as closely as possible to even the wording of journalistic or scientific sources or to insert in the mouths of fictional characters the words of real people (we may be reminded of those twentieth-century collages in which, along with bits of lifelike drawings, have been included fragments of actual photographs, newspaper clippings, etc.); the devices obviously meant to produce the illusion that we are witnessing the events narrated at the instant that they occur, as though through the eye of a camera[12]—everything, in short, that helps the fiction writer in love with the reassuring solidity of fact explode the barrier between raw reality and art.

For example, it was not enough for Zola simply to take all Bonnemort's bodily traits from a description of a typical old-style coal miner in Dr. H. Boëns-Boissau's *Traité pratique des maladies, des accidents et des difformités des houilleurs* (1862), along with several of Boëns-Boissau's words; he was compelled to adhere quite closely to the order in which Boëns-Boissau distributes the details of his description. Like the Belgian doctor, he evokes first the hair, then the paleness of the face, its blotches, the neck, the curvature of the legs in that order.[13] Nor was it enough for Zola to model Souvarine partly on Bakunin. The passage, in Part IV, Chapter iv, where he summarizes Souvarine's goal largely consists of verbatim quotations either from Laveleye's résumé of Bakunin's theories of pan-destruction in *Le Socialisme contemporain* or from a brochure by Bakunin himself, *Les Principes de la Révolution:*

> "To destroy everything. . . . No more nations, no more governments, no more property, no more God or religion. . . . a new world. . . . By fire, by poison, by the dagger. The outlaw is the true hero, the avenger of the people, the revolutionary in action—someone who has no need of fancy phrases from books. . . . All discussions about the future are criminal because they prevent pure destruction and impede the march of the revolution."[14]

Similarly, the habitual remarks of the Company doctor, Vanderhaghen, as he makes his rounds are those of a real company doctor whom Zola had observed in Anzin: (to the women) "Don't bother me! You drink too much coffee!" and (when the woman mentions her husband's chronic pains) "That's because you're wearing him out. Stop bothering me!" (V, 98; Sig., 84).[15]

But if *Germinal* strongly testifies to Zola's extraordinary appetite for facts, it also does so just as strongly to his desire, grounded in his positivism, to make his fictional world conform to scientific truth (or, more precisely, to those scientific assumptions, hypotheses, and theories that he tended to regard as truths).[16] Not only does Etienne partly serve as yet another demonstration of Prosper Lucas' theories (specifically the principle that drunkenness in a parent can produce a streak of madness in his or her offspring);[17] there is a definite hint of transformism in the novel. In Part IV, Chapter vi, we study through Etienne's eyes Jeanlin "who—with his greedy muzzle, his green eyes, his large ears, his abortive intelligence and savage cunning—was slowly reverting to an ancient animality" (V, 222; Sig., 221). Toward the end of the concluding chapter the possibility of a specifically Darwinian interpretation of society and history is raised. "Could Darwin be right?" Etienne wonders as he meditates on all that has happened during his stay in Montsou. "Was the world merely a battlefield, with the strong devouring the weak for the sake of the beauty and perpetuation of the species?" (V, 403; Sig., 426).[18]

Moreover, I suspect that Zola was still influenced when he wrote *Germinal* by the view of man propounded by Charles Letourneau, a leading anthropologist of Zola's day, whose *Physiologie des passions* (1868) was one of the scientific works that he had most assiduously consulted while planning the *Rougon-Macquart* series in late 1868 and early 1869.[19]

A thoroughgoing materialist and reductionalist, Letourneau saw everything in man's higher nature as nothing but the development of something in man's lower nature. He was convinced that what poets, philosophers, and theologians termed (as he said) "the unfathomable mystery of life" was actually astonishingly simple—nothing but a "phenomenon of organic assimilation and disassimilation." Man, "envisaged sanely," and not through "the tinted glass of metaphysics," he maintained, was "like all other organized beings, nothing but an aggregation of histological elements, fibers, or cells, forming a living 'federal republic' directed by the nervous system and constantly renewing itself." Descartes's "I think, therefore I am" should, he proposed, have been "I feel, therefore I am." The highest, most complex human activities, including religion, were nothing, in his opinion, but extended developments of activities originating in the simplest cells. When all the veils were stripped away, he declared, it would be seen that the sole true motive of humanity is to attain pleasure and avoid pain through the satisfaction of organic desires. Our moral and intellectual needs are essentially as organic as our need for food, and, among all our needs, that for food is the strongest and most indispensable and our moral and intellectual needs the weakest and least essential. As he succinctly put it, "The stomach often imposes its laws on the brain."[20]

The view of things that emerges from *Les Rougon-Macquart*, including *Germinal*, could in part be taken as an illustration of Letourneau's doctrines. It is possible, for example, that Letourneau's influence helped confirm Zola's stylistic insistence on depicting reality as something that comes to us—and can be explored by us—only through our nerves. Starting out with the very first page, with its evocations of the flatness of the plain, the blackness of the March night, the coldness of the wind, the numbness of Etienne's bleeding hands, the redness of the flames burning in the braziers, the novel bombards us with sensations. The story is, indeed, largely presented to us through them.

Zola's deliberate downgrading of the brain in *Germinal* as only one among many organs[21] and his equally conscious attempt in this novel (as often elsewhere) to demonstrate, as he put it in a letter to Gustave Geffroy, that thought is nothing but "a function of matter" (XIV, 1443) may also be partly due to the continuing influence of Letourneau.

Most notably, however, *Germinal* would seem to reflect the supreme importance that Letourneau gave to the biological organism's need for food. In fact, Zola himself points out in his original notes for *Les Rougon-Macquart* that its leading characters are largely creatures of appetite.[22] More than one of the titles of other individual *Rougon-Macquart* novels shows the same preoccupation with the theme of alimentation: *La Curée (The Quarry)* with its evocation of the hunt ceremony in which parts of the game are distributed to the hounds, *Le Ventre de Paris (The Belly of Paris)* with its metaphorical transformation of Les Halles into a giant stomach. Not only does the title of *Germinal* (through its historical connotations as well as the association established in the text between the idea of germination and growing wheat) fall into this category, but so also do some of the titles that Zola considered giving the novel before settling on *Germinal: Le Grain qui germe (The Germinating Grain), Moisson rouge (Red Harvest), Les Affamés (The Hungry).* Within the novel itself, which Marcel Girard has rightly called "a drama of hunger,"[23] images connected with the ideas of hunger and nourishment abound. It is impossible not to be struck by them–the winds crying famine, Le Voreux with its voracious maw, the Maheus' breakfast in Part I, the Grégoires' breakfast (including Cécile's famous brioche) in Part II, the Hennebeaus' elaborate luncheon the day the strike breaks out in Part IV, the marching mob's famished shouts of "Bread! Bread! We want bread!" and the tardy arrival of the Hennebeaus' *vol-au-vent* in Part V, the scenes of mass starvation reaching a climax in Alzire's death in Part VI. As in *Le Ventre de Paris*, class conflict is thus poetically reduced to a battle between the fat and the lean–terms that actually recur in *Germinal*, in Part VII, Chapter ii (V, 349; Sig., 366). In short, humanity's struggle to attain social justice would indeed appear to be primarily motivated in *Germinal*, just as Letourneau would have said, by its need to satisfy its most fundamental organic desire.

Yet these are, of course, not the only indications or possible indications of Zola's positivistic, scientific side in *Germinal*. No summary would be complete that did not point out to what a considerable extent this novel probably reflects, in addition to these specific scientific thinkers, the scientific determinism that Zola, like most other positivists of his day, tended to take for granted.[24] Although I believe that many older critics tended to exaggerate Zola's scientific (as opposed to, for example, his Tainian)[25] determinism and that it is impossible to prove beyond any shadow of a doubt that *Germinal* is a deterministic novel in the strictly scientific sense, it cannot be denied that there is nothing in the text to prevent such an interpretation and a great deal that would seem compatible with it. As many critics have already noted, Zola's characters generally tend to lack that unpredictability which would indicate the possession of a free will;[26] and Etienne, Catherine, Maheu, La Maheude, Jeanlin, and the other characters of *Germinal* are no exceptions. They do not act so much as they react or are acted on. They are essentially products of natural and social forces. For example, Jeanlin is the product of a hereditary degeneracy combined with the shaping action of the mine. As Zola characteristically remarks in Part IV, Chapter vi, "The mine, which had formed him, had applied the finishing touches by breaking his legs" (V, 222; Sig., 221). Etienne's impression that he is the strikers' leader turns out to be only an illusion: "Actually, he had never led them–it was they who had led him. . . . At every outbreak of violence he had remained stupefied by the turn of events, for he had neither foreseen nor wanted any of them" (V, 347; Sig., 363). Given his heredity, Etienne has no choice but to kill Chaval: "A need to kill came over him, an irresistible physical need, like the violent fit of coughing that follows on the irritation of a bleeding mucous membrane. It rose in him, burst beyond his control under the pressure of his inherited taint" (V, 387, 388; Sig., 409). La Maheude is finally reduced by economic necessity to a mere machine endlessly maneuvering back and forth a little ventilator in the over-a-hundred-degree heat of a deep gallery close to Tartaret. Nor are the novel's bourgeois characters any freer than its proletarians. Hennebeau, for example, would live a very different life if he had his way; but, as he painfully realizes, this, of course, cannot be. Moreover, the repeated suggestions in the novel that no one is to blame for the disasters recounted in it can also be cited as evidence of Zola's determinism. If Deneulin cannot, upon reflection, hate the Montsou bandits who have ruined him, it is because he realizes that "everybody was to blame—the fault was general, centuries old" (V, 261; Sig., 264). La Maheude echoes the same principle when she confesses to Etienne: "Oh, there was a time after all those deaths when I could have killed you, but after a while you get to thinking and you begin to realize that it's really nobody's fault after all. . . . No, no, you're not to blame, everybody's to blame" (V, 401; Sig., 423).[27]

Still other reflections of Zola's factualistic, positivistic side may be perceived in the attitudes that he expresses in *Germinal* toward certain widespread contemporary ideas incompatible with philosophical positivism, notably humanitarian utopianism and Christian socialism.

His treatment of humanitarian utopianism may, indeed, particularly remind us of several of the journalistic essays that he fired off in the late seventies and early eighties, when his adherence to the tenets of philosophical positivism was at its peak—the period of *Le Roman expérimental* (1880), *Les Romanciers naturalistes* (1881), and *Documents littéraires* (1881). In these ardently positivistic essays, he especially attacks those aspects of humanitarian utopianism which he associated with the romantics, above all Victor Hugo. In *Le Figaro* of November 2, 1880, he remarks about Hugo's dream of "the universal kiss of peoples, the end of war, the arrival of humanity in a city of light where all would live in a state of utter bliss" that it is a product of Hugo's senility (XIV, 463). In *Le Figaro* of November 2, 1880, once more condemning Hugo's "starry-eyed humanitarianism lost in a dream of universal love" (XIV, 610),[28] he asserts that he himself infinitely prefers to Hugo the great positivist Littré: "One is my youth, the other my maturity. They clash with and exclude each other" (XIV, 609). In *Germinal,* he carries on in apparently the same positivistic vein, repeatedly presenting the predominantly humanitarian utopian ideas that he ascribes to Etienne and his Montsou converts—the "great kiss," or "universal embrace," that would soon end all misunderstanding between the classes and usher in a new golden age of fraternity, equality, and justice—as a revery or hallucination of ignorant, credulous minds. In Part III, Chapter iii, he stresses the superficiality of Etienne's socialistic education before setting forth the humanitarian utopianism that had resulted from it, and he invests them with a decidedly fairy-tale quality. As Etienne's passionate voice goes on, he tells us, the misfortunes of his wide-eyed listeners disappear, "as if swept away by a burst of sunlight and justice descended from the sky in a fairylike dazzle." The new city that springs up in their imaginations is "as splendid as a mirage." The dream grows "more and more beautiful and more and more seductive" as it soars "higher and higher into the impossible" (V, 146; Sig., 136, 137). In Part IV, Chapter viii, which relates the strikers' nocturnal meeting in the Plan-des-Dames, he adopts the same critical attitude. Etienne, expounding once again the same humanitarian dreams, once again exceeds, he comments, all rational bounds. "Only the single-mindedness of the fanatic" remains. "The scruples of his sensibility and common sense" are "swept away" (V, 231; Sig., 230). Undoubtedly to emphasize the utter lunacy of it all, he bathes the whole scene in the light of a rising full moon.

The novel's highly critical portrayal of Christian socialism, embodied by Abbé Ranvier, with his feverish voice and glittering eye, apparently betrays the same positivistic bias; for here again, what is stressed is the lack of any firm factual basis for the ideas in question. Carried away by his vision of a Christian Utopia effectuated by the clergy with the support of the proletariat, Ranvier has, Zola remarks, such a superb disregard for "mundane facts" that he is "able to go through the villages without alms and pass through that army of starving people with empty hands, himself only a poor devil who saw suffering as a spur to salvation" (V, 307; Sig., 318). Bursting unannounced into the Maheus' house just before Alzire expires from hunger, Ranvier pays no attention to the moribund child. He is indifferent to the darkness, the cold, the empty larder. He also fails to grasp the realities of his own situation, to perceive how tight the Church's alliance was with the propertied classes and how utterly alienated the proletariat was from Christianity.

I suspect, moreover, that Zola's decision to have both Etienne's effort to lead the strike to a successful conclusion and Ranvier's campaign to persuade the workers to throw in their lot with the priesthood fail may also be interpreted as an expression of his positivism; for, as those familiar with Zola's essays know, he was convinced that the only way to bring about desirable social change was to develop a truly scientific politics.[29]

However, the novel's extraordinary abundance of true details, its encyclopedic qualities, its mathematical precision, its sharply photographic traits, its closeness in many instances to the texts of its documentary sources, its straining toward a scientific vision of the world, its implied critiques of humanitarian utopianism and Christian socialism are not, of course, the only reflections that we may find in it of Zola's factualism and positivism. They may, finally, also be expressed in the structural relationship between the fictional story that he narrates in the novel and the principal documentary study that he incorporated into it: i.e., the general investigation that he undertook while planning it of the awakening of the modern industrial proletariat, proletarian types, mores, and beliefs, the social condition of the proletariat during the Second Empire, the conflict between the proletariat and capitalism, bourgeois attitudes toward the proletariat, the whole social problem which, he rightly foresaw, would become the most important social problem of the twentieth century. Indeed, I can think of no other work by Zola that might seem to come closer to his naturalistic (i.e., factualistic, positivistic) ideal of a truly scientific novel, a novel consisting of a plot squarely based on a scientific research project.[30] *Germinal*'s central dramatic theme—"the revolt of the working class, a nudge against society, which cracks open for a moment, in a word the conflict between capital and labor"[31]—is directly inspired by the study which I have just briefly summarized. The main outlines of the characters, setting, and central dramatic action, as well as many of the dramatic subtopics, are also dictated by it, either directly or through the secondary study—a veritable anthropological dissertation on coal mines and coal miners—which primarily serves as a frame for it. In fact, there is very little in the story which Zola relates in *Germinal* that cannot be interpreted as a synecdochical, metonymical, or metaphorical representation of this or that element of the novel's principal documentary study.[32] I need hardly point out, for example, to what a considerable degree Etienne, Maheu, Bonnemort, Levaque, Pierron, and the other miners in the book are synecdochical embodiments of the general typological classes of workers to which they belong—the Rising Young Socialist Labor Leader, the Typical Worker, the Old Worker, the Firebrand, the Political Indifferent. Or the awakening of the Maheu family in Part I, Chapter ii, a metaphor for the historical awakening of the proletariat. Or the Catherine-Etienne romantic subplot, an allegory of the struggle of revolutionary socialism to win the allegiance of the proletariat. Or Deneulin's story, an illustration of, as Zola puts it in his notes, "the triumphant reign of money, big money, over . . . even the endeavors of individual capitalists."[33] Or the bloodstains that La Maheude notices on Catherine's shift just after the troops have fired on the strikers, a signal not only of the advent of puberty, but also of the progression of the working class to a higher, possibly more fecund stage of revolutionary development.

Even *L'Assommoir*, Zola's first great working-class novel and surely one of his most naturalistic works, cannot quite compare with *Germinal* in these respects; for whereas the main dramatic theme of *Germinal* is, as I have just recalled, dictated by its principal underlying scientific study, the main dramatic theme of *L'Assommoir*, the arclike rise and fall of Gervaise Macquart after her first abandonment by Auguste Lantier, was suggested to Zola by the curving horizon of the sea at Saint-Aubin, where he planned part of that novel.[34] Another major plot element of *L'Assommoir*, Lantier's return, has its roots not in the scientific subject, but in Zola's old obsession with the theme of the Returned Lover. As for most of Zola's other novels, they conform even less completely to Zola's factualistic, positivistic conception of what a work of fiction should be. For example, the immediate predecessor of *Germinal* in the *Rougon-Macquart* series, *La Joie de vivre* (1884), grew out of a long meditation on the question of whether or not life was worth living. *L'Œuvre* (1886), composed just after *Germinal,* rests primarily, I believe, on a personal myth, Zola's identification of his own artistic struggle against nature with the biblical story of Jacob and the angel.[35] The following novel, *La Terre* (1887), is, as everyone who has read it knows, first and foremost a vast quasi-religious "poem." Only the plot of *La Débâcle* and possibly those of *Lourdes* and *Rome* are as exclusively derived as that of *Germinal* from scientific observations.[36]

2

The Black Poem

But if *Germinal* contains many reflections or possible reflections of the factualist and positivist in Zola, the Zola of "Le Catholique hystérique," "Gustave Doret," "Deux définitions du roman," and *Le Roman expérimental*, the Zola intent on capturing, as he once said, that "naked, living reality" which "this life of suffering, of doubt . . . makes one deeply love" (X, 74), it also contains many reflections or possible reflections of the pessimist in Zola, the Zola of "Doute," "Aventures du grand Sidoine et du petit Médéric," *La Joie de vivre, La Bête humaine,* and *Lazare,* the neurotic Zola, the tormented skeptic, the black poet, the disciple of Musset,[1] the friend of Flaubert, the young Huysmans, and Céard, the Zola whom Edmond de Goncourt, writing in 1880, waspishly described as "more unhappy . . . more disconsolate . . . more gloomy than the most disinherited student who has failed to qualify for a profession,"[2] the Zola who frequently sank into deep despair, indulged in what he calls in a youthful letter to Baille, the "blasphemies of a heart ulcerated by doubt,"[3] cried out broken-heartedly in "Doute," "Alas! How dark it is in the valley of mankind!" (XV, 923), vainly longed for "that one and entire Truth which alone can cure my sick soul" (IX, 182), was obsessed with "the horrors of life," would lie awake brooding on death, sometimes so frightened by the thought of its grim specter pursuing him that he would suddenly jump out of his bed and stand there quaking beside it "in a state of inexpressible terror,"[4] the Zola who, despite his cult of fact and positivistic persuasions, frequently invested reality, like Goya or Kafka, with the qualities and archetypes of nightmare and succumbed to more than one of the specific pessimistic ideas about man, nature, and history that were so widespread in France in his time.

Like *L'Assommoir,* for example, or *La Joie de vivre, Germinal* tells a story of undeserved suffering, unmerited failure, gross injustice. The tragic character of its protagonists is never more apparent than in our farewell glimpse of them—"black, silent shadows that never laughed or raised their eyes . . . the teeth clenched in anger, the hearts swollen with hate, the resignation due solely to the demands of the belly" (V, 396; Sig., 419). It is true that the novel concludes with Etienne's often cited vision pointing to the ultimate realization of the humanitarian ideal: "Slowly the light spread, and the life of earth was rising with the sun. . . . There was a whispering rush of overflowing sap, the sound of seeds spread in a great kiss. . . ." But those readers intent on discovering in *Germinal* expressions of Zola's pessimism could argue, quite logically, that if Zola chose to conclude the novel in this way, he did so only because the very brightness of this dream, which, as we have seen, he strongly intimates in Part III, Chapter iii, and again in Part IV, Chapter vii, is nothing but a dream, serves to bring out through contrast the darkness of the reality of the miners' defeat.

In *La Joie de vivre*, which, we recall, Zola wrote just before *Germinal*, one of his objectives had been to portray nothing less than the whole range of human misery. Bonneville, the small fishing village slowly crumbling into the sea, is, he specifies in his preparatory notes, "the abominable world in miniature." The Houtelards, Prouanes, Cuches, Gonins, and Tourmals symbolically resume all the major sins—including the seven capital sins—and all the principal ills besetting humanity.[5] In *Germinal*, we encounter the same emphasis on the grim side of life, the same compulsion to write a summa of man's wretchedness. Like *La Joie de vivre*, *Germinal* parades before us all the capital sins: Chaval's lust, jealousy, and anger, Maigrat's lust and greed, the Levaques' laziness and jealousy, the Pierrons' covetousness and gluttony, Mme Hennebeau's pride. . . Idolatry, murder, adultery, theft, are also richly represented: the bourgeois's worship of capital, that "monstrous idol gorged with human flesh" (V, 234; Sig., 234); Jeanlin's murder of Jules; Mme Hennebeau's adulterous affair with Négrel; La Levaque's theft of the shoes presented by Cécile to old Bonnemort . . . Quite as much as any of Zola's other novels, including *L'Assommoir* and *Paris*, *Germinal* shows us the appalling uncharitableness of the society of Zola's day—e.g., the sleek Abbé Joire's refusal to stop when La Maheude greets him on the Joiselle road in the hope that he will give her something to help feed her hungry family or Mme Hennebeau's utter indifference to the miners' poverty as she shows her elegant Parisian visitors around Village Number 240 as if it were some kind of zoo.

Like *La Joie de vivre*, *Germinal* is also a compendium of the major evils to which mankind has always been subject, everything that Zola found most lamentable in the human condition, poverty, hunger, disease, the rigors of heat and cold, ignorance, loneliness, unrequited love, natural disasters, the smallness and frailty of man, decay, and death: The immense plain engulfing the village. The vast night submerging everything. Bonnemort's cough. The Maheus' overcrowded house with its thin walls. Alzire's hump. Jeanlin's hereditary degeneracy. Lénore and Henri's too big heads. The coffee so diluted it looks like rusty water. The smoky slag in the stove. The miners pitted against the giant mine, much as the fishermen of Bonneville are against the sea. Hennebeau's loneliness. Maigrat's lifeless eyes staring heavenward while angry women stuff clay into his mouth. The pink cardboard box that La Maheude is finally forced to sell. Alzire's incessant quaking and soft, delirious laughter. Jeanlin's knife buried to the hilt in Jules's throat. Trompette's abandoned corpse. The violent deaths of Bébert and Lydie, Mouquet and Mouquette, La Brûlé, and Richomme. The red froth spilling from Maheu's lips into the puddle of melted snow where he has fallen face down. Bonnemort, his eyes wide and staring, nailed to a chair in front of the fireless chimney. The miners crushed by falling planks or hurtling to their deaths down the Voreux mine shaft or drowned by the flood. Bataille's death cry. Catherine and Etienne trying to subside on worm-eaten wood. Chaval's bloated corpse. Catherine's motionless body stretched across Etienne's knees . . .

Germinal might also serve as an excellent example of Zola's tendency to transform real objects into terrifying dream images or myths. Here as elsewhere in his writings, he is obviously bringing out in a symbolic way what he must have perceived in his darker philosophical moods to be the inherently nightmarish quality of reality. The black, gloomy night, the wailing, buffeting winds, the sea imagery of the first chapter, while perfectly consistent with his factualistic, positivistic objectives, are a modern variation on verses 25-33 of Canto V of Dante's *Inferno*:

> Now I began to hear the doleful notes.
> I had at last come to the place
> Where a great lamentation beat against me.
> I had come to a place where light was mute,
> A place that bellows like a stormy sea
> When it is battled by contrary winds.
> This storm of Hell which never is at rest
> Drives forward all the spirits in its fury,
> Beating, overturning, molesting them.[6]

The Unknown God gluttonously devouring his own offspring, the modern industrial proletariat, has all the unforgettable fearfulness of Goya's nightmarish Cronus. Etienne, like some modern Theseus, has no sooner entered Le Voreux than he finds himself in "a labyrinth of stairways and dark corridors" (V, 43; Sig., 27). The comparison, in Part I, Chapter iv, of Maheu lying on his side between two layers of rock to "a plant-louse caught between two pages of a book, in constant danger of being completely crushed" (V, 50; Sig., 33) prefigures Kafka's *Metamorphosis*. The death of Bataille—"His cry of distress never ceased; even when the flood covered his mane it issued only the more hoarsely from his raised and gaping mouth" (V, 383; Sig., 403)—anticipates in some ways (the constricted subterranean space, the woman holding a lamp, the screaming equine figure) Picasso's *Guernica* and just as much as *Guernica* is surely one of the supreme artistic expressions of the violence, fear, and anguish at the heart of modern culture.

But whether or not we can go so far as to infer that *Germinal*—or any of Zola's other writings for that matter—actually equates reality with nightmare, we can, I suspect, detect in this novel reflections or possible reflections of certain pessimistic ideas of a decidedly philosophical character which we do know he entertained—ideas concerning the nature of history, for example, or of humanity or the relationship between man and the rest of the cosmos.

In his blacker moods, Zola not only rejected on positivistic grounds the more glowing idealistic conceptions of mankind's future that many of his contemporaries embraced; he veered toward a philosophy of history sharply at odds with them. There were moments when he found himself in agreement with the view that nature never changes and that history, whether human or natural, will always be a grim, bloody, endlessly repeated kaleidoscopic process. In "Aventures du grand Sidoine et du petit Médéric," he derides the messianic hopes of his age, opposing to them a nightmarish vision of reality reminiscent of Bruegel's *Big Fish Eat Little Fish*: "A sort of fearful round, an immense circle filling the skies; this circle was made out of all living creatures placed one behind the other, devouring each other; it turned without stopping, pushed on by the fury of the terrible feast" (IX, 154). In the same grim tale, after relating how the lions, tigers, and other wild beasts that its hopelessly idealistic heroine, Primavère, tries to "civilize" in a model school also end up consuming one another just like the creatures in the vision, he sarcastically comments: "Perhaps this is the unity of which mankind is vaguely aware, the final goal, the mysterious labor of the worlds tending to merge all creatures in a single creature" (IX, 177). In *Le Messager de l'Europe* of October 1879, he quotes the following remarks of Sainte-Beuve:

> One has only to penetrate ever so little under the veil of society to see that, just as in nature, there are only wars, struggles, destructions and recompositions. This Lucretian view of criticism is hardly cheerful; but when one has attained to it, it seems preferable, even with its profound sadness, to the cult of idols.

He then comments approvingly: "This last sentence is profound and superb. It contains the whole philosophy of scientific criticism" (XII, 456).

Nothing in *Germinal* would permit us to assume that Zola had in any way renounced when he wrote this novel the historical pessimism implicit in these statements. Indeed, he specifically alludes in Part III, Chapter iii, to "the eternally recurrent misery" (V, 146; Sig., 136) which characterizes his miners' reality as opposed to their utopian reveries. In a letter to Edouard Rod discussing *Germinal*, he clearly specifies that it was to illustrate, among other things, "the eternal injustice of the classes" (XIV, 1440). The spectacle that the novel offers us of the strong feeding on the weak can certainly be interpreted as yet another episode of the terrible feast evoked in "Aventures du grand Sidoine et du petit Médéric." Could one not, moreover, even discern in *Germinal,* as in one after another of Zola's other works, an illustration of the "Lucretian" vision of history that he so admired in Sainte-Beuve? Conflict, struggle, destruction, and recomposition—incessant class warfare, the destruction of Le Voreux, the recomposition of Montsou society after the strike, the vision of an army growing up through the soil "for the harvests of the coming century"—are of the very essence, it could be argued, of the harsh, black world portrayed in this bleak novel.

Numerous images and episodes in Zola's other writings depict nature as aggressively cruel: e.g., the unmerited destruction visited by the Durance on the hero of Zola's short story "L'Inondation" (IX, 655-76), the sudden fierce snowstorm that pelts Gervaise in *L'Assommoir*—despite her entreaties to God not to let it snow—as she wanders half-dead through the Paris streets in search of help (III, 923),[7] the Atlantic relentlessly undermining Bonneville in *La Joie de vivre,* or the hailstorm that destroys a harvest in *La Terre* (V, 840-43). In *Germinal,* nature repeatedly assumes the same role of cosmic bully—in, for example, the freezing March wind that makes Etienne's hands bleed as he first approaches Montsou, the sudden downpour that drenches the anguished crowd watching the collapse of Le Voreux, or the firedamp explosion that kills Zacharie during the rescue operations.

But elsewhere in *Germinal,* as in more than one other writing, Zola also develops the equally pessimistic theme of nature's indifference. In "Doute," he already expresses the idea that nature is supremely impassive, impersonal, incapable of sympathizing with our human woes:

> And the azure dome that regards the earth
> Contemplates, indifferent, its misery and shame,
> Cares little whether the divine rays
> Are a new torment in the night of man
> And expands, proud, selfish, in the clouds,
> Image of this God who regulated space. (XV, 924)

In *La Terre,* he asserts: "The earth takes no part in our maddened insect-struggles; she pays no more attention to us than a nest of ants. . . . What does our happiness count for in the great system of the stars and sun?" (V, 1142). In *La Débâcle,* he stresses how little concerned nature seemed to be with the horrors of Sedan. As Emperor Wilhelm stands high up on La Marfée looking down at the battle, the sky above this scene of carnage is serenely blue. The men locked in combat are nothing more than dust—"that human dust, a few black specks, lost in the midst of eternal, smiling nature" (VI, 845). In *Germinal,* nature seems no more interested in the miners' troubles than she would be in the French defeat of 1870. During the tempestuous meeting at the Plan-des-Dames, the moon shines calmly down on the shouting, shoving, surging crowd. The forest responds to the cries of massacre with deep silence.

Only the frozen moss crackled underfoot, and the beeches rose powerfully, the delicate tracery of their branches black against the white sky, neither seeing nor hearing the miserable creatures swarming at their feet. (V, 236; Sig., 236)

The miners' frantic march across the frozen plain the next day leaves the sky as indifferent as it does at first a group of bourgeois picnickers returning to Montsou "in the dying light of the beautiful clear winter day" (V, 275; Sig., 280). As Lucie, Jeanne, Mme Hennebeau, and other sightseers peer down curiously into the crater of the engulfed mine, where Etienne and Catherine are still trapped alive, it is a beautiful spring day, Zola tells us; the sky is a "delicate blue" (V, 376; Sig., 396). We are reminded of Hugo's "A Villequier":

> The months, the days, the ocean's waves, and eyes that weep
> Pass under the blue sky . . .

Or the moon of "Paroles sur la dune":

> And we both stared at each other fixedly,
> She who shines and I who suffer.

Or we may recall Flaubert's irritation at nature's unperturbed calm: "What a scoundrel this old nature is! . . . What serenity, in contrast to our agitations!"[8]

As those familiar with Zola's other writings know, he was also tormented throughout his career by a pessimistic view of human nature. In "Doute," he denies that man is made in the image of God, calling him, rather, a mere "child of the void," "a shapeless rough outline where nothing can be read." In the same poem, he decries mankind's utter ignorance of higher truth. He compares men to "herds upon the plain / Living off the sewers that surround a crumbling wall" (XV, 923). In "Aventures du grand Sidoine et du petit Médéric," he again posits the absolute nothingness and ignorance of man, going on to assert that our exaltation of ourselves is a joke that has gone on too long and that if we could ever bring ourselves to admit frankly what we really are, we would probably all commit suicide "each in his own corner" (IX, 182). Defending his repeated insistence on the essential brutishness of man, he remarks in *Le Roman expérimental*:

People should realize that if our analyses are inevitably cruel, it is because our analyses probe deep down into the human cadaver. Everywhere we look, we encounter the brute. To be sure, there are more or less numerous veils; but when we have described them all, one after another, and lift the last one, we always find behind it more things which repel us than things which attract us. (X, 1321)[9]

Read in the context of this pessimistic conception of man, *Germinal* might well be taken as an illustration of it—a conception which sharply contrasts, we may note in passing, with the Christian, humanistic view of man that still prevails in Zola's earliest writings.[10]

Totally earthbound, wholly ignorant of higher truth, lacking a spiritual dimension, bereft of free will, ruled primarily by physical need, instinct, and emotion, the characters of *Germinal* are just as much "children of the void" as any of Zola's other fictional characters. Indeed, even his heavy use of darkness imagery throughout the novel would seem to emphasize this nihilistic view of man; for, like so many others before and since, he tended to use words like "darkness" and "nothingness" interchangeably.[11] Not only does the story begin in absolute darkness; it largely unfolds in darkness. As Marcel Girard has pointed out, of the forty chapters, only ten take place in daylight. Six transport us into the depths of the earth. The other twenty-four occur at night.[12] Furthermore, not only Etienne but most of the other members of the major cast, the inhabitants of Village Number 240, are plunged in darkness when we first encounter them. The first workers whom Etienne glimpses are only "moving shadows" (V, 24; Sig., 6). Bonnemort's features are only partially visible in the obscure light of flames. The faces of Catherine and the rest of the Maheu family emerge into view only after she has lighted a candle. The other miners whom Catherine, Maheu, Zacharie, and Jeanlin join on their way to work through the darkened village are only "a slow stream of shadows moving under the gusty wind" (V, 37; Sig., 21). Just as they begin in darkness, they also end in darkness. As Etienne departs from Montsou in the final chapter, the miners whom he passes in the streets on their way to work are again only "black, silent shadows" (V, 396; Sig., 419). Our last glimpse of La Maheude is of her being swallowed up by darkness: "The cord was pulled to hammer out the meat signal, the cage started and dropped into the darkness" (V, 402; Sig., 424). Jeanlin, the last inhabitant of Montsou whom we see in the novel, disappears "into the rising cloud of black dust" that he makes as he cleaves with his hammer a large block of coal (V, 402; Sig., 425).

Surely *Germinal* is also one of those novels in which Zola most forcefully reasserts his pessimistic conception of man as a brute, a "human beast." Not only does he, as many critics have noted, make extensive use of animal comparisons in his descriptions of human characters—as when, for example, he portrays La Maheude's enormous, tired breasts "hanging free and bare, like the udder of a huge cow" (V, 192; Sig., 186); he concentrates even more exclusively than in most of his other works on the instinctive, brutish, bestial side of human nature. No doubt we can think of novels—*La Bête humaine,* for example— where his picture of humanity is even bleaker. There are moments when we even find ourselves admiring this or that moral attitude or action of this or that character. The mine disaster in particular brings out the best in many of them, including Zacharie and Négrel. But it must be admitted that the overall conclusion that the novel invites us to draw concerning man's moral nature is a depressing one. The members of the bourgeois cast are in general a sorry lot, smugly self-satisfied and indifferent to social injustice. The workers, despite Zola's more sympathetic handling of them, are hardly more admirable as a group—at best only "an enormous, blind . . . mass" (V, 347; Sig., 363). Etienne himself is anything but a true hero, his laudable devotion to justice hopelessly compromised by his lust for personal power and glory. Even those characters who come closest to enlisting our full sympathy and respect as human beings, Maheu, La Maheude, and Catherine above all, lack that higher humanity that they might have acquired if they had emerged from, let us say, the pen of a Dostoevski.

Germinal also reflects another idea fundamental to Zola's pessimism: the notion, currently so widespread in Western culture, that death means total annihilation. He repeatedly defines death in this manner in other writings, including some of those which are most obviously autobiographical. One of his fictional alter egos, the unnamed narrator of "Printemps: Journal d'un convalescent," refers to death as "the annihilation of my being . . . a void . . . a black hole" (IX, 907). Another, Olivier Bécaille, the narrator of "La Mort d'Olivier Bécaille," alludes to it in similar terms: e.g., "a black abyss," "the void" (IX, 742-44). So also do Lazare Chanteau, the spiritually tormented hero of *La Joie de vivre,* and still another avatar of Zola's, the Lazare of the opera libretto of the same name. That Zola was also laboring under this same conception of death when he wrote *Germinal* is particularly evident in Part VII, Chapter v, where he recounts Catherine's death and Etienne's near death. The whole passage is marked by recurrent images of extinction. When the young couple's lamp finally goes out, they are enveloped by "complete, absolute night—the dark night of the earth in which they would sleep without ever again opening their eyes on the light of the sun." Catherine, associating the event with her own approaching death, takes refuge in Etienne's arms, as if, Zola tells us, "she had suddenly felt the shadows grab for her," and repeats in a low voice the common miner's saying: "Death blows out the lamp" (V, 389; Sig., 410, 411). The legendary Black Man, whom she now "sees" in an hallucination, becomes in this context very definitely a symbol of annihilation, "blacker than the darkness" (V, 393; Sig., 416). After her death, as Etienne himself grows progressively weaker, everything fades away, Zola tells us before adding: "he was nowhere, beyond space, beyond time" (V, 394; Sig., 417). Death, in *Germinal,* would seem in this context to be the same "night," the same "void," "black hole," "black abyss," "deep, black sleep," or "black immensity" that it is in the other works just mentioned.

When Catherine cries out in terror after the appearance of the Black Man, "Oh, I'm afraid, I'm afraid!" she is voicing, of course, one of Zola's own deepest feelings. Yet Zola's well-known necrophobia, with its concomitant belief that life was worth living despite all its horrors,[13] was countered by certain other elements of his pessimism. Quite as much as Huysmans, Laforgue (whose *Complaintes* appeared the same year as *Germinal*), or any of the many other French Schopenhauerians of their period, the black poet in Zola believed in the universality of suffering. Like them, at least occasionally, he longed for the utter extinction brought by death, regarding it as man's only sure deliverance from life's pain. "I am out of my mind with grief," he confessed to Céard just after hearing about Flaubert's death on May 8, 1880. ". . . Oh, my friend, it would be better if we could all pass away! It would be over sooner. All things considered, there is nothing but sorrow, and life is not worth the pain it brings" (*Corr.*, III, 461). When Gervaise supplicates Bazouge during her final agony to take her away—"Oh, take me away, I've had enough, I want to go. . . . Oh, yes, the time comes when you're happy to croak!" (III, 929)—it is this quasi-Schopenhauerian side of Zola's thought which she is probably expressing. Certainly Lazare Chanteau is when, toward the end of *La Joie de vivre*, he feverishly recites by heart the most violent passages in Schopenhauer and, embracing his master's ideal of universal suicide, speaks of stamping out the will to live "in order to put an end to life's barbarous, imbecile parade" (IV, 1265). So also is the Lazare of the opera libretto of the same name when, instead of thanking Jesus for resurrecting him, he begs to be allowed to die again:

> It was so good, O Jesus, this deep, black sleep, this deep, dreamless sleep. . . . Live again? Oh, no, no, no! Haven't I paid with enough suffering my frightful debt to life? I was born without knowing why, I lived without knowing how; and you would have me pay it twice, you would have me start all over again my term of pain on this sorrowful earth!

"To live again," he concludes, "would only be to feel oneself dying once again a little bit each day, to be endowed once again with an intelligence condemned to suffer the relentless pangs of doubt, a will doomed to continual frustration, a tender heart inflicted with unending grief" (XV, 537-39).

When, in Part V, Chapter v, of *Germinal*, Zola has Hennebeau, stung by fresh evidence of his wife's infidelity, reflect, "a bitter, poisonous taste" in his mouth, on "the pointlessness of everything, the eternal pain of existence" (V, 279; Sig., 285), he is again expressing indirectly much the same dark thoughts. This is also true of the doleful conclusion he ascribes to Hennebeau in a subsequent paragraph, that "the only good was not to be at all, or if be one must, to be a tree, a stone, or even less—a grain of sand that cannot bleed under the heels of passersby" (V, 280; Sig., 286).[14]

As David Baguley has suggested, Souvarine would seem to arrive at a similar conclusion. When we first encounter Souvarine, he still clings to his anarchistic faith that destruction of the present social system may result in the creation of a better world. But as Baguley points out, he is torn between this essentially optimistic doctrine, with its assumption of the essential goodness of human nature, and a mystical, utterly despairing nihilism. The slaughter of his pet rabbit, Pologne, by Madame Rasseneur, who, to his utter horror, serves it up to him in a stew, is the turning point. The last tie that binds him to any living being has been sundered. He is well on his way to having lost all his illusions as to the possibility of resurrecting the lost virtues of a more natural past. Confronted by Etienne with the possibility that the new world rising from the ashes of the old might be no better than the one it has replaced, he protests at first, but, when Etienne presses him, his triumphant nihilism asserts itself in a great cry of despair:

> Faced with this vision of eternal misery the engineman cried out in a terrible voice that if justice was not possible for mankind then mankind would have to disappear. As long as there were rotten societies there would have to be massacres, until the last human being was exterminated. (V, 349; Sig., 366)

This hunger for absolute, definitive destruction, this longing to see the whole of creation collapse back into the night from which it came, whose creature it is, constitutes, according to Baguley (and I cannot but agree with him), Souvarine's true motive for sabotaging Le Voreux. As Baguley concludes, this is the unmistakable meaning of the images of darkness and silence with which Zola constantly associates Souvarine in the scenes culminating in this final symbolic act of violence. Here too, as Baguley also points out, we probably have to do not only with a reflection of the nihilism that had become in Zola's day a conspicuous feature of much Russian thought, but also with an attempt on Zola's part to give fictional expression to his own fundamental doubts and fears.[15]

In short, those looking for expressions—or at least possible expressions—of Zola's pessimism in *Germinal* may find them in the tragic aspects of the epic events it relates; the panoramic view that, like *La Joie de vivre*, it offers us of human sinfulness and all the other major evils to which mankind is subject; its strongly nightmarish qualities; its emphasis on the themes of the eternal suffering caused by the passions and the eternal injustice of the classes; its portrayal of the strong devouring the weak; the "Lucretian" vision of history into which its narration of the Montsou strike might seem to some observers to fit; its partly figurative depiction of nature as either actively cruel or supremely indifferent to human woes; its concentration on the bestial side of human nature underlined by animal comparisons; its heavy use of darkness imagery and other figures (e.g., the "abyss" of the mine) to suggest the nullity of man and/or the nothingness beyond the grave; and the rejection of life and longing for extinction ascribed to Hennebeau and, it would appear, Souvarine as well.

Jules Lemaitre's definition of the plot and underlying philosophical vision of *Germinal* has been so frequently cited that I hesitate to close this chapter without at least mentioning it:

A herd of poor wretches aroused by hunger and instinct, attracted by a crude
dream, moved by fatal forces, and surging forward with a great deal of commotion
only to collide with a superior force; this is the drama. Men appearing like waves
on a sea of shadows and unconsciousness; this is the very simple philosophical
vision into which this drama resolves itself.[16]

Obviously this is a vast oversimplification. It takes into account only those
aspects of this amazingly ambiguous novel which were most in accordance
with the fashionable pessimism of Lemaitre's and Zola's time, mostly inspired
by Schopenhauer and von Hartmann. Nevertheless, it is still intriguing. It
resumes, if not the whole drama and the whole philosophical vision of
Germinal, much of what is most central in them. In doing so, it takes us very
close to the heart of Zola's pessimism in general, which, after all, largely drew
from the same sources as most of his contemporaries.[17] Significantly, Zola
himself, despite his disagreement with Lemaitre on one or two other points
concerning the novel, did not object to this summary of it. He even went
on in his letter thanking Lemaitre for his review to say that he quite willingly
accepted Lemaitre's definition of the whole *Rougon-Macquart* series as "a
pessimistic epic of human animality" (XIV, 1439).[18]

3

Pan

Yet the more deeply we explore *Germinal* in the light of Zola's philosophical and religious thought, the more we become aware of all the multitudinous reflections or possible reflections that this great novel contains
of still other aspects of his complex, confused, paradoxical genius: the
optimistic dreamer, the seeker after reassuring higher truths, the mystic,
the man of faith, the prophet.

Zola had—as anyone at all familiar with him knows—quite as sharp a need
for what he once called, in a youthful work, "the sweet deceitful hopes that
dreams inspire" (I, 9) as he did for the solidity of fact and scientific truth.[1] He
tended just as much as anyone else to take refuge from the harshness of existence in consoling reveries;[2] and, as a study of these reveries will show, almost
all were of a wholly or partly metaphysical or religious character.[3] Moreover,
despite his initial failure after his rejection of Catholicism to develop a secular
faith that he could truly believe in,[4] he kept on doggedly trying to do so.
In 1865, apropos the hero of his first novel, his fictional alter ego Claude,
he had remarked: "He will fall down on his knees perhaps someday. He is
looking with immense despair for a truth capable of sustaining him" (I, 10).
Just as revealingly, Zola had observed in an essay composed during the same
early period: "Every powerful intelligence, recognizing in itself the need
for truth and finding it nowhere, is obliged to create for itself a faith out of
bits and pieces of faiths picked up all over the place" (X, 506). Over and
over again in Zola's works we find evidence of a persistent struggle to meet
these needs for, on the one hand, escapist reveries, and, on the other hand,
a serious new faith: a large stock of heterogeneous ideas that possessed spiritual
value for him and—fashioned out of them—a whole array of more or less
different daydreams, visions, professions of faith, idealistic philosophies, "new
religions" leaping far beyond the restrictions imposed by his positivism and
strongly contrasting with his pessimism.[5]

It was undoubtedly some of the earliest of these dreams, visions, creeds,
etc., that he was referring to when, in the luminous ending of *La Confession
de Claude*, he had had Claude exultantly proclaim:

I will be young again, I will have something to believe in again, I will be able to start out life again with new dreams. Oh, I can feel all the thoughts of my youth crowding back, filling me with strength and hope! Everything had disappeared in the night I had entered. . . . I was blind; now I understand myself again. . . . I am going to start working again, get my strength back, fight for the things I believe in, the things I love. (I, 110)

Moreover, as we know from Zola's early correspondence and other youthful writings, he had started out his career fired by the romantic belief in the sacred mission of poetry. Poetry, he had written Baille, was synonymous with God. Art was "a splendid torch lighting humanity's path" (*Corr.*, I, 223). Poets, "luminous beacons in human life" (*Corr.*, I, 223) had been placed by God on earth "to show man the way to Heaven" (*Corr.*, I, 223). The ancient Hebrew prophets and the modern artist therefore performed, he maintained, the same function, all of them bearing on their brows the same mark made by God's finger (*Corr.*, I, 223). The young Zola realized, of course, that not everyone who wanted to play this role succeeded, that one had to be divinely chosen. "But it is always glorious to try; if you lack the breath, what difference does it make! You may fail, but you will still be great, thanks to your audacity" (*Corr.*, I, 224). "If God will only grant me the inspiration I need, I am ready" (*Corr.*, I, 206), he had already remarked, in an earlier letter. In the Prologue to *La Genèse*, an immense verse epic that he had first conceived in 1857 and never finished, he is consumed by the same prophetic aspiration: "Creative Principle, unique First Force . . . Give me the golden wing of the inspired prophet" (XV, 937). It is evident from his subsequent writings—including *Les Rougon-Macquart* and *Les Trois Villes*, not to mention his last major work, *Les Quatre Evangiles* (of which he completed only the first three volumes, *Fécondité*, *Travail*, and *Vérité*, before he died)—that he never lost this ambition. Throughout his career, it constantly reinforced his compulsion to indulge, on the one hand, in glowing metaphysical or religious fantasies and, on the other, to find a secular faith to which he could seriously commit himself.

Of course, a secular faith does not necessarily have to be religious in any of the narrower senses of the term, and it is true that many of the ideas Zola invested with religious or quasi-religious worth may not seem to most readers particularly religious.[6] Like many other nineteenth-century thinkers, he seemed at times to use such words as *religion, religious, sacred,* and *holy* loosely.[7] Yet we cannot study this side of his character without being impressed by its authentically religious dimensions. An atheist only in the sense that he had rejected the Christian deity, he never denied the existence of some kind of supreme being. On the contrary, he was always, to borrow Tillich's terminology, vitally concerned with that ultimate reality to which we give the symbolical name of God.[8] Even during the period, in the late 1870s and early 1880s, when his self-identification with pure philosophical positivism had been most pronounced, he had asserted that discovering the true nature of God was the ultimate goal, or highest aim, of naturalism.[9] He not only wanted to know God in the manner of philosophers, as an object of cognition; he also desired that "I-thou relationship" with the Deity which, as Martin Buber has insisted, constitutes an essential element of most religions.[10] Moreover, it would seem that Zola was subject at certain privileged moments to genuinely religious experiences: overwhelming urges to worship, Kierkegaardian leaps of faith, divine revelations, beatific visions, mystical union with the supreme forces of reality.[11] Anything short of a true religion was incapable of permanently satisfying him, and this was one of the reasons, we may gather, why he was always moving restlessly from one of his new personal "religions" or religious-substitutes to another.

His persistent tendency to sacralize his central values—nature, love, life, force, work, science, progress, humanity, France, etc.—or even at times, as we shall see, to deify one or another of them is also indicative of the essentially religious orientation and thrust of his thought. So also is his compulsion to employ traditional religious models. He had a penchant for basing characters on biblical figures—e.g., Adam and Eve, Jacob, Lazarus, or Christ—or for introducing into his fiction variations on biblical events (e.g., the Flood) or parts of the Christian cosmos (e.g., Paradise or Hell). Commencing with the still partly Christian profession of faith in his letter of August 10, 1860, to Baille (*Corr.*, I, 226), he more than once cast his beliefs of this or that moment in forms reminiscent of Christian creeds, the best known being Pascal's Creed, in *Le Docteur Pascal*.[12] Not only in such early works as "Paolo," "Doute," "Religion," and the Prologue to *La Genèse*, but here and there throughout his writings, we discover him composing prayers for himself or his fictional alter egos. A good example would be Sandoz' prayer in Chapter v of *L'Œuvre* (V, 567) or Luc and Josine's orison in *Travail*—partly a variation on the Golden Rule.[13] Zola also created rites reminiscent of Christian rites like the elaborate public religious ceremony modeled on the Eucharist in *Travail*.[14] In *Vérité*, his last novel, posthumously published in 1903, he imagined a "scientific catechism" meant to replace the Catholic catechism.[15] If he included in his last fictional series four "Gospels" instead of three, as originally planned, it was in order to match the four Gospels of the New Testament, Matthew, Mark, Luke, and John.[16] Not surprisingly, the heroes of the three "Gospels" that he completed are Mathieu, Marc, and Luc, and the hero of the fourth, "Justice," would have been named Jean.

The degree of seriousness with which Zola may have embraced any of the visions, creeds, and whole new faiths that he created or associated himself with over the years is debatable. Some he may never have thought of as more than purely escapist dreams. Each of the credos he inserts in his writings has an air of conviction about it; yet we cannot help but notice that he never repeats the same credo twice. Two of his new faiths, he even went so far as to propose quite solemnly and earnestly to the public—the first in *Le Salut Public* of October 14, 1865 (X, 100, 101), the second in an address to a student group on May 18, 1893 (XII, 681-83). The major premises of the latter, however, are repeated in *Les Quatre Evangiles*, which, in a letter to a friend, he characterizes as the reveries of his old age (VIII, 516).[17]

Yet whether he ever absolutely believed in any of these visions, creeds, and whole new faiths, there can be no question as to their importance to him both as a man and as an artist—or as to the urgency of his desire for an acceptable secular faith or the sincerity of his commitment to his prophetic vocation. Like Michelet, one of the principal sources of his thought,[18] he accepted the Viconian thesis that religion is the central feature of any civilization— or of any individual personality, for that matter. "It is impossible to know a people," he had once observed, we recall, "without a complete knowledge of its religious beliefs. . . . I am convinced that an archeologist and a scientist, an historian and an artist must know the gods before they can know men. Tell me whom you worship, and I will tell you who you are" (X, 569).[19] For such a man, it was essential that a civilization which, like his own, was in the process (or so he believed) of losing its traditional faith should have a new one to replace it. At issue was nothing less than an existential *sine qua non.* More than one of his earliest works are already "gospels" in the same sense as his last series of novels, that is to say, works conceived of as means of promulgating ideas of religious value, if not the rudiments of a new faith. Think above all of "Paolo" or "Un Coup de vent."[20] As he approached first middle and then old age, his absorption in his struggle to create and impose an acceptable new religion or philosophical religion-substitute became an increasingly central, patent part of his creative activity. This is especially noticeable in many works written after the extraordinarily grave existential crisis reflected in *La Joie de vivre. L'Œuvre, La Terre, Le Rêve, L'Argent, Le Docteur Pascal,* are all novels with profound religiometaphysical dimensions. Indeed, the primary function of *Le Docteur Pascal,* which Zola thought of as the "philosophical conclusion" of the entire *Rougon-Macquart* series, is to set forth Pascal's Creed, a confession of faith with unmistakably religious overtones. *Les Trois Villes,* the massive trilogy that forms a kind of sequel to *Les Rougon-Macquart,* turns on the struggle of a spiritually troubled priest, Pierre Froment (another spokesman of Zola's) first to regain his lost Catholicism, then to champion a modernized version of Christianity reminiscent of Francesco Nitti's "Catholic socialism" (VII, 1130), and finally to find a new religion capable of filling the void left by the collapse of Christianity. At the end of *Paris,* the third volume, Zola unveils what, during the period when he was writing *Les Trois Villes,* he believed this new religion would be, and he shows Pierre ecstatically embracing it. This whole religiopoeic process in Zola, of which we may trace the beginnings all the way back to the outset of his career, culminates in *Les Quatre Evangiles,* a fireworks display of his philosophical and religious optimism as it was evolving in his last years.

Among other things, I am tempted to agree with those critics, starting out with Gustave Geffroy, who have perceived in *Germinal* expressions of the pantheism which is one of the chief attributes of this whole side of Zola.[21] The word *pantheism* has, of course, often been used rather loosely with respect to nineteenth-century artists and writers, sometimes to designate little more than a reverence for and vague sense of unity with nature. Yet—as I shall show in the remainder of this chapter—the Zola whom we are discussing here was indeed a true pantheist at heart, and there is much in *Germinal* which can be construed as reflective of the pantheism, or, more precisely, several forms of pantheism, he associated himself with at one time or another.

Pantheism, as we know, can be defined as the tendency to view the world as a single whole of closely interrelated parts, with nothing beyond it, and either to regard this whole as divine and the proper object of worship or to assume that it contains some divine indwelling principle.

The tendency to conceive of the world as a single whole of closely interrelated parts, with nothing beyond it, was undoubtedly one of Zola's most persistent traits. Following in the footsteps of Hugo and the other romantics, he took part in the modern endeavor to break down traditional distinctions between subject and object, the self and the world, the material and the spiritual, the conscious and the unconscious, the divine and the profane, the world and its creator. He had as much as any other modern thinker a sense of the continuity between man and nature and the presence of God. He wanted to see everything in everything, to relate every element of the universe to larger patterns, to proceed from the Many to the One. The kaleidoscopic transformations of symbols and synesthetic apperception characteristic of much of his writing,[22] the compulsion that led him to write novels that are not so much distinct wholes as parts of larger wholes contituting a still greater whole, like sections of an immense fresco, the basically synecdochic structure of his fiction are all symptomatic of the same unitism, or monism. As he indirectly informs us, through Sandoz, his fictional spokesman in *L'Œuvre,* the vision toward which his works point is that of the immense ark of being, the great, soaring, self-sufficient totality of all things (V, 567).[23]

This monistic bent, an essential element of his pantheism, may also be seen in his attachment to a number of traditional concepts presupposing the unity, or close-knit coherence, of nature. As we can see in "Paolo" (XV, 898-913), "Du progrès dans les sciences et dans la poésie" (X, 310-14), and some of his later writings, he clung to the ancient, now largely abandoned notion of universal, or world, harmony.[24] Especially at that moment in his youth when the overall outlines of his major works were beginning to take shape in his

mind, he had been very much drawn to another ancient idea, the great chain
of being. The original title of *La Genèse*, the ambitious unfinished epic to
which I have already referred, was indeed precisely that: *La Chaîne des êtres*
(*Corr.*, I, 182); and throughout his twenties he had kept coming back to the
same metaphysical notion. For example, in February 1869 (the year he had
begun the first volume of *Les Rougon-Macquart*), he had mentioned with
obvious approval the impression that Edgar Quinet's epic *La Création* gave him
of "a divine ladder up which the entire universe is ascending" (X, 796). In
making Dr. Prosper Lucas' doctrines of heredity into one of the main scientific
bases of *Les Rougon-Macquart*, he had also made his own the equally ancient
philosophical conception of the microcosm and the macrocosm; for, as we can
see from the following passage from the Preface of Lucas' *Traité*, it was an
essential element of Lucas' theory:

> MAN . . . is at the highest rank of those works of life instituted by NATURE in
> accordance with settled laws of which he retains at once the energy and the imprint.
> Symbol of her thought, word incarnate of her force, in which she repeats herself,
> he repeats her, perpetuates her in perpetuating himself; he is the MICROCOSM. In
> him lives, breathes, and acts the principle which creates in the universe. Successfully
> to grasp and define the elementary forms of human activity is, therefore, in a
> certain sense to grasp and define the elementary forms of THAT of which it is
> at once the organ and the image.

The young novelist had, in fact, been so impressed by these remarks that he
had taken the trouble to summarize them in his preliminary notes for *Les
Rougon-Macquart*, citing more than one verbatim.[25] It is probable that they
were still in his mind when, more than two decades later, he wrote in his notes
for the concluding volume of the series: "Heredity is a communicated movement. . . . heredity makes the world, and if we could intervene, understand it
in order to make use of it, we could make the world."[26] Even in his old age, he
continued to think of nature as a giant organism, on the model of the individual
organisms within it.[27]

The same monism was also undoubtedly among the factors that attracted
Zola to Hippolyte Taine, whose disciple he declared himself in 1865, and that
led him, that same year, to come out as a journalistic champion of Taine's
favorite philosopher, Spinoza (X, 684).

This tendency to conceive of the world as a single whole can be seen also
in Zola's rejection of the old dualism between body and soul, matter and spirit.
Except for those brief moments when, under Bernard's influence, he discarded
both *materialism* and *spiritualism* as terms that no longer had any place in the
language of science (X, 1198),[28] he adopted during his most productive period
an ever more complete materialism. In his preliminary notes for *Les Rougon-
Macquart*, he characterizes the underlying philosophy of the series as a kind
of vague "materialism."[29]

His enthusiastic acceptance of the scientific supposition that, as he put it, "the same determinism must rule a roadway stone and a man's brain" (X, 1182) is still another indication of his monistic bent.

But most of the tentative "new religions" that he created or appropriated in the course of his career were also monistic. In connection with more than one, he uses the monistic term "the great whole."[30] In outlining the "new religion" prophesied in the conclusion of *Paris* (1898), he actually employs the word *monism* itself:

And already was this religion not beginning to disclose itself, the idea of duality, of God and the universe, set aside, the idea of unity, of monism, more and more evident, unity implying solidarity, the unique law of life flowing, by evolution, from the first speck of ether which condensed in order to create the world? (VII, 1561)

Not only in the "new religion" adumbrated in *Paris*, but over and over again in his other writings, Zola also insists on the tight bonds of kinship uniting everything in reality. Recall, for example, the moving episode in Part III, Chapter v, of *La Terre*, in which scenes graphically depicting the birth of Lisa's infant alternate with scenes portraying in just as vivid detail the birth of La Coliche's calf (V, 946-56). Zola even shared Michelet's well-known distaste for killing insects; for, as he confesses in an essay composed in Gloton in June 1868, he agreed with Michelet that these "tiny existences" draw their life from the same source as we, "the great common hearth" (XIII, 114). In his letter of March 14, 1885, to Lemaitre, concerning *Germinal*, he once again insists on the fraternity uniting man and beast (XIV, 1439); and he again emphasizes the same idea—an essential part of his monistic view of the world— in *Le Docteur Pascal*:

And animality, the beast that suffers and loves, that is like a rough outline of man, all this fraternal animality that partakes in the same life as we! . . . Yes, I would have liked to include it in the ark, to have allotted it its place in our family, to have shown it ceaselessly mingling with us, completing our existence. (VI, 1243)[31]

Inspired by the same monistic vision, Zola also emphasizes just as frequently the numerous affinities that he perceived between the animal and vegetable kingdoms. In "Printemps: Journal d'un convalescent" (1866?), which is probably a veiled account of his own recovery from a serious illness, the fictional narrator supposes that the flowers in his garden are trying to speak to him and imagines that he has become a plant, absorbing like a plant the life-giving rays of the sun and feeling sap coursing through his own veins (IX, 914). In the aforementioned essay composed in Gloton, Zola reports a similar experience, influenced by Michelet's *L'Oiseau*, *L'Insect*, and *La Montagne*. Resting in the grass under some poplar trees on a remote island in the Seine, he feels rooted, like the poplars, in the soil. He can feel surging through his rejuvenated flesh the same vital juices that he could hear trembling under the bark. Immobile and mute, he becomes, like them, absorbed in the worship of the sun and participates in their long reveries about the secrets of the earth (XIII, 114). The same or similar sentiments of oneness with plants are expressed over and over again in Zola's novels, including such major works as *La Faute de l'abbé Mouret, La Terre,* and *La Débâcle.* For example, those who have read *La Débâcle* may remember how, under the bombardment of the Prussian cannon during the battle of Sedan, an ancient oak in the Garenne Forest topples with the tragic majesty of a hero; the screams of wounded men mingle with the sobs of shattered trees; and fallen trees endowed with human traits figure along with the human casualties in epic descriptions of the dead:

> Everywhere, felled trunks were lying, denuded, full of holes, ripped open like breasts; and this destruction, this massacre of branches weeping sap, was just as horrible and heartbreaking to see as a human battlefield. Then there were also some corpses, soldiers fallen fraternally with the trees. (VI, 976)

Throughout Zola's writings, images suggesting resemblances between human beings and seeds, human lives and the life cycles of plants, point in the same metaphysical direction. In "Printemps" and *La Faute de l'abbé Mouret,* the efforts of convalescents to regain their health become, in their deliriums, the painful struggles of seeds to work their way upward toward the sun (IX, 908, 909, 912, III, 103). In *La Terre,* the old peasant Fouan is buried at seed time. Glimpses of Fouan's interment alternate with evocations of sowers, and as Fouan's son-in-law, Pierre, peers down at the casket descending into the grave, the color of the fresh pinewood reminds him of wheat (V, 1136, 1137). In *Paris,* the whole French capital is transformed into a shining wheatfield: "It seemed that the same upsurge of life, the same flowering, had re-covered the whole town, making of it one great harmony, turning it into nothing but a single, limitless field covered with the same fecundity. Wheat, wheat everywhere, an infinitude of wheat of which the golden swell rolled from one end of the horizon to the other" (VII, 1567). In *Vérité,* once again we come across, in the final pages, essentially the same vision of men metamorphosed into plants, germinating, springing up from the soil (VIII, 1470).

But if Zola liked to think that men, animals, and plants are united, he also tended to think of even so-called inanimate objects as part of the same tight unity of all things. In the article written in Gloton in June 1868, he specifically includes in the living oneness of the world the warm, sun-bleached stones on the shore of his island retreat (XIII, 114). In the letter mentioned above to Lemaitre, apropos *Germinal,* he insists that even the humblest pebble is part of the same animated whole (XIV, 1439). His well-known tendency to animate everything in his fiction—Gervaise's working-class tenement on La Rue de la Goutte-d'Or, Octave Mouret's department store, Paris, Jacques Lantier's locomotive, La Lison, the moon, the sun, and the stars—far from being a mere poetic conceit, originates in this religiometaphysical vision of the world as a single whole of closely related parts.

There can be no question, moreover, as to the fundamentally pantheistic character of this monism. As an adolescent, Zola had taken from the romantics the conception of nature as God's temple,[32] and throughout the rest of his life he kept on thinking of romantic nature, bucolic nature, as a kind of church, a sacred place where he could take refuge from the profane city.[33] In his mind, the place of priest and altar in a Christian cathedral was occasionally taken by, for instance, a majestic tree.[34] But during most of his adult career, nature was for him not only God's dwelling place; nature, all nature, *was* God. God, matter, spirit, were one. It was no coincidence that many of those other nineteenth-century writers who had the greatest impact on him, those to whom he was the most strongly attracted, were men with pantheistic leanings—e.g., Hugo, Lamartine, Michelet, Taine, Renan, Lucas.[35] The Spinozism Zola championed in 1866, no doubt under Taine's influence, was, as his own definition of it shows, definitely of the pantheistic variety.[36] Writing on Pissarro, Jongkind, and Corot in 1868 (the year he began planning *Les Rougon-Macquart*), he enthusiastically equated the pantheistic vision of nature that he perceived in their landscapes with truth.[37] Years later, in 1896, respecting a volume of essays by the young Naturist writer Saint-Georges de Bouhélier, *L'Hiver en méditation,* he could still confess: "I infinitely love the pantheistic inspiration that reigns in it" (XII, 715).

In the proposal for a new religion that he included in an article published in *Le Salut Public* of October 15, 1865, he capitalizes the word *whole* in the expression "the great Whole" and, as the context confirms, clearly identifies it with God (X, 100, 101). In his preliminary work notes for *La Terre,* the same equation between the great whole and God occurs.[38]

The strongly pantheistic cast of Zola's thought is most evident, however, in his persistent identification of the whole of reality, symbolized by the soil, or earth, with the divine Terra Mater, or Great Mother. This pantheistic trait may already be clearly seen in "Les Quatre Journées de Jean Gourdon" (1866). At one point, Jean, the fictional narrator, lyrically recalls how, one glorious spring day in his boyhood, as he lay on the ground, pressing his body hard against it, he had actually felt the energies of our great common mother surging up through his breast (IX, 457); and that we have to do here with a divinity is undeniable, for elsewhere, in the same story, Jean's mentor, his uncle Lazare, a country priest, substitutes the pantheistic notion of man created in the image of eternal Earth for the Judeo-Christian view of man as having been made in the image of Jehovah: "Man, my child, has been created in the image of the earth. And, like the common mother, we are eternal" (IX,

471). In Zola's subsequent writings the concept of a divine Mother Earth, or Great Mother, recurs repeatedly. For example, he says, obviously with great emotion, in the "Causerie" he wrote in Gloton in June 1868, that Michelet will remain forever glorious for having been one of the first modern thinkers to "have fallen down on his knees before our great common mother" (XIII, 115). In *L'Œuvre*, no doubt remembering the mystical experiences recounted in this essay and in "Les Quatre Journées de Jean Gourdon," the novelist gives vent once again to his own innermost mystical longings when he has Sandoz passionately pray Earth to take him and absorb him into her divine self:

> Ah, good earth, take me, thou who art the common mother, the unique source of life! Thou who art eternal, immortal . . . Yes, I want to lose myself in thee, it's thou I feel here, under my limbs, embracing me and inflaming me, it's thou alone who shalt be in my work the first force, the means and the end, the immense ark. . . . (V, 567)

In *La Terre*, which Zola wrote just after *L'Œuvre* (which, as I have already noted, immediately follows *Germinal* in the *Rougon-Macquart* series), his exaltation of Earth, the Great Mother, as the symbol of the Great Whole, of God, is stronger than ever. As those familiar with *La Terre* know, it is, indeed, first and foremost a prose poem celebrating Earth, culminating in a great hymn to Earth where, once again, the words *Earth, Great Mother*, and *God* are used interchangeably (V, 1142).

But it must be noted that if Zola often tended to regard the great whole as divine, he also persistently posited, although not always at the same time, three major universal principles each of which he sacralized and even at certain moments equated with God.

One of these three principles, perhaps the earliest, is life.

Recalling his boyhood in Aix, he wrote in 1874 that he and his close friends Cézanne and Baille had conceived during their promenades through the Aixois countryside "a great disdain for the world and a tranquil faith in the forces of life alone" (IX, 348). In his adult years, this faith blossomed into a veritable cult, a cult which received its fullest expression in *Le Docteur Pascal* and *Fécondité*, but which is already reflected in many of his earlier works.

By the word *life*, used in this general sense, he meant much more, of course, than just the sum of all individual lives, a mere abstraction. Having abandoned in his early twenties, it would seem, the traditional Judeo-Christian belief in individual souls, he had soon afterwards replaced it with the concept of a universal life, or universal soul. (The two terms, in his mind, were interchangeable.)[39] The whole of nature, beyond which nothing else existed, assumed for him the character of a single living creature, of which mankind was only one of an infinitely diverse, ceaselessly changing multitude of forms.[40] Lying in the tall grass of his wooded island retreat near Gloton on June 25, 1868, he had lost the sense of his separateness, felt his individual consciousness reabsorbed into the universal self, "drawing a fraternal soul from the sap that the trees shared with me," becoming mystically one with "the infinity of life" (XIII, 115). Still possessed by essentially the same vision of life during the period that he wrote *Germinal,* he had remarked in his letter of March 14, 1885, to Lemaitre: "You isolate man from nature; I cannot conceive of him apart from the earth, from which he comes and to which he returns. The soul that you shut up in a human being, I sense spread out everywhere, in the human being and outside the human being, in the animal whose brother he is, in the plant, in the pebble" (XIV, 1439). The same unanimism is an important feature of the religiometaphysical ideas that Zola ascribed to his spokesman Sandoz, in *L'Œuvre.* "How stupid it is to suppose that each one of us has a separate soul," Sandoz exclaims as he lies, as his author had before him, on his stomach in the tall grass of an island in the Seine, "when there is this great soul!" (V, 567). Life, for Zola, was "all things" animated "by the breath of all beings" (V, 567). It was the sap of the earth (XIII, 114). It was a restless, infinitely dynamic and powerful force. Sometimes he compares it to a flood (XII, 608), a torrent (VIII, 969), or a sea (XII, 608). In his later works, starting out with *Le Docteur Pascal,* he repeatedly insists that life is nothing but a movement.[41]

Starting out with the idea of universal life, or soul, Zola had also arrived at the notion of the universal consciousness which must be one of the attributes of this soul—a consciousness which, he speculates in a youthful writing, we may all ultimately share, if not in our individual lifetimes, after death, as parts of the Great Whole (X, 100). This may, I suspect, partly explain one of the most noteworthy peculiarities of his optic: the extraordinary profusion of points of view which we find in his major series of novels, especially *Les Rougon-Macquart.* For by multiplying points of view, as it were, ad infinitum, by placing eyes, as he does, everywhere, by endowing, as he also does, even objects—the moon, a cathedral window, a train headlight, for example—with sight, he comes very close indeed to making us see the world of his fiction as the eye of the universal soul itself might see it.[42]

Driven by his longing for immortality and abhorrence of death, he habitually emphasized, moreover, the irrepressible persistence of life. In writing "Printemps: Journal d'un convalescent," he had thought in terms of "the great battle, the eternal battle, of life against death" (IX, 909), but as he grew older and his fear of death more obsessive, he was tempted more and more to regard death as not so much the foe of life as an essential part of the life process and therefore good and acceptable, always preparing the way for new life, fertilizing the ground.[43] He also liked to think that, since life is universal, therefore omnipresent, it must be present even in death—that death is not annihilation as he sometimes assumed, but, like birth, just another phase of life. "Birth, death, these are only states, words; she [Earth] creates only life.

... Corpses, seeds, they are next spring's germination," he jotted down in his preparatory notes for *La Terre*.[44] In the scene recounting Luc's death in *Travail*, he concludes: "And Luc expired, entered the torrent . . . of eternal life" (VIII, 969).

Zola's exaltation of fecundity—women, children, potent males, the acts of procreation and giving birth—and his concomitant obsession with seminal imagery (including the equation of sap with semen)[45] are also deeply rooted in his cult of life. He always regarded as of great worth everything that contributes to the life process: rivers irrigating the land, for example, or the warm springtime sun.[46] At those moments when exaltation of life dominated his thinking, he tended to assume, whatever he might maintain at other moments, that the supreme task of every man, woman, and other being is to reproduce, that the unique purpose of life must forever be to bring forth ever more abundant life. He already expresses this idea in "Les Quatre Journées de Jean Gourdon,"[47] but in later works he does so more emphatically, especially in *Le Docteur Pascal* and *Fécondité*.[48]

His chief motive in writing, as he confessed in *Le Bien Public* of September 24, 1878, was to defeat death by creating works through which he could attain immortality (X, 1338. Cf. V, 650). It was only fitting that these works and the aesthetics behind them should reflect his cult of life as strongly as possible. As Richard Grant has put it so well, Zola's main aesthetic principle is "that the force of life is truth and is beauty."[49] "Life is everywhere," Zola wrote in 1869, "and art is nothing other than life" (X, 884). In his notes for *Le Docteur Pascal*, he told himself: "But above all incarnate in the doctor what I want to have the whole series express. . . . love of life, of health, of sacred energy, of force."[50]

A stubborn, instinctive (or so it has seemed to such critics as Anatole France) confidence in life and tendency to revere, worship, deify life were indeed among Zola's most persistent traits. In moments of despondency, he turned to his faith in life for succor. "The height of wisdom is to accept life as it is," he wrote Cézanne on June 25, 1860 (*Corr.*, I, 191). Barely more than ten months after his mother's death in October 1880, months during which he had been engaged in a struggle to free himself from a near suicidal mood, he had asked, in *Le Figaro*, "Why not have faith in life . . . ?" (XIV, 651). In the conclusion of *La Joie de vivre*, a product of the same struggle, he has Pauline, despite all the terrible things that have happened to her and those she loves, laugh with joy as she nurses little Paul, a living symbol of life's persistence (IV, 1322). Old Chanteau, despite his everlasting gout, exclaims at the news of their housekeeper's suicide, "How idiotic people who kill themselves are!" (IV, 1322). Several of the works that Zola wrote in his fifties and sixties, as the dreaded spector of death approached, proclaim his faith in life even more resoundingly. *L'Argent* (1891) ends on the word *life*. So does *Le Docteur Pascal* (1893) and consequently the whole *Rougon-Macquart* series. So also do his last short story, "Angeline ou La Maison hantée" (1899), and his second "Gospel," *Travail* (1901).

In the essay composed in Gloton in the spring of 1868, he specifically refers to life as "the first force that rules the world" (XIII, 115). In his notes for *Le Docteur Pascal*, he states: "Life is God, the great motor, the only one, the soul of the world."[51] In *Le Figaro* of May 23, 1896, he says that he wants life to be worshipped "like the good goddess" (XIV, 790). In *Fécondité* (1899), he preaches what he calls quite simply "the religion of life" (VIII, 499), expressing the hope that this "religion" will eventually triumph over Christianity. In *Travail*, he imagines how this victory might actually come about (VIII, 954), once again explicitly equating life with God: "Life, in the final analysis, is nothing but matter at work, a perpetually active force, the god of all religions" (VIII, 669). No one in Zola's generation, in fact, would seem to have taken more seriously than he the exhortation by Eugène Pelletan, one of the leading spiritual guides of that generation, in his *Profession de foi du dix-neuvième siècle* (1852): "Live, and live ever more abundantly. This is God's law and his commandment. Let us breathe in, attract to us, infinite life, that is to say, the Divinity, at every step, at every instant. . . . Life! Life! Let us get drunk on this word, for we have to do here with a sacred drunkenness."[52]

However, alongside Zola's pantheistic cult of life, we can also discern in many of his works a veritable cult of love.

This cult, too, had strong pantheistic characteristics. Love, as Zola defined it, was first and foremost passionate love, love between the sexes. But he defined the word very broadly, denoting by it not only passionate love, maternal love, filial love, fraternal love, friendship, love for God, the sense of solidarity binding human groups together, the affection that we feel for animals—an affection which, he insisted, was a distinct form of love, not to be confounded with any other (XIV, 737)—but also every kind of attraction. Love, in Zola's opinion, included "the great fraternity of the trees and the waters" (XIII, 108), the "loves of a flower" (XIII, 115), and "the tranquil, universal love of the earth, which gives nourishing juices to every seed" (IX, 914). Love, in Zola's opinion, even included universal gravitation. He liked to think of all the celestial bodies held in place "by a law of love" (X, 325). "The invisible particles of life that populate matter, the atoms of matter themselves, were making love, coupling, causing the ground to shake voluptuously" (III, 174), he affirms in *La Faute de l'abbé Mouret*. In *Paris*, he even goes so far as to propose (through one of his fictional mouthpieces, the chemist Guillaume Froment) the theory that the whole universe was created by the lovemaking of the atoms: "Was this not the only scientific theory, the unities creating the worlds, the atoms creating life by the attraction of gravity, ardent, free love?" (VII, 1317).

Moreover, just as, at certain moments, Zola liked to suppose that life is the chief principle of all being, at other moments, he conceived of love (which, it must be admitted, he often treated as synonymous with life) as fulfilling the same cosmic function. This idea, which was probably as deeply rooted in his childhood Christianity as in his classical education and adolescent romanticism, is implicitly or explicitly expressed in many of his writings, including writings from every major period of his career. We already encounter it in "Paolo" and "Religion":

> This love that burns within me is the divine flame
> That has ruled this universe for the last six thousand years. (XV, 912)

> If love is the law of all nature,
> If it burns in your heart like a devouring flame,
> Then to love is why each creature is born.
> So love! Love! That's the secret word.
> ....
> Everything follows the great law: appears, loves, and fades away. (XV, 925)

In "Du progrès dans les sciences et dans la poésie," his first major literary manifesto, he speaks of the immediate intuition poets have of the ultimate moral truth—"love, the greatest love, the *caritas* of the Latins" (X, 312). In *La Faute de l'abbé Mouret,* his conception of love as the unique imperative, the great end of all being, is reflected in Serge's answer to Albine's question as to why he loves her: "Well, we have no other business. We love each other because our whole purpose in life is to love each other" (III, 153). Identifying sap not only with life, but also with love, Véronique, the heroine of *Messidor* (1894), proclaims to her son Guillaume and his bride Hélène: "Dear son, dear daughter, it's love that makes life, love alone is the sap of the world. Love each other, be each other's joy, strength, and fecundity" (XV, 580). In *Fécondité* (1899), love is more than ever extolled as the primal universal force:

> From the limitless sky, from the palpitation of the stars, descended the law of universal mating, the attraction that rules the worlds. . . . The whole soul of the universe resides in desire, the force that sustains matter, that makes out of the atoms an intelligence, a power, a sovereignty. (VIII, 91)

The novel's hero and heroine, the archetypal lovers Mathieu and Marianne, had loved each other, Zola tells us, "with that inextinguishable fire with which the universe burns, so that there may be continual creation" (VIII, 500). In *Vérité,* he is still expressing much the same idea: "The central hearth of the world is in this universal flame of desire and union" (VIII, 1148). In an interview published in *La Revue Blanche* of March 1, 1902, only six months before he died, he said, once again voicing essentially the same conviction, "Desire is what sustains the world, what engenders . . ." (XII, 745).

It is not surprising that his cult of love, in itself or in combination with one or more of his other cults, also tended to assume in his thought the proportions of a veritable religious faith. In "Un Coup de vent," the young lovers Stephen and Mimi are united by love into a single soul and transported "in a divine transport to the feet of God" (IX, 887). In "Religion," the truth that love is the supreme law of nature is presented in the form of a divine revelation (XV, 925). In *La Faute de l'abbé Mouret*, when Serge and Albine copulate under the sacred Tree of Fecundity, they become one with "the begetting forces of the world . . . the very forces of the earth" (III, 175). In a review of Maupassant's *Des vers*, Zola accuses those who had objected to the eroticism of Maupassant's poetry of committing a sacrilege: "In our shivering morality, we have come to look upon the coupling and engenderings of the earth as shameful. How absurd! It is God himself for whom we blush, because desire comes from God!" (XII, 615). In *Fécondité*, Mathieu and Marianne are metaphorically transformed whenever they make love into a temple—the holy dwelling place of "divine desire" (VIII, 500). In *Travail*, Luc makes the cult of love into one of the main components of the "Religion of Humanity" that he founds as a substitute for Christianity, replacing the Lord's Prayer with his and Josine's regularly repeated prayer to Divine Love (VIII, 849).

The third great indwelling principle in Zola's monistic reality was work. We have to do here with still another nearly lifelong cult[53] which developed at times into a form of pantheism. According to Zola, work was not only, as for Voltaire's Martin, a means of distracting oneself from metaphysical anguish by productive labor,[54] but also the source of all health and strength.[55] Moreover, we often find Zola giving in to a tendency to "tie in" work, as R. J. Lifton might say,[56] ever more inextricably with his other cults, including his cults of nature, life, and love. He defined *work* very broadly. *Work* meant in his vocabulary not only what we usually think of as work, but also labor in the physiological sense—the labor of childbirth.[57] Furthermore, it is evident in a number of his writings that not only childbirth, but all activities, human or nonhuman, contributing to the perpetuation of life were, for him, forms of work: lovers mating to produce a child, flowers manufacturing seeds, seeds thrusting up through the soil, leaves growing, rivers flowing, the sun rising. "Look at this flower at our feet," Jean Gourdon's uncle Lazare tells him. "For you, it is a delightful fragrance. For me, it is a form of work. It is doing its job by producing its share of life, a little black seed that will work in its turn, next spring" (IX, 456). Throughout Zola—*La Faute de l'abbé Mouret*, *L'Œuvre*, *La Terre*, *Fécondité*, or *Travail* for example—we encounter reflections, amplifications, and variations of the same basic idea.[58]

But in the tradition of Saint-Simon, Zola also conceived of society as a giant "workshop," "building yard," or "concert of industries."[59] He repeatedly expands this family of metaphors, moreover, to include all nature: "The earth is a vast workshop which never shuts down," Jean's uncle remarks in the same passage from which we have just quoted (IX, 456). In *Travail*, Luc, inspired by the same image, rhetorically asks: "Is not the universe an immense workshop which never lies idle, in which the infinitely small workers accomplish every day gigantic amounts of labor, in which matter ceaselessly bestirs itself, fabricates, engenders everything from the simplest ferments to the most perfect creatures?" (VIII, 668, 669). Participation in this great common task is, he insists in his later works, the prime raison d'être of each of us. Life, indeed— he was sometimes led to assert—has no other meaning, no other aim. Even if we did not want to take part, we could not but do so. No one, no thing, can remain idle. We are all, whether we like it or not, caught up, swept along, assigned a function, put to work. Whoever does not work, whoever drops out of the great common labor, ipso facto is doomed to disappear, to be rejected like a defective tool or machine part, in order to make way for a more indispensable worker. Each of us is, like a bee, born only for the infinitessimal—yet useful—sum of energy that he or she can contribute to the hive. If nature created each of us, it was because she still needed one more worker. Any other explanation of why we are here, Zola tended to believe when his cult of work was paramount in his thought, is as erroneous as it is prideful.[60]

If, as he stated in his notes for *Le Docteur Pascal*, life is movement,[61] then it follows, as he himself was quick to point out, that work is the very movement of life.[62] Since in the same notes he equates life with God, he would have had to admit, therefore, that work is, if not God also, at least the movement of God. But he had hardly finished *Le Docteur Pascal* before, in his speech of May 18, 1893, to the Association Générale des Etudiants, he was already making work itself into the center of his religious faith, proposing what he would call in *Travail* "The Religion of Work" (VIII, 669). And it is clear from *Travail* that at least by the time he wrote this second "Gospel" he had very definitely come to think of work and God as one: "savior, creator, and regulator of the world. . . . work our king, work our only guide, our only master, our only god" (VIII, 954, 955).

Can we not quite legitimately discern reflections of one or more of these same interrelated yet somewhat divergent pantheistic visions in *Germinal*? Can we not regard this novel as in part a product of the same tendency, first of all, to conceive of the world, nature, reality, as a single whole of closely interrelated parts with nothing beyond it and, secondly, to look upon either this Great Whole or one or another of its three leading indwelling principles— life, love, and work—as identical with God?

Certainly, even those critics who may question whether *Germinal* can be absolutely proven to be a pantheistic work strictly speaking must admit that it expresses quite as unmistakably as most of Zola's other major novels the same monism which in many of his writings does assume an unmistakably pantheistic form. Indeed, in no other major novel does he employ more intensively most of the poetic procedures that he uses elsewhere to suggest the tight kinship, the strong affinities, the common destiny uniting everything with everything else.

The epically vast cast of characters includes numerous animals—Bonnemort's yellow horse, the chaffinches competing in the singing contest, the red cat that startles us as it leaps out of the shadows just before the collapse of Le Voreux, the dog howling during the same disaster, Souvarine's pet rabbit, Pologne, and the two mine horses Bataille and Trompette. Zola, true to his monistic vision of reality (and the immense sense of solidarity with animals that went along with this vision), gives these dumb creatures an important place in the narrative, thoroughly integrating them, as he would have said, into "the great ark." As if to drive home the point of our common nature, he shows them, like all his other fictional animals, suffering and loving along with his human characters, sharing with them some of the same sentiments and dreams, completing them, confounded with them, caught up in the same life, subject to the same fate. The same bitterly cold March wind that makes Etienne's hands bleed in the opening scene blows up on end the hair of Bonnemort's long-suffering horse's coat. Both the old man and the horse move with the same somnambulistic motions. The hundred and eighty finches, blinded, each in its darkened cage, egged on to sing in such furious rivalry that some collapse and die, are victims of the same exploitative system as their owners, the Marchiennes nailworkers, and the Montsou miners cheering them on. Bataille and Trompette labor along with the human workers in the endless subterranean night, and their friendship with each other has something nobly human about it. They share with the human workers the same longings for deliverance, the same obsessive dreams of sunlight and green fields. Bataille's and Catherine's death scenes complement each other, reinforce each other. Each is as memorable as the other. Pologne's suffering as Jeanlin drags her along with a piece if string tied round her neck, "on her belly or her back, just like a pull-toy" (V, 225; Sig., 224), is as excruciating to watch as any human martyrdom, and when Souvarine pales at the thought that he has just, without knowing it, devoured his pet, cooked up in Madame Rasseneur's stew, there is nothing funny about it. We sympathize with his shock and grief.[63]

But the cast of *Germinal* not only contains animals; it also includes, quite as much as any other Zola novel, representatives of the vegetable and mineral kingdoms: the beets and wheat, the thick vegetation around the abandoned Réquillart mine shaft (V, 114), the giant beeches and frozen moss of the Forest of Vandame, the mines, the wind, fire, and rain, the Torrent, the clouds, moon, sun, and stars. And here, too, Zola, undoubtedly spurred by the same monism, poetically erases the distinctions separating the different categories of reality, decompartmentalizing creation, endowing plants and so-called inanimate objects with attributes we normally ascribe to man or beast. As we have seen in Chapter ii, the giant beeches, the moon, the sky, are capable of feeling, if nothing else, at least a vast indifference to human woes. Marcel Girard is probably right in intimating that the thick vegetation, full of copulating couples, around the rim of the Réquillart shaft represents in Zola's imagination the mine monster's pubic hair (V, 114, 115; Sig., 102).[64] The engine of Le Voreux squatting solidly on its masonry base becomes in Part VII, Chapter iii, a reclining giant. Nor must we forget the train of carts and the black flood water that turn into reptiles, or how, toward the end of the novel, the vision of the mines as hell gives way to that of the earth as a giant womb, still another biological image.[65]

Moreover, like La Lison, Jacques's beloved locomotive in *La Bête humaine*, for example, or the heroic shattered oaks in *La Débâcle*, plants and objects in *Germinal* are caught up in the same drama as man and beast. In this hungry novel, we recall, even the winds in Part I, Chapter i, cry famine. In the mob scenes in Part V, even the sun shares in the carnage, soaking the rampaging strikers in the blood of its dying light. At the sight of the murdered soldier Jules, the clouds flee in horror (V, 323; Sig., 335). Just before Le Voreux goes down, watched by the aghast crowd, the weathercock on the headframe creaks in the wind "with a tiny shrill cry—the single, sad voice of these huge buildings destined to die" (V, 367; Sig., 384). Then the square tower housing the "gasping" drainage pump falls over "on its face like a man cut down by a cannonball." The engine, torn from its masonry base, its limbs outspread, struggles against death. "It moved," Zola tells us, "it stretched its connecting rod, its giant knee, as though to rise, but then it died—was shattered and engulfed" (V, 368; Sig., 386). The Montsou strike is not just an isolated human event, but a universal disturbance, a giant storm involving all nature as well as man, foreshadowed in the sea-tempest imagery of the overturelike first chapter—the wind coming in "mid-sea bursts," the "blinding darkness of the shadows" buffeting Etienne on the jetty-straight road (V, 23; Sig., 5)—and reaching two climaxes in the human flood thundering across the plain in Part V and the cosmic deluge evoked in Part VII.

Furthermore, Zola not only brings out the animality of man (as we have seen in Chapter ii), but also transforms human characters into vegetables and minerals. In Part IV, Chapter viii, the crowd of strikers is poetically turned into a wave, a flood, a stormy sea. Elsewhere, Bonnemort becomes "an old tree twisted by the wind and the rain" (V, 310; Sig., 321). La Brûlé, her breast torn open by a soldier's bullet, falls forward, "crackling like dry firewood" (V, 337; Sig., 351). Just after Le Voreux drops into the abyss, members of the fleeing, shrieking crowd are swept along by horror "like piles of dry leaves" (V, 368; Sig., 386). Chaval's corpse looks like "the black hump of a pile of slack" (V, 388; Sig., 409). Along with endowing beasts, plants, and so-called inanimate things with qualities of beings higher up on the scale of creation, Zola obviously felt obliged to do the reverse. Here, too, we are justified in perceiving possible evidence of his monism—with its attendant compulsion to emphasize with metaphor and simile and every other poetic device at his disposal the essential oneness of all being. In *Germinal*, just as much as in many of Zola's other writings, we are introduced, it would seem, into a monistic reality, a reality in which everything is related, everything shares in the attributes and destiny of everything else, everything is part of the same unity.[66]

Along with Zola's monism—and monism, as I have noted, is an essential part of any pantheistic conception of the world—*Germinal* also very probably expresses Zola's pantheistic worship of nature.

On a certain level, the chief protagonist of the novel is not, as some would say, Etienne or, as others have maintained, the embattled colliers of Montsou (or, more precisely, the whole modern industrial proletariat, for which they stand), but Nature, Earth, the Great Whole. The mass lovemaking that constantly goes on around the abandoned Réquillart mine shaft is, Zola explains, Nature's own doing:

> They would settle down, elbow to elbow, without paying any attention to their neighbors, and it was as though all around this lifeless machine, next to this shaft weary of spewing forth coal, the powers of creation were taking their revenge— unbridled love, under the lash of instinct, planting babies in the bellies of girls scarcely more than children themselves. (V, 115; Sig., 102)

Reviving forgotten beliefs, the miners entrapped by the inundation of Le Voreux invoke the earth, "for," as Zola goes on to say, "it was the earth that was avenging itself, making the blood flow from the vein because one of the arteries had been severed" (V, 381; Sig., 401).[67] Twice in the text, the proletariat is referred to as "a force of nature":

> Yes, all this was what was passing along the road like a force of nature, and the terrible blast of it was striking them [the bourgeois] full in the face. (V, 277; Sig., 283)

> . . . he [Etienne] was afraid of them, of this enormous, blind, irresistible mass of people rushing onward like a natural force, sweeping everything before it, overriding rules and theories. (V, 347; Sig., 363)

Earth, Zola's symbol par excellence of Nature, the Great Whole, also dominates the concluding vision of the novel, with its evocation of men and plants surging forth from earth's womb. Since Zola seems, as we know, to have chosen very carefully the last word of each of his novels, it is also significant that *Germinal*, like *La Terre*, that great canticle to Goddess Earth, ends with the word *earth*.

But as we study *Germinal* in the light of Zola's pantheism, which, as he possibly would have been the first to admit, was not at all systematic, we would also seem to find him exalting the three major indwelling principles of his monistic universe, life, love, and work, each of which, as we have observed, he tended to sacralize and even in turn to deify.

To say that *Germinal* expresses Zola's rejection of the traditional Western belief in numerous individual lives, individual souls, in favor of the concept of a single, universal life, a single, universal soul, simply because he himself as much as says so in his letter of March 14, 1885, to Jules Lemaitre would be to succumb to what has rightly been called the intentional fallacy. Obviously, works of art do not always do exactly what their creators want them to do. Yet we do not have to know of this letter to come away from a reading of *Germinal* with the impression that it is indeed a unanimistic novel, a novel portraying the world as endowed with a single all-pervasive life, a single all-pervasive soul—Sandoz' "immense ark, where everything is animated by the breath of every being" (V, 567).

Most of the poetic procedures which, as we have seen, Zola uses in *Germinal* and elsewhere probably to suggest the tight kinships, the common movements, the shared destiny uniting all things might also, needless to say, be cited as expressions of his pantheistic vitalism, or unanimism: the winds endowed with voices, the sun's light turning into blood, the mutual reveries of men and beasts, the absorption of individuals into larger entities—e.g., a wave, a sea, a starry serpent, "a single, compact, swarming mass" (V, 276; Sig., 282).

Is it not also significant in this respect that in the last paragraph of *Germinal,* where the symbolic mode is clearly ascendant, there appears, along with the word *earth,* the word *sap,* which, as we have seen, connoted for Zola as for many other poets, the cult of universal life? (". . . There was a whispering rush of overflowing sap . . .") Is it not just as noteworthy that the word *life* itself, clearly used in a collective sense, also figures in the same resounding *gerbe* of words sacred to Zola?

> . . . Now the April sun was high in the sky, blazing gloriously, warming up the teeming earth. Life was springing from her nourishing flank, buds were bursting into green leaves, fields were trembling under the push of the grass. (V, 405; Sig., 428)

As we read this, can we not almost hear Zola once again exclaiming: "Why not have faith in life!" Do we not have here, as Henri Mitterand has suggested, part of one of the possible morals of the novel?[68]

It is true that those critics who question whether *Germinal* is a unanimistic work could point out that the word *soul* employed in senses associated with traditional psychology occurs (if my count is correct) four times in *Germinal*:

> . . . the daredevils who were bold enough to look down these cracks at night swore they could see flames—the condemned *souls* roasting in the fire below. (V, 244; Sig., 245)

Slowly his vanity at being their leader, his feeling that he constantly had to think for them, was setting him apart and creating within him the *soul* of one of those bourgeois whom he so despised. (V, 296; Sig., 305)

In the center of the great empty area rose Le Voreux. Not a living *soul*, not a sound—a desert; the doors and windows, left open, showed the emptiness inside ... (V, 367; Sig., 384) `

Forgotten superstitions reawakened in their terrified hearts [literally, "these frantic *souls*"]. (V, 381; Sig., 401)

However, the first time that the word *soul* is used, it is, as we can see, in indirect discourse. Zola himself does not see the souls of the damned roasting in Tartaret; he is simply reporting the testimony of those superstitious individuals who claim to have done so. The second and third times he uses the word, it is clearly in the sense of *spirit, character, set of mind,* or, simply, *person* or *living being.* A belief on Zola's part in the existence of individual souls is no more implied necessarily than a belief in Woden, the Ptolemaic system, or the physiology of the four cardinal humors is when we say, "Wednesday," "sunrise," or "a man of sanguine humor." The phrase "frantic souls" in the fourth sentence just cited is harder to explain. But here again we must not necessarily infer a reversion by Zola to traditional psychology. If there was such a lapse, it was certainly inadvertent as well as momentary. Raised in the Christian religion, writing in a language molded by the Judeo-Christian and Greco-Roman traditions, Zola could hardly have completely eliminated all vestiges of these traditions from his writings. It is more likely, however, that we have to do in this fourth instance once more with nothing but a common usage, a mere linguistic convention. As the translator suggests, the word *soul* is probably synonymous here with *heart.*[69]

Our impression that *Germinal* does indeed reflect Zola's religious—or at least quasi-religious—vitalism is reinforced, moreover, by other considerations. Only two or three years after he composed this novel, he conceived the idea of writing a novel exalting fecundity and pleading the right to life of every potential human being,[70] a project that ultimately bore fruit in the first of his "Gospels," *Fécondité.*[71] The intuition at the core of this later work, that the capacity to produce or propagate life abundantly is essential to social progress, is certainly already shadowed forth in *Germinal.* The characters representing capital are infecund. Deneulin has only two children, Lucie and Jeanne. Cécile, the Grégoires' only child, is a late arrival. Monsieur and Madame Hennebeau, that "Ceres gilded by autumn" (V, 168; Sig., 160), are childless. In contrast, the proletarians are constantly multiplying. The Maheus alone have seven children. Herein undoubtedly lies the chief source of that new blood, that superior freshness and strength which, as Etienne speculates in the final pages of the novel, could ensure the proletariat's ultimate victory. Surely this hope is also implicit in the book's concluding images: workers growing up through the soil like wheat, seeds bursting everywhere, sap flowing in torrents. Is it not symptomatic of Zola's cult of life, furthermore, that it is indeed precisely with *these* images that the novel ends—not with the destruction of the mine, Catherine's death, the failure of the strike, the humiliation of the defeated strikers, but with these symbols of the enduring strength of life, life pouring forth even in the midst of defeat and death, life stronger than ever, making the earth throb and tremble, filling it with new strength, hope, and joy?

Furthermore, it need hardly be pointed out that *Germinal* contributes just as much as any other *Rougon-Macquart* novel to the creation of that pantheistic optic which I have associated with Zola's cult of life and which, as I have noted, is one of the chief peculiarities of the *Rougon-Macquart* considered as a single work of art. As elsewhere in the series, Zola would seem to be striving in *Germinal* to make us see his fictional world not through just one, two, or three pairs of eyes, like most other novelists, but through a veritable host of eyes, symbolically evoking thereby the Argos-like vision of universal life, or universal soul, itself. Etienne may be the character with whom we are most frequently led to identify ourselves in *Germinal,* but he is by no means the only one. Throughout the novel, Zola is constantly shifting from one viewpoint character to another, Etienne, Bonnemort, Etienne, Catherine, Etienne, Maheu, Etienne, and little by little as the novel progresses the overall number of viewpoint characters becomes legion. We witness events not only through the eyes of individuals, but also through the collective eye of crowds— in the Plan-des-Dames, the heart of Montsou, an entrance to Le Voreux. Especially during the mob scene in the heart of Montsou, in the street just outside the Director's house, in Part V, Chapter vi—the scene that reaches a climax in the castration of Maigrat's corpse—Zola succeeds in making our vision truly multiple, all pervasive. We have the illusion of viewing the events which transpire during this scene not only from various points within the crowd, but also from various points around it—the window from behind which peers Madame Maigrat, for example, or the door of Tison's, where Rasseneur, Zacharie, and Philomène are standing, or the shuttered windows of the manager's house, where the Hennebeaus and their guests are looking on. It is as though Zola had been determined to include in this group optic all the major types and classes affected by the strike, just as, in *Les Rougon-Macquart* taken as a whole, he induces us to observe its central event, the Second Empire, through the eyes of all the various principal types and classes of people involved in it. The same, I suspect, may be said of the entire novel, not just some of its major episodes. We experience its central drama, the Montsou strike, through the widest possible range of subjectivities. We stand in the shoes of all the main sorts of participants—the young and the old, men and women, bourgeois, proletarians, soldiers, priests. As elsewhere in Zola we are even invited to identify ourselves with animals—Bataille, for example, or Pologne—and so-called inanimate objects are, as we have seen, endowed with sight—the two huge yellow eyes formed by the headframe lamps in the receiving shed, the clouds fleeing in horror after Jules's murder. The total effect is indeed almost that of universal life watching itself.

Yet if *Germinal* reflects Zola's pantheistic cults of nature and life, does it not also express his equally pantheistic cult of love? Pierre-Henri Simon was surely right to suspect that this cult—which Simon refers to as Zola's "eroticism" or "Dionysiac pantheism" (V, 19, 20)—is a major aspect of *Germinal.* Not only does *Germinal* strongly communicate to us Zola's idea of passionate love ("the sovereign, the eternal love"), exemplified in Catherine and Etienne's love idyll. The novel also provides us with memorable illustrations of several of the other kinds of love which, as Zola saw it, were also part of Universal Eros: Etienne and Souvarine's friendship, for example, or Deneulin's paternal love for Lucie and Jeanne, Négrel's sense of human solidarity brought out by the mine disaster, Souvarine's love for Pologne, Bataille's friendship with Trompette, not to mention the universal embrace, the "great kiss," of the book's final paragraph.

It is evident, moreover, that Zola has spared no effort to impart an erotic significance to the central events of the novel. From beginning to end, its political, social, and economic themes are associated with dramatic and poetic elements having to do with love. The mob violence related in Part V climaxes in the Dionysiac vision of the castration of Maigrat's corpse by a group of working-class women. The knife with which Jeanlin kills Jules has the word *Love* engraved on its handle. The strikers' clash with the troops is linked with the arrival of Catherine's puberty. The account of the mine disaster in Part VII ends with Catherine and Etienne's "honeymoon" and the suggestion that she may have died pregnant.[72] The embrace of these two lovers in the entrails of the earth is followed almost immediately in the text by the fraternal embrace of Etienne and Négrel, the proletarian chieftain and his capitalist rescuer,[73] and this event is followed in turn by the evocation of the aforementioned universal embrace. The message would seem to be clear: even the rise of the proletariat, the principal theme of *Germinal,* is a manifestation of the primordial Eros, the ceaselessly creative divine force that burns eternally at the heart of reality.

Finally, can we not also regard *Germinal* as an expression of Zola's cult of work, which also grew in his mind, as we have seen, into a veritable pantheistic religion? As in "Le Forgeron," *L'Assommoir, L'Œuvre, Travail,* and the other short stories and novels that he wrote while under the influence of this cult, *Germinal* exalts work. We may be particularly tempted to compare it in this respect to *L'Assommoir.* Like Gervaise, Coupeau, Goujet, and the other characters of *L'Assommoir,* Etienne, Catherine, Maheu, La Maheude, and the other members of the proletarian cast of *Germinal* would, as Erich Auerbach has reminded us, have been considered by Boileau as suitable only for low farce. Yet as Auerbach also points out in the same study, Zola has made them into the leading figures of great historical tragedy—thus ascribing to them roles reserved traditionally for persons of high rank or birth.[74]

Indeed, could it not even be argued that of all Zola's supreme values, nature, life, love, and work, each of which he tended to make into the deity of his monistic world, none is more central in *Germinal* than work? *Germinal* is above all a novel about work and workers. It strongly suggests that the destiny not only of modern society, but also of the cosmos, is bound up with that of the working class and the holy principle which this class comes closer to embodying than any other. The strike, as we have noted, is a storm involving the whole of nature. Furthermore, is there not, especially in the final paragraph, to which I must refer again here, a resurgence of Zola's conception of all of nature as one vast workshop? It is, in fact, hard to believe that he could have written the novel's ending without having had in mind the entire lyrical, mystical passage in "Les Quatre Journées de Jean Gourdon" where he first expresses this concept through Jean's uncle Lazare:

> Spring itself teaches you this lesson. The earth is a vast workshop which never shuts down. Look at this flower at our feet. For you it is a delightful fragrance. For me it is a form of work. It is doing its job by producing its share of life, a little black seed that will work in its turn, next spring. And now interrogate the vast horizon. All this joyousness comes from taking part in the life-creation process. If the countryside is smiling, it's because she's starting all over again her eternal task. Can you hear her now breathing hard, active, impatient to get on with it? The leaves are sighing, the flowers are hurrying, the wheat goes on growing without ever pausing to take a rest. All the plants are competing to see which can grow the fastest. And the water, the river, which is also alive, hastens to help out in the common task, and the young sun rising in the sky is in charge of enlivening the eternal labor of the workers. (IX, 456)

In both this passage and the final paragraph of *Germinal*, we come across similar or identical constellations of images and ideas: spring, rising sun, joy, seeds, wheat, birth, growth, even black (the little black seed that will work in its turn, next spring, and the black avenging army germinating in the furrows, sprouting for the harvests of the coming century)—all associated with the idea of work, of labor.[75]

It may, of course, be objected that nothing in this chapter conclusively resolves the question as to whether *Germinal* may be termed a pantheistic novel in a strict sense. It is true that nowhere in the text does Zola explicitly identify nature or any of its chief indwelling principles as God. It is also true that Zola's metaphysical and religious thought was extraordinarily unstable, as we have already begun to see in this book. Even the fact that both *L'Œuvre* and *La Terre*, the two novels that Zola wrote just after finishing

Germinal, are indisputably pantheistic works does not, therefore, absolutely prove that *Germinal* must be one also. Those readers who do not wish to see in *Germinal* an expression of Zola's pantheism are consequently free to do so. But at the very least it must be admitted that *Germinal could* express Zola's pantheism, that there is much in it which *could* point toward the overt pantheism of several of his subsequent works, including *L'Œuvre* and *La Terre,* or echo the equally overt pantheism of some of his earlier writings, the short story from which I have just quoted, for example. In this connection, Zola's insertion of the word *sap* in the final paragraph of *Germinal* seems to me particularly significant. For it is a word which not only in Zola but also in many other writers ancient or modern, including Hugo, his first literary hero, is weighted with pantheistic connotations.

4

The Geological Gospel

There is, moreover, a strong probability that Zola was particularly influenced in *Germinal* by the very specific quasi-religious vision of man, nature, and history that he had derived in his youth primarily from geology. I have in mind the complex of ideas which we may already find him developing in his plans for *La Genèse* and which he expresses most completely and systematically in the proposal for a new philosophical and religious faith that he first published in *Le Salut Public* of October 14, 1865.

As we know from his letter of June 15, 1860, to Baille, the idea for *La Genèse* had occurred to him at least as early as 1857—the same year that he had won the top prize for excellence in physics, chemistry, and natural history at the Collège Bourbon in Aix.[1] According to the brief summary of his intentions that he had included in the same letter, this impossibly ambitious epic, of which he would never write more than the first eight verses, would have covered nothing less than the whole story of creation, past, present, and future. It would, moreover—or so we may gather—have been very much in accord with some of the most current philosophical, historical, and scientific ideas of the time: continuous, universal progress; a temporalized Great Chain of Being; the hypothesis that man is just the latest in an immense series of life forms and will be succeeded by a superman; a catastrophism largely rooted in the theories of Cuvier and his followers;[2] and the Kantian notion that, contrary to what the Bible tells us, the divine labor of creation is still going on.[3] "It will have three cantos, which I shall be pleased to call: *The Past, The Present,* and *The Future,*" the young poet had written Baille.

The first Canto (*The Past*) will cover the successive creation of all the life forms that preceded man. In this part, I shall recount all the cataclysms that have taken place on the globe, everything that geology teaches us about the whole regions that have been destroyed and the animals that have been swallowed up in their debris. The second Canto (*The Present*) will take humanity at its inception, in the savage state, and will follow its story all the way up to civilized times; what physiology teaches us about physical man, what philosophy teaches us about man's spiritual, intellectual nature, will be included, at least in an abridged form, in this part. Finally, the third and last Canto (*The Future*) will be a magnificent divagation.

Using as my basis the fact that the object of God's handiwork has done nothing
but improve from the moment that the first forms of life, those zoophytes, those
shapeless, barely alive beings, were created, up to man, his most recent creation,
I shall imagine that this creature is not the Creator's last word and that after the
extinction of the human race new, more perfect beings will come to inhabit this
world. A description of these beings, their mores, etc. (*Corr.*, I, 182)[4]

The poet's supreme purpose, as we may see from the first eight verses of *La
Genèse*—the only part of this epic which, as I have said, he had managed to
compose—would have been to glorify the handiwork of God, the divine Creative Principle, or First Force, and, by discovering his thought as revealed in
his laws, achieve closer communion with him:

THE BIRTH OF THE WORLD

I

Creative Principle, unique First Force,
Who with the breath of life made matter animate,
Thou who livest, knowing neither birth nor death,
Give me the golden wing of the inspired prophet.
I shall sing of thy work and on it traced
In time and space I shall read thy thought.
I shall rise toward thee, borne upwards on thy breath,
To offer thee this mortal song of immortality. (XV, 937)

When precisely Zola had abandoned this project, which would have taxed
the genius of even a Hesiod or a Lucretius, we shall probably never know.
Indeed, it could be argued, with much justification, I think, that Zola never
really did abandon it, that any study of the genesis of his major later works,
Les Rougon-Macquart, Les Trois Villes, and *Les Quatre Evangiles* (which
are really one vast single work), must take *La Genèse* into consideration as an
important starting point, that they are partly an outgrowth or realization of
it, that, in other words, it did not die, but only metamorphosed, merging
with other projects inspired by other visions.[5] But whether or not every
student of Zola is prepared to accept this hypothesis, it must be admitted
that, if nothing else, the themes and subject matter of *La Genèse* continued
to obsess Zola and evolve in his mind long after he had given up the idea of
completing this epic as originally conceived. Although in his mature years
he would, as we know, identify himself primarily with physiology, his first
great love among the sciences was obviously geology, a newly born science
which, for him and many of his contemporaries, including many specialists
as well as laymen, was still more or less identical with natural history and
solidly encased in a natural theological and metaphysical framework.[6] The
would-be bard of *La Genèse* is very much in evidence in Zola's two early,
largely identical poems "Religion" and "Doute" (c. 1861), with their long,

anguished questions concerning the origin of the world and the purpose of creation. "Du progrès dans les sciences et dans la poésie," Zola's first published literary manifesto (1864), also evinces the same preoccupation with geology and its metaphysical and theological implications. It is true that by the time he wrote "Du progrès dans les sciences et dans la poésie" his philosophy of nature had somewhat evolved. What he stresses in this essay above all is the notion of the earth's ceaselessly circulating flood of life. Furthermore, whereas in *La Genèse* he would have attempted to prophesy the ultimate shape of things to come, he has now relinquished this ambition. He now dares speak only of life's "mysterious goal." Yet it is evident from this essay that at the time he wrote it the vision that he then wanted to spend his life trying to express was still profoundly geological, or natural historical, in character. The first sentence of the following excerpt would seem to echo in particular the first eight verses of *La Genèse*:

> ... in the depopulated heavens, I would show the god Infinity and the immutable laws that descend from his being and rule the worlds. The earth, divested of her coquettish attire, would no longer be anything for me but a harmonious whole where the flood of life circulates without ever diminishing, always tending toward the mysterious goal. Must I say it? I would be a scientist. I would borrow from the sciences their vast horizons, their hypotheses which are so admirable that they may perhaps be true. (X, 313)

A review published in December 1864 of two popular scientific works, Amédée Guillemin's *Le Ciel* (1864) and Alfred Frédol's *Le Monde de la mer* (1864), attests once again to the young Zola's passion for geology and its related sciences and reflects still another stage of his own evolving ideas on the subject. Regarding Laplace's theory of the origin of the universe as expounded by Guillemin, he confides that he knows of nothing more grandiosely poetic "than this scientific genesis" (X, 326). Discussing Frédol's panorama of undersea life, he cannot resist the temptation to share with us his own conception of natural history and does so in a style barely concealing the enthusiasm which it was still capable of arousing in him. He still clings to the concept of the Great Chain of Being, which had inspired the original title (or at least one of the original titles) of *La Genèse*; and he still insists on other natural historical notions that he had earlier embraced in connection with that project. But he now emphasizes the, for him, new idea that the world is the product of the colossal collective labor of *all* its creatures, starting out with the amoeba and the humble polyp. He has also embraced by now the assumption that these and all the other relatively simple creatures of the sea were designed first by nature in order to test her basic organic principles, that these primitive beings must be regarded as rough outlines of higher, more complex forms of animality. It is evident, moreover, that the hypothesis that progress has had no beginning and will have no end, that the world has always been and always will be in the process of creation, that there is no limit to the perfectibility of nature now also particularly appeals to him.

The proposal for a new secular philosophical and religious faith which, as I have said, had first appeared in *Le Salut Public* of October 14, 1865 (in a review, I should add, of Victor Duruy's *Introduction générale à l'histoire de France*), had grown out of the same long meditation as these earlier writings. In this proposal, Zola repeats most of his previous ideas on the subject but, at the same time, clearly reveals a pantheistic tendency less evident, if present at all, in his earlier formulations. In some respects, we may note in passing, the vision that this proposal for a new faith conveys to us would seem to anticipate, if not Henry Drummond, Raymond Sabatier, or, as Henri Mitterand has suggested, Teilhard de Chardin,[7] Madame Ackermann's verse epic "La Nature à l'homme," planned in mid-1864 and dated 1867, or Quinet's prose epic *La Création*, published in 1870.[8] As we read this proposal, we are also reminded of Renouvier's definition of the philosophy which, under the guise of positivism, was in fact dominant during the Second Empire: "Its spirit, its character consist of a kind of pantheism and fatalism animated and developed by the hypothesis of continual, universal progress"—to which he adds: "It is like a religion which one is trying to invent for oneself all the while pretending that one is not doing so, but that it is being imposed by history."[9] For Zola's "new faith," while retaining vestiges of the old natural theology, must definitely be placed within this mid-nineteenth-century tradition.

Since this proposal is not only one of the major expressions of Zola's philosophical and religious thought, but also, as I am maintaining in this chapter, probably an important key to the understanding and appreciation of *Germinal*, I shall reproduce it here in its entirety:

> The history of the world began with the first meeting of two atoms. For historians, the annals of a country start out with the origins of a nationality; for thinkers and philosophers, these annals go back all the way to God, the first force, and embrace the history of the formation of the soil and also the history of the creation and improvement of life forms. . . .
>
> The annals of the earth during the epochs preceding the present age are truly awe inspiring. We reckon that our own age began 6,000 years ago;[10] the creatures that came before us could trace theirs back several million years, years of conflagrations and convulsions ceaselessly going on in the bowels of the earth. There stretches out behind us a frightfully long past, more than a score of vastly different worlds, billions of peoples, an unknown, terrifying history. The world, before it got around to making us, had already existed a long time, transforming and perfecting itself. Here, no doubt, is the truly important story to be told: our few centuries of human troubles are nothing compared to the eternities that the earth and its inhabitants have traversed in the midst of flames and ruins. What is the human period to God, when he considers the ages that have preceded it? It is good to meditate on this long preface to our history: it humbles us and helps us to discern the truth.

I see in the study of geology the basis of a new faith, a faith at once philosophical and religious. No doubt, we have to do here with nothing but a hypothesis; but this hypothesis has a truer ring to it than all those other hypotheses that have been accepted as truths. Theodicies, human religions relate everything to man; they make him into the center, the supreme aim of creation. In our attempts to explain the universe, we have been guided by our human pride, and what proves that the world's religions are our inventions is that each and every one of them tends to exalt man and sacrifice the entire work of creation to his interests. God, in his justice, must view through a different eye this earth which has already cost him so many centuries. We who were born only yesterday are just another small part of the immense family of his creatures and become the creature of the moment, the most perfect, if you like, but possibly not the last.

Instead of affirming that the earth and the sky have been created exclusively for our use, we ought, rather, to consider ourselves as having been created for the use of the Great Whole, the work which has gone on elaborating itself ever since the beginning of time. We are moving toward the future, a simple manifestation of life, another phase of the same creature, making creation advance one step further toward the unknown goal. There is a certain indefinable grandeur, a supreme peace, a profound joy in the idea that God is working in us, that we are preparing the earth and beings of tomorrow, that we are part of the creative process, and that on the final day we will be present to see with the entire universe the completion of the work.

It would be impossible, at the beginning of a history of man, to bring up more grandiose thoughts. I love to see our haughty struggles, our beginning and our end, confronted by what has gone on before us and what will no doubt go on after we have disappeared. The annals of the ages that have preceded us assign us our veritable place in creation, and the hypotheses that we can make about future ages are a call for justice, a summons to us to do our duty, an appeal for universal peace.

M. Victor Duruy recounts, cataclysm after cataclysm, the history of the former stages of the earth's surface. He studies the world and its life forms both at the same time, retracing step by step the formation of the soil and the formation of man. Each upheaval brings with it fragments of a continent, each race brings with it when it appears its share of life. Little by little, France takes shape, the human race is born. This took centuries and centuries. Sometimes the land was once again engulfed by the seas. Its inhabitants were destroyed. Life flagged. Finally, shortly before the last deluge, the country that we call France assumed its present configuration, "man appeared *and God rested.*"[11]

No, God did not rest. Yesterday, today, always, he is working in us and all about us. The creation continues, the work goes on, grows. The labor of the worlds is eternal. We can feel the earth in childbirth trembling under our feet. We can feel matter purifying itself in us. There are still other geographical regions waiting to be born in the earth's womb. There are inside of us, in our vague aspirations and our longing for the infinite, still other, purer, more perfect beings.[12] It is absurd to maintain that God can rest and that he lives in idleness in some corner of the sky, contemplating himself in our image, satisfied with his handiwork and unaware of the need for perfection by which we ourselves are driven.

The history of the worlds that have preceded us makes us hope for other worlds to come. We who are the present should, I repeat, find in this belief a great source of strength; for if the past reduces us to the rank of transitional creatures, the future promises the earth of which we are a part indefinite progress in the ages that lie ahead. (X, 99-101)

As it turned out, this "new faith" had unfortunately been no more capable than any of the others that Zola had developed or would develop of permanently satisfying all his spiritual needs. After he had formulated it, his metaphysical and religious ideas, as well as his scientific conceptions, had gone on evolving. Among other things, he had, as we know, become appreciably more susceptible in the following years to the influence of Darwin, who, while granting natural catastrophes a certain role in biological change, did not give them anything like the crucial importance that they had acquired in other naturalist systems, most notably, those of Cuvier and his followers. Nevertheless, the quasi-religious philosophy of universal earth history that formed the basis of this "new faith" would seem to have retained for Zola throughout much of the rest of his career a good deal of its original philosophical and religious as well as poetic appeal. He had liked this "new faith" founded on geology so much, in fact, that he had included the article in which he had set it forth, reentitled "La Géologie et l'histoire," in *Mes haines,* his first volume of selected essays, published in 1866. In January 1867, reviewing Edouard Barbier's translation of Sir John Lubbock Avebury's *Prehistoric Times,* he had observed, undoubtedly recalling "La Géologie et l'histoire": "Geology, born yesterday, will certainly become the basis of a new philosophy" (X, 709). Discussing, in February 1869 (the year he had completed his initial plans for *Les Rougon-Macquart*), Edgar Quinet's *La Création* (1870), of which he had seen the proofs, he had summarized this vast prose epic in terms strongly reminiscent of his own geological vision of universal history, observing with obvious admiration, "A simple and grandiose idea that the author has tried to make accessible to all. It is a sort of natural philosophy, a superb, broadly inclusive explanation of man and nature," and concluding (with, we may imagine, a touch of jealousy): . . . M. Edgar Quinet has found the infinity which he needed if his poet's wings were to spread freely. The book, in my opinion, will enjoy a big success" (X, 796).

Moreover, many of Zola's writings composed after "La Géologie et l'histoire" reiterate most of the principal ideas comprising the "new faith" that he proposes in it. The vision of reality that emerges from his works considered as a whole is profoundly colored by these ideas. His pantheistic belief in the unity and divinity of nature, exaltation of the universal soul, cult of work, refusal to regard man as a creation apart from the rest of animality, and insistence on the smallness of man in the great scheme of things are all elements of this "new faith." So also is his frequently repeated trust in the inevitability of progress. "I believe in the day that is now passing, and I believe in the new day that will dawn tomorrow, certain of an ever vaster expansion" (XIV, 655), he had proclaimed in *Le Figaro* of September 5, 1881. In 1892, planning

Le Docteur Pascal, the philosophical conclusion of the *Rougon-Macquart* series, he would enthusiastically adopt as his own Renan's progressionist creed as summarized by Melchior de Vogüé:

> ... Two elements, time and the tendency to progress, explain the universe. A kind of inner spring, a nisus, propels everything toward life and toward an ever more highly developed life. There exists in the universe a central consciousness which is progressively taking shape and which is capable of an unlimited "becoming."[13]

As we proceed through Zola's works, we come across over and over again expressions of the same confidence, the same almost blind faith, culminating in *Les Quatre Evangiles.* "I want a dazzling optimism," he remarks in his preliminary notes for this last series of novels. "It is the natural conclusion of all my writings" (VIII, 506).

The related notion that the act of divine creation is still not over, that the genesis of the world is still going on, that all of universal history is a cosmogony, also continued to haunt him. Before settling on the definitive title of the novel that he wrote just after *Germinal, L'Œuvre,* he considered such possible other titles, reminiscent of *La Genèse* and "La Géologie et l'histoire," as *Faire un monde (Making a World), Création (Creation), Etre Dieu (To Be God), L'Œuvre vivante (The Living Work), Les Créateurs de monde (The World Creators), La Force créatrice (The Creative Force), L'Ebauche (The Rough Outline).* The same conception of a still continuing cosmogony resurfaces in still later works such as *Le Docteur Pascal* and *Les Quatre Evangiles.* It is taken for granted by Pascal's niece Clotilde, for example—as when she passionately exclaims, "Oh, living, living, this is the great task! This is the work carried on, to be completed no doubt some evening!" (VI, 1277). It also underlies Luc's definition of the world as "the common work" and his obsessive dream of "the completed work of happiness for which we all feel within ourselves the imperious need" (VIII, 669).

The idea that the goal of universal progress, or world creation, has not been divulged to us by the divine creator, another important element of the "new faith" expounded in "La Géologie et l'histoire," also recurs in several of Zola's writings, including *La Terre* (V, 1142), *L'Argent* (VI, 658), and *Le Docteur Pascal* (VI, 1277).

There can be no doubt whatsoever, furthermore, that *La Genèse* and "La Géologie et l'histoire" are the major sources, within Zola's writings, of the catastrophism which is such a persistent feature of his vision of reality. He kept on all his life envisaging history as a bloody, violent process. The disasters of the present day and those he foresaw in the world's far-off future were, in his imagination, simply the continuation of the unending succession of eruptions, earthquakes, floods, and disasters of every other sort that had occurred in the primeval past. For example, in a short story first published in the June

1877 issue of *Le Messager de l'Europe*, he asserts that "war is like those cataclysms of the antediluvian world which prepared the world of man" (IX,
1013). Moreover, he seems to go out of his way in novels like *La Débâcle* or
Travail to imply through all the poetic resources at his command that the
upheavals of the present are just as awe inspiring as any in the earth's past.
It is as though he always had before his mind's eye while writing about the
present the fearful, Cuvier-like vision of the past eons of earth history that
he had resumed in "La Géologie et l'histoire." Even so relatively minor an
event as the collapse of the fortune of the Contesse de Guédeville and her
father, Baron Nathan, in *Vérité* is magnified in Zola's prose into "the final
tremors brought about by the end of a world" (VIII, 1437).

Furthermore, Zola not only, as we have just seen, kept on all his life portraying history as a cataclysmic process; he also clung to the assumption, also
basic to *La Genèse* and "La Géologie et l'histoire," that catastrophic violence
is cosmogonically useful, even necessary. He generally tended throughout the
rest of his career to associate the act of creation, of giving birth, with travail,
torment, convulsion, blood. It was always hard for him to imagine any significant advance occurring without atrocious dislocation and suffering. "Each
cataclysm brings with it a fragment of a continent," he had said, we recall, in
"La Géologie et l'histoire." ". . . We can feel the earth in childbirth trembling
under our feet. We can feel matter purifying itself in us." Three years later,
when he came to draw up his initial plans for *Les Rougon-Macquart,* he made
one of its principal themes the "troubled gleams of the moment," the "fatal
convulsions that attend the birth of a world."[14] Over and over again in subsequent writings, he makes much the same linkage of the idea of progress,
or world creation, and the idea of violence, as we can see from the following
examples:

> If the present moment still seems troubled . . . it is the rumbling made by the
> ceaseless rise of democracy. Democracy is the future. . . . And above all we must
> not tremble at its approach, however fierce the storm that brings it may be. The
> world was created in the midst of cataclysms. (*Le Figaro,* September 5, 1881,
> XIV, 651, 652)

> Scientifically, socially, I accepted the hypothesis of slow, simple evolution. . . . And
> it was then that first in the history of the earth, then in the history of society, I
> had to make room for the volcano, the sudden cataclysm, the sudden eruption,
> which has marked each geological phase, each historical period. One comes this
> way to realize that never has a single step forward been taken, any progress
> achieved, without the help of frightful catastrophes. (*Paris,* 1898, VII, 1322)

This geological view of history, with its insistence on the necessity, indeed
the utility, of great upheavals, made it possible for Zola to reconcile his painful
awareness of the harsh, bloody side of the unfolding history of his own day

with his belief in progress. Faith in the usefulness of violence, the dogmatic assertion that what might seem to us to be an evil is a good when properly understood in the context of universal history (of which human history is only a small part) enabled him to remain an optimist without closing his eyes to the grim aspects of nineteenth-century life. In the face of the despair voiced by the decadents and other doomsayers of his day, he could strike an attitude of hope and courage. Like a sinner eagerly embracing the purifying flames of purgatory, he could even, in a way, welcome the upheavals produced by the political, social, economic, and intellectual revolution through which Western society was going in his time. His scientific catastrophism, extended to include the history of society as well as natural history, thus fulfilled much the same consoling, reassuring function for him that the religious catastrophism of the apocalyptic tradition always has for many others.

We sense the lingering presence of this earlier Zola in *Germinal* even more than in most of Zola's other novels—the young would-be epic writer and religious innovator in love with geology and intent on communicating to us the grandiose visions that geology had inspired in him, the Zola of *La Genèse* and "La Géologie et l'histoire," especially the latter.

Germinal is to a considerable extent a geological novel. It not only, as I pointed out in the last chapter, ends with the word *earth*; it also shows us once again to what a great degree Zola possessed, along with his other scientific preoccupations, the concerns of a geologist—not to mention that aesthetic taste for mines which had been formed by the impact of geology and its related science of minerology on the romantic—or, more precisely, preromantic—sensibility.[15] He portrays in *Germinal* in comprehensive detail the geological features of the partly real, partly fictional northern French coal mining region in which the plot action unfolds: the interiors of Le Voreux and other mines, the various coals, schists, and other minerals that the miners have to deal with, the disposition of the veins, the temperature of the earth at various depths and localities. At the same time, his poetic imagination obviously delights in the same geological and mineralogical subject matter. The epic account that he gives us in Part I, Chapter iv, of Maheu, Zacharie, Levaque, and Chaval laboring in the Guillaume vein of Le Voreux is as much a masterpiece of sustained animated description as, let us say, Homer's celebrated account of Hephaestus' creation of Achilles' shield in Book 18 of the *Iliad*. But whereas in Homer we have to do with a work of art, a marvelously decorated silver shield, in Zola our eyes are fixed on a brute mineral, coal. Better than any other novelist that I know of, he shows us coal, its cruel resistance to the miner's pick, its harsh sonority under the striking steel, its heaviness, the way it crumbles as it falls, its occasional shimmer under the glow of the miners' lamps, its extraordinary blackness, its smeariness, its invasive dust. Any geologist not completely indifferent to the peculiar poetry of his profession should,

moreover, be delighted by Zola's report of Etienne's first descent into Le
Voreux, in Part I, Chapter i, or the following description of Tartaret, the burning mine, in Part V, Chapter i:

> Tartaret, at the edge of the forest, was an uncultivated wasteland of volcanic
> sterility, under which a coal mine had been burning for centuries. Its beginning
> was lost in legend, and the local miners told the following story: a fire from heaven
> had once fallen on this Sodom in the bowels of the earth—where the haulage
> girls used to indulge in obscene abominations—and it had happened so quickly
> that the girls had not had time to get out and were still flaming away at the bottom
> of that hell to this very day. The dark-red calcined rocks were covered with an
> efflorescence of alum, like a leprosy. Yellow flowers of sulfur spread from the
> edges of the fissures, and the daredevils who were bold enough to look down these
> cracks at night swore they could see flames—the condemned souls roasting in the
> fire below. Flickering lights moved along the ground; hot vapors stinking of filth
> and of the devil's foul kitchen smoked day and night . . . (V, 244; Sig., 244, 245)[16]

Nor must we forget how Zola makes one of the huge underground lakes in
the Valenciennes coal basin into another major feature of the novel's setting, the Torrent, metaphorically transforming it into a mysterious underground sea, "that subterranean sea which was the terror of the mines of the
Nord—a sea with its storms and shipwrecks, an unknown, unsounded sea that
rolled its dark waves almost a thousand feet below the sunlight" (V, 353;
Sig., 369).[17]

But if Zola shows in *Germinal* his fascination at once scientific and poetic
with the internal structure of the earth, i.e., its morphology, he also lets us
see once again in this novel something of his old obsession with the history of
the earth. His development of the storm theme culminating in the inundation
of Le Voreux could be interpreted as still another expression in his mature
works of the same geological catastrophism, reminiscent of Cuvier, that is such
a notable feature of the quasi-religious vision of history first fully set forth in
"La Géologie et l'histoire." On the one hand, spurred no doubt by recollec-
tions of Vulcanism, he metaphorically transforms the yawning, fifty-foot deep
cavity formed by the collapse of Le Voreux into the "crater of an extinct
volcano" (V, 368; Sig., 386). On the other hand, inspired, we may suppose,
by Neptunism, he links the inundation of Le Voreux with the primordial
floods that he had long ago evoked in "La Géologie et l'histoire":

> They could hear the thunderous sound of cave-ins at every moment. The entire
> mine was shaken, its narrow guts bursting with the immense flood that was gorging
> it. Forced back into the ends of the galleries, the air accumulated, became com-
> pressed, and exploded with great violence among the splintered rocks and the
> churned-up soil. It was the terrifying din of internal cataclysms—like a part of the
> prehistoric struggle when floods were turning the earth upside down, burying the
> mountains under the plains. (V, 384; Sig., 404)[18]

It could be argued that *Germinal* also reflects, like most of Zola's other novels, the rejection of anthropocentric creation theories that is another major feature of the "new faith" proposed in "La Géologie et l'histoire." Far from glorifying mankind, far from holding that man is a creation apart, that the world was made for man, that man is the lord of creation, Zola does everything possible in *Germinal,* as we have seen, to reintegrate man in nature, to demonstrate that man is not necessarily superior to other forms of life, and to suggest that man is being used by nature for her own transcendent aims. Indeed, there may be some readers for whom the most admirable and one might almost say "human" characters in the novel are not human characters at all, but Bataille and Trompette, particularly Bataille, the "old philosopher" as the miners call him, endowed as he is with a gift far superior to theirs for finding his way around in the darkness of the mine.

Moreover, as in "La Géologie et l'histoire," *La Terre, La Débâcle, Le Docteur Pascal,* and other writings, *Germinal* leaves the ultimate goal of history wrapped in obscurity. It is impossible to read the novel without being compelled to ask questions concerning the meaning, the course, the outcome of history. No other work of fiction gives us a stronger impression of being caught up in history, rushed onward by history, overwhelmed by history. Just as someone who has fallen into a raging uncharted river and is swept on by it urgently wants to know where it is taking him, we want to know where the great historical events with which the novel is concerned are taking mankind. What is more, Etienne, Souvarine, and other central characters are tormented by the same pressing need. As we glimpse Etienne for the last time, walking off into the April sunrise, he is still struggling to make sense out of history, still looking for some more satisfying explanation of what the world is all about than Darwin's:

> Could Darwin be right? Was the world merely a battlefield, with the strong devouring the weak for the sake of the beauty and perpetuation of the species? The question continued to trouble him, though he had supposedly, with scientific smugness, settled it. (V, 403; Sig., 426)

As we know, Zola was himself as susceptible as any of the numerous other prophets or would-be prophets of his age to the urge to prophesy the future. "The great force of genius," he said in *Le Voltaire* of October 14, 1879, "consists in being at the head of one's century, of going in the same direction, in outdistancing it even" (XII, 369). In *Le Figaro* of June 6, 1896, he said that he was not a scientist or an historian, if the truth were told, but only a novelist whose task was to "gather together on a subject everything floating in the air . . . and to resume and create things and creatures to such a point that it becomes possible to formulate the hypothesis of tomorrow, to announce the future" (XIV, 800). At the outset of his preparatory notes for

Germinal, he states, "I want it to predict the future."[19] His intentions in
La Terre were equally prophetic: "Say that I have the outlandish ambition to
write a book that will contain everything about peasant life, their life, loves,
politics, religion, past, present, future" (XIV, 1452). *Les Quatre Evangiles* was,
from the start, to be his prophetic work par excellence: ". . . the natural
conclusion of all my works: after the long investigation of reality, a prolonga-
tion into the future" (VIII, 506). Again, as toward the end of his life he drew
up plans for still another important work, a vast series of plays to be entitled
La France en marche, he aspired to rend the veil concealing the shape of things
to come. He concluded his initial summary of what he wanted to do in this
new series with the words, "Where we are, where we are going" (XV, 844).
And we know that his prophetic ambitions were not limited to deciphering
just the immediate future. Dr. Pascal, his alter ego in the novel of the same
name, is obsessed with the question of the final end of things. So also is Pierre
Froment, the hero of *Les Trois Villes* and another major fictional incarnation
of Zola. In fact, one of the main purposes of this huge trilogy was, in Zola's
mind, to treat the subject of, as he put it, "What humanity can hope to gain
through evolution . . . the ultimate goal . . . What we can hope for."[20] In short,
Zola liked to imagine that he had the genius to provide the chaotic, rapidly
changing society of his day with a true vision of what it was to be and, going
still further, to relate the transformations that he and his contemporaries saw
taking place around them to the great scenario of natural history. Yet in
Germinal, as in *La Terre* or *Le Docteur Pascal,* for example, this prophetic
urge was effectively countered—or so we may infer from his refusal to commit
himself on the matter in these novels—by his suspicion, going back to "La
Géologie et l'histoire," that the ultimate goal of history was something that
the human mind could never know.

Both *Germinal* and "La Géologie et l'histoire" communicate to us, furthermore, much the same sense of temporal and spacial immensity—that acute
awareness of the vastness of time and space which, as we know, modern
geology has brought with it, revolutionizing traditional Western concepts
of the universe and its temporal setting. The flat plain drowned in darkness
over which Etienne approaches Montsou in Part I, Chapter i, seems to go on
forever. As Zola points out, the miners laboring in the depths of Le Voreux
are only ants in a "giant anthill" (V, 48; Sig., 32). During the strike meeting
at the Plan-des-Dames, the "profound silence of the deep forest" embraces the
crowd's "cry of Massacre"; the "hurricane of the three thousand voices"
fades away "in the pure light of the moon" (V, 236; Sig., 236). The destruction of Le Voreux, symbolic of the revolutionary upheavals to be brought
about by the revolt of the proletariat, is, as he suggests by identifying it metaphorically with the great cataclysms of geological history (thus also identifying
the time of the novel with geological time), just another in the vast series of
catastrophes which has transformed the globe repeatedly over countless millions

of years and will no doubt go on doing so for countless millions of years to come.[21]

Moreover, was not Zola, when he wrote *Germinal*, still intrigued, as he so clearly is in *Le Docteur Pascal*, for example, by the Kantian notion, central to the "new faith" expounded in "La Géologie et l'histoire," that the genesis of the world, contrary to what the Bible tells us, is still going on? In "La Géologie et l'histoire," he had written, we recall:

> No, God did not rest. Yesterday, today, always, he is working in us and all about us. The creation continues, the work goes on, grows. The labor of the worlds is eternal. We can feel the earth in childbirth trembling under our feet, we can feel matter purifying itself in us. There are still other geographical regions waiting to be born in the earth's womb. There are inside of us, in our vague aspirations and our longing for the infinite, still other, purer, more perfect beings.... (X, 101)

The same vision of the world as a still unfinished piece of work, a work still in a state of genesis, would seem to lie behind the numerous analogies that *Germinal* suggests between the rise of the modern industrial proletariat and Judeo-Christian and Greco-Roman myths of Creation. No one brought up in the Judeo-Christian tradition can fail to compare Zola's epic description of the inundation of Le Voreux to the Great Flood of Genesis. But, as I have pointed out elsewhere,[22] a careful reading of the novel will also show that nearly all the explicit classical mythological allusions scattered throughout its text—the comparison of the women mutilating Maigrat's corpse to Furies, of Mme Hennebeau to Ceres, the naming of the burning mine, Tartaret, after Tartarus, the obvious parallels between the Dieu Inconnu and Cronus, or, to mention another example, between the new society prophesied in the conclusion and the Golden Age—suggest particularly Greco-Roman stories of the Creation and the War of the Gods: the cosmic struggles between Uranus and Cronus, Cronus and Jupiter. The Furies leaped into being from the blood of Uranus after he had been grievously wounded by Cronus' iron sickle. The golden-haired Ceres was, like her father Cronus, connected with the institution of the golden harvest and, like her daughter Proserpine, associated with rites of death and of the lower world. Tartarus was the profound abysm of the earth where Uranus thrust his fearful children the Hecatonchires and Cyclopes, who were released by Jupiter at the advice of their mother, the earth-mother Gaea, to take part in his war against Cronus. It was here, also, that after ages of struggle the Titans were consigned in their turn, making of Tartarus a symbol of the revolutionary forces that eternally exist deep within the earth itself. Just as the dreadful children of Uranus were called up by Gaea to fight their elder brother Cronus, the proletarians, those new instruments of mother nature, well up out of the depths of the earth about Tartaret to wage revolutionary warfare on capital. As I have already noted in Chapter 3, there is perhaps an even more obvious analogy between Zola's Unknown God, one of the most recurrent images in the novel, and Cronus—especially since, as we know, both are shown as devourers of their children. Again, while, as I say, the metaphorical storm in *Germinal* may remind us in some respects of the biblical Deluge, the violence of the Montsou strike may be even more reminiscent of the catastrophes of the war between Cronus and Jupiter. Indeed, Zola's description, in Part VII, of the destruction of Le Voreux, transformed, as we have noted, into a giant slowly collapsing into the abyss, strongly recalls mythological images of the defeat of the Titans. In some respects, the novel's concluding vision, a new generation of men rising up with the wheat out of the earth after the inundation of Le Voreux, may remind us of the myth of Deucalion and Pyrrha. There are, in addition, such an impressive number of analogies between the Greco-Roman mythical cosmos and the setting of *Germinal* (Oceanus and the Torrent, the Elysian Fields and Catherine's dying hallucination, the Vale of Enna and Côte-Verte) that it is almost impossible not to believe that Zola had classical mythology, which he knew well, more or less in mind when he wrote the novel and that consciously or unconsciously he was tempted to conceive of the modern social cataclysm that he recounts in it in terms of these ancient myths treating of the succession of the primordial ages, the metamorphoses of primitive gods, and the origins of man. Was he not trying to suggest in this poetic manner that this modern cataclysm is, like the mythic events to which he compares it, a cosmogonic event, that the world of Etienne, Catherine, Maheu, and La Maheude, the world of the awakening proletariat, is quite as much as the world of Noah, Cronus, or Deucalion and Pyrrha, a world in which, as he says in "La Géologie et l'histoire," "we can feel the earth in childbirth trembling under our feet"?

5

Romantic Humanitarianism

But the conception of man, the world, and history expressed in *Germinal* has obviously been influenced by another, largely contrasting complex of ideas which, as we know from many of Zola's other writings, also strongly appealed to him. As we have just seen, his "new faith" founded on geology takes a cosmic view of earth's past, present, and future. It conveys to us the geologist's sense of temporal and spatial immensity. It focuses not on France or any other country, but on the whole globe. It reckons time in thousands or millions of years and attaches no special importance to any particular century. By "past," it means the prehuman past, by "present," the age of man, by "future," the ages that will follow the disappearance of man. Embracing the doctrine of catastrophes which since Cuvier and Buckland had been practically synonymous with geology in the popular mind, it regards the social as well as natural upheavals of the present as no more than an infinitessimal part of the series of cosmogonic cataclysms which stretches back to the dawn of time and will possibly go on forever. It considers progress as a very slow process indeed, involving countless eons, regards the world as in a perpetual state of cosmogony, or, to use the biblical term, genesis, and, while assuming that history has a goal, admits that this goal, or ultimate purpose, is unknown to man. As we have also just seen, this "new faith" founded on geology is, moreover, absolutely opposed to all anthropocentrisms. The other complex of ideas which I have just mentioned originates, however, less in the scientific or pseudoscientific thought of Zola's age than it does in the romantic humanitarianism that had acquired in France by the time Zola was born, in 1840, the character of a secular religion.[1] When Zola was primarily under the influence of these ideas, which he had absorbed through his youthful readings of Hugo, Michelet, Lamennais, George Sand, and other romantic writers, his thought was much more parochial. He was concerned first and foremost with humanity. He identified the past with traditional human culture, especially the feudal culture predominant in Europe before the French Revolution; the present with the period of transition between traditional culture and modern, scientific, democratic culture, especially his own nineteenth century; and the future with a mythical "twentieth century," the new golden age that would, he liked to suppose, commence when this transitional process was complete.[2] By "progress," he now meant society's march out of the darkness of the pre-nineteenth-century human past into the light of the hoped for new era.[3] Forgetting his rejection of anthropocentrisms in "La Géologie et l'histoire," he had even gone so far sometimes as to exalt, if not individual human beings, humanity as a whole, even to the point of identifying it, like Comte, with the Deity.[4] Zola's humanitarianism also led him to glorify the nineteenth century. Comparing it, like many of his like-minded contemporaries, to the dawn of a new day or a mother great with child or actually in the process of giving birth, he regarded it as an object of faith and worship:

> People reproach us for being disbelievers. I would like to stand up and recite in a loud voice my own confession of faith. I believe in my century, with all my modern heart. . . . (XIV, 655)[5]

Like the other French humanitarians and the foreign thinkers who had succumbed to their influence (for example, Heine), he also exalted France, conceiving of it as the sacred land of the Revolution, a Christ among nations, the New Messiah,[6] and characterizing Paris, in similar humanitarian images, as the capital of progress, the spiritual successor to Rome, the volcano of the Revolution, the wine vat in which the society of the future was being brewed, the wheat field in which the shining harvest of the coming summer was growing.[7] Whereas, moreover, he had, in "La Géologie et l'histoire," left the goal of history undefined, referring to it only as "the unknown aim" of creation, he now tended, like his fellow humanitarians, to conceive of the ultimate stage of progress as the perfect realization of those values which underlay humanitarian idealism: truth, justice, fraternity, love, work, fecundity, harmony. For example, even though, as we have seen in Chapter 1, he could not, as a positivist, regard the humanitarian dream of, as he put it in an article on Hugo, "the universal kiss of peoples, the end of war," as anything but the sheerest wishful thinking, he now made it his own. For instance, recall Luc's dying words on the last page of *Travail*: ". . . the final stage has come at last, the fraternal embrace, at the end of this long voyage, which has been so rough, so painful" (VIII, 969).[8]

Furthermore, although Zola usually tended at those moments when he was under the sway of his romantic humanitarianism to retain something of the scientific catastrophism of "La Géologie et l'histoire," he was also even more obviously influenced at such times by the socialistic apocalypticism which was another major feature of romantic humanitarian thought.[9] He would then picture the passage of society from the hateful past to the socialist paradise of the future in terms of an apocalyptic drama of world destruction and renewal, or, as he phrased it in a newspaper article, "the immense and grandiose

spectacle of this age which is surely in the process of giving birth to a world"
(X, 947).[10] He would recount the great, earth-shaking transitional upheavals of
his time, real or prophetically foreseen, in a violently colored poetic language
not only comparing them to geological cataclysms, but also suggesting parallels
with the disasters foretold by the apocalyptists of old. As I have already
pointed out, in Chapter 1, the fall of the Second Empire and the Paris Commune of 1871 are metaphorically linked in *La Débâcle* with the Apocalypse
of Saint John; and *Travail*, largely set in the "twentieth century," is full of
apocalyptic elements. He and his contemporaries, the novelist would intimate,
were living in the End Time, the Time of Troubles, the Reversion to Chaos
which precedes the Coming of the Kingdom of God. He was haunted by,
among other things, the apocalyptic myth of the Great Final Conflict. We can
see this in Maurice's "black dream" in *La Débâcle*, for instance (VI, 1121);
or we can see it in the final chapter of *Travail*, with its apocalyptic account
of the "last war," here envisaged as the worldwide struggle between capitalism
and socialism which will end in the definitive victory of the latter.

> ... Oh the last war! The last war! ... There was no time left even to carry away the
> dead; they piled up in great walls, behind which new regiments, inexhaustible,
> came to die in their turn. The battle raged on even at night.... From the sky itself,
> bombs rained down from balloons, reducing the towns in their paths to ashes.
> Science had invented explosives, engines capable of spreading death throughout
> prodigious areas, of suddenly swallowing up entire populations, like an earthquake.
> ... And what a monstrous massacre, on the last day of that giant battle! ... One
> could walk hour after hour, encountering an ever more massive harvest of slaugh-
> tered soldiers, with their eyes wide open, proclaiming the immensity of human
> folly through their black, gaping mouths. (VIII, 967-69)

During the Dreyfus affair, Zola, clearly obsessed by an equally apocalyptic
vision, even went so far as to exhort his future son-in-law, Maurice Le Blond:
"Action! Action! Everyone should act, everyone understands that it is a social
crime not to act, at such a grave moment, when the nefarious forces of the past
are engaged in a final conflict with the energies of tomorrow" (XIV, 1532).

Moreover, in conformance with the same humanitarian apocalypticism, he
referred to the society of the future as "the Kingdom of Heaven on earth"
(XII, 731). As we have seen in Chapter 1, he reincarnated in his fiction more
than one of the dramatis personae of the Apocalypse. Etienne's sister, Nana,
as I have suggested, is probably in some ways a naturalist embodiment of the
Red Whore of Babylon (if not, as Paul Arène supposed, the Great Beast of
the Apocalypse himself). The herds of riderless horses thundering across the
battlefield of Sedan after the French defeat, in *La Débâcle*, have a strongly
apocalyptic quality, reminiscent of the horses of the Apocalypse. Nor must
we forget the apocalyptic longing for the New Messiah which Zola shared
with other humanitarians—a longing reflected, for example, in Clotilde's

messianic reveries in the final pages of *Le Docteur Pascal* or the messianic fantasies that Zola plays out in *Les Quatre Evangiles.*[11]

This quasi-religious conception of the past, present, and future, glorification of humanity, France, the nineteenth century, the socialist dream, this apocalypticism—all grounded, as I have said, in Zola's humanitarianism—had an enormous impact on his definition of his own situation and role as an artist. Of all his artistic motives, few were stronger than, for example, his aspiration to wield his art as a weapon or tool in the service of his humanitarian ideals. To help build the society of the future, to be a "soldier of the avant-garde that precedes the nation" (XIII, 43), was always one of his chief prophetic ambitions.[12]

But these elements of his humanitarianism not only supplied him with his poetic mission; they also stimulated his poetic imagination as few other subjects could. Like dozens of other nineteenth-century writers before him, he wanted to write the great humanitarian epic.[13] As early as 1860, he was already turning the subject over and over in his mind, along with his project for *La Genèse.* "The epic poem—I mean an epic poem of my own invention, and not some stupid imitation of the Ancients—appears to me an original path to follow," he wrote Baille toward the beginning of September of that year.

> . . . The hopes for the future, the breath of liberty which is arising everywhere, religion in the course of purifying itself: these are certainly powerful sources of inspiration. The trick is to find a new form, to sing in fitting fashion the peoples of the future, to show in a grand manner humanity mounting the steps of the sanctuary. You will have to admit that there is something sublime to be found there. (*Corr.*, I, 233)

Nearly a year later, absorbed by the same dream of a humanitarian epic, he wrote Baille of his growing conviction that those writers of their generation who aspired to greatness could do no better than draw their inspiration from the great leap forward that humanity was taking in their day. "This is what your century offers you; take as much of it as you want!" he said that he would like to tell them. "Become great with this subject matter!" (*Corr.*, I, 306).

In his mid-twenties, still fired by the same literary ambition, but now deeply ensconced in journalism, he conceived the idea of a vast series of newspaper articles chronicling the transitional spectacle of his time as a reporter like himself could observe it unfolding in each of the various major social sectors: "the great battle of our century . . . this conflict of all interests, both human and divine . . . this laborious childbirth of a new society" (XIII, 47). The objective of this proposed series would have been not only to satisfy his contemporaries' curiosity as to where their society was heading, but also to record for their descendents, the society of the future, "how they were born, in what gigantic suffering and travail" (XIII, 47).

Probably because of his failure to find a sympathetic editor, he never actually wrote these articles. There can be no doubt, however, that the *Rougon-Macquart* series and its sequels, *Les Trois Villes* and *Les Quatre Evangiles*, grew in large part out of his determination to realize this epic humanitarian ambition in a fictional frame. When we stand back and contemplate the twenty-six novels that comprise them as a whole, it immediately becomes apparent that the prophetic humanitarian vision that we have been concerned with here, with all its apocalyptic qualities, is far and away the principal ingredient of the vision of history, past, present, and future, that emerges from them.

This same vision—humanity ascending the steps of the temple of progress, the struggle between the forces of the past and the forces of the future, the tumultuous birth of a new world, the socialist paradise, etc.—would have also been at the heart of *La France en marche,* the series of plays he wanted to write in his old age. "I would like," he jotted down in his preliminary notes,

> to do for the Third Republic what I have done for the Second Empire: a series of works treating once again the natural and social history of our epoch. . . . I would take the Third Republic at its inception. Then, abruptly, I would put my finger on its characteristic trait: a nation with its long clerical and monarchical past which has had such a terrible time trying to liberate itself. . . . From then on, the main lines would take off from there, the slow struggle, forever obstructed, to attain liberty, truth, justice. . . . On the one hand, the forces of the past, the monarchical spirit, the clerical spirit, in action. . . . On the other hand, all the forces of progress. That is the whole battle, and therein lies the whole interest. . . . It is France, in accordance with her destiny, who will lead the fight for progress, for the just city of tomorrow; at least, that is my premise, and hence my dramas, the episodes of humanity marching on, at a given moment. (XV, 843, 844)[14]

Essentially the same scenario, the same apocalyptic vision, the same conception of humanity and its salvation, obviously obsessed Zola when he wrote *Germinal.*

Etienne's socialistic millennialism reminiscent of 1848, his apocalyptic vision of the proletariat "waking up down there . . . germinating in the earth just like a real seed" (V, 144; Sig., 135) and finally growing up out of the ground one fine morning to destroy the old world, to reestablish justice, to build "humanity of the future . . . the edifice of truth and justice that would grow up in the dawn of the twentieth century" (V, 231; Sig., 230)—this is a dream that Zola himself had had, the very dream that would culminate in *Les Quatre Evangiles.* It is true, as I have noted in Chapter 1, that in the novel itself, starting out in Part III, Chapter iii, he denigrates this dream, characterizing it as a feverish hallucination of ignorant minds. The positivist, the pessimist, the author of "La Géologie et l'histoire," not to mention the Darwinian, in Zola were, to be sure, obliged to reject it.[15] But the still partly romantic humanitarian in him obviously sympathized with Etienne and even shared his revery.[16] We are reminded of Zola's similarly ambivalent attitude toward the reveries of the equally naive, half-educated young republican insurgent Silvère, in *La Fortune des Rougon*.[17]

It could be maintained that, as the title *Germinal* implies, Etienne's dream of the revolt of the masses and its Utopian sequel is, in fact, the central vision of the novel. The main lines of the plot, it could be argued, are an amplification of it: the awakening of the proletariat (the awakening of the Maheu family in Part I, Chapter ii); the growing spirit of revolt (the increasing resentment and anger of the miners at the injustices of the Company in Parts I, II, III, and IV); the emergence of the proletariat from the lower regions of society (the emergence of the Montsou strikers from the mines); the destruction of the unjust old world (the rampaging mob of Part V, the destruction of Le Voreux in Part VII); the advent of the new socialist golden age (the symbolic April sunrise of the book's final chapter); the whole overall movement from the wintry darkness and cold of the first chapter to the springtime light and warmth of the denouement.

Moreover, even those readers who insist on seeing *Germinal* as primarily an expression of Zola's positivism or pessimism must be struck by the fact that he ends this ambiguous work with passages setting forth this same humanitarian conception, that the last paragraphs of the novel are, indeed, nothing less than a recapitulation of it in the strongest lyrical terms. Although Zola takes care, through his use of a device akin to what the French call "free indirect discourse," to suggest that it is Etienne's thought he is communicating to us, not necessarily his own, those of us who are familiar with Zola's other writings are not fooled. Etienne's cry, "Ah, how truth and justice would then spring awake!" (V, 404; Sig., 427), is Zola's cry. The humanitarian dream of "a great kiss"—

There was a whispering rush of overflowing sap, the sound of seeds spread in a great kiss. (V, 405; Sig., 428)

—is, of course, Zola's dream too. The men springing up in the wheat through which Etienne passes as he leaves Montsou on his way to join Pluchart in Paris—"the black, avenging army ... slowly germinating in the furrows, sprouting for the harvests of the coming century" (V, 405; Sig., 428)—are the hosts that will defeat capitalism in the "last war" recounted in the concluding chapter of *Travail*.

Furthermore, even as we note the extent to which the vision that emerges from *Germinal* may reflect Zola's humanitarianism, we are impressed by the degree to which he has made of this novel a weapon in behalf of the humanitarian cause. He not only communicates to us his humanitarian dream, he obeys his own exhortations to fight for it. Nowhere, not even in "J'accuse," is the embattled humanitarian prophet in Zola more alive and active than in *Germinal*—the Zola who had written Baille more than two decades earlier:

"the poet's role . . . is that of a regenerator, that of a man who devotes himself to the progress of humanity. What he proposes are, I admit, dreams, but they are dreams which must be fulfilled" (*Corr.*, I, 185). Quite as much as, for example, that great late-sixteenth-century epic inspired by the Wars of Religion, *Les Tragiques* by Agrippa d'Aubigné, a poetic genius who was also, we recall, a Calvinist general, *Germinal* is, indeed, from beginning to end, a fighting work. Although it never quite falls into the excesses of outright propaganda, it has despite its naturalism something of the same fulgurant partisan fury as Agrippa's epic, something of the same sustained, violent baroque tendentiousness, something of the same persuasiveness, partly realized through some of the same baroque techniques—the deliberate use of shock, the glaring oppositions and contrasts, the resounding, mutually reinforcing metaphors, the strong colors, the theatricality, the effects of light and shadow, the cosmic imagery, the grandiose personifications, the marriage of reality and hallucination, the exaggerations, the dynamic rhythms. As Zola himself confessed, *Germinal* is a "cry for pity and a cry for justice" (XIV, 1449). In it, he not only plays on his largely bourgeois public's fears of the disasters that would surely occur if the required reforms were not made; he seeks to arouse compassion for the victims of capitalist injustice. The account of the Grégoires' "charity" in Part II, Chapter ii, for example, exposes what usually passes for Christian charity in modern society for the detestable, self-serving thing it really is and makes us long for that authentic charity which calls out for an end to the social inequities at the root of poverty.[18] The Montsou miners' martyrdom disquiets us just as much as Aubigné's account of the atrocities of the Wars of Religion. The gaiety of the victorious bourgeoisie, symbolized, in the last chapter, by the "white plume faintly tinged with carmine" of a steam exhaust above the dark silhouette of the refurbished Jean-Bart pit (V, 397; Sig., 420), is as enraging in its own way as the high spirits of the French court watching the massacre of Saint Bartholomew from the windows, battlements, and terraces of the Louvre.

If, furthermore, Zola tried so hard in *Germinal* to be ruthlessly scientific, to present the public with the cold, hard *facts*, to show the harsh reality of nineteenth-century working-class life as it really was, it was not only, we can be certain, to satisfy his own intellectual need for scientific realism—that hunger for solidity originating largely, as we have seen, in his metaphysical uncertainties; it was also because, like his fellow humanitarians, he firmly believed that only through the application of the scientific method to all fields of activity, including the writing of fiction, could significant social progress be achieved. As he had Bertheroy (modeled on the famous chemist Berthelot) put it in *Paris*, scientists were the only true revolutionaries:

Wasn't science enough? What was the use of trying to speed up events, when one step forward by science resulted in more progress for humanity . . . than a hundred years of politics and social revolt. Only science sweeps away dogmas, rids us of

the gods, brings light and happiness. I, the decorated member of the Institute,
am the only true revolutionary. (VII, 1268)

One of Zola's fondest hopes had, indeed, always been that by baring with his
anatomist's scalpel the evils of society for all to see, he could provoke legislators into taking the steps necessary to heal them. "If my fiction accomplishes
anything," he had written in his preliminary notes for *Les Rougon-Macquart*,
"this is what it will be: to say the human truth. . . . It will then be up to the
legislators and moralists to think about dressing the wounds that I have
shown."[19] With respect to *L'Assommoir* in particular, he had commented
in the same notes: "It would be an act of courage to tell the truth and to
solicit, by the frank exposition of the facts, air, light, and instruction for the
lower classes."[20] In writing *Germinal*, the sequel of *L'Assommoir*, he was
spurred on by essentially the same belief in the humanitarian utility of the
scientific method as applied to fiction. To those critics who accused him of
distortion, he replied:

> Don't try to contradict me with sentimental reasons. Take a look at the statistics
> for yourselves. Go and investigate yourselves the locale. And then you will see if
> I have lied or not. Alas, if anything, I have attenuated the facts. When the day
> arrives when we can finally bring ourselves to recognize poverty for what it really
> is, with all its pain and degradation, it will not be long before something will be
> done to improve the condition of the poor. . . . Why would anyone suppose that
> I would want to calumniate the unfortunate? I have only one desire, to show them
> such as our society has made them and provoke such a great outpouring of
> pity, such a great demand for justice, that France will finally stop letting herself be
> devoured by the ambition of a handful of politicians and pay attention to the
> physical and material well-being of her children. (XIV, 1441)

But at the same time, the author of *Germinal* performs his humanitarian
function as a regenerator of society in another, astonishingly primitive way.
The scientific reformer in this novel goes hand in hand with a kind of tribal
initiation master. Indeed, when we look at the text from the point of view
of a student of primitive religion, it immediately becomes apparent that we
have to do with, in effect, nothing less than a rite of passage. Like a primitive
initiator leading a boy through a symbolic death and resurrection intended
to mark and facilitate his transition from boyhood to manhood, Zola would
appear to have attempted in *Germinal* to mark and facilitate ritually the
advance of his society from one stage of progress to another, higher stage.
Whether or not he was fully aware that he was doing this is, of course, not
a question that can be settled here. It is not, however, we may note in passing,
the only instance of the survival in Zola's fiction of elements going back to
early periods of human culture.[21]

In particular, as we read *Germinal*, we may recall those initiation rituals
which in many primitive cultures involved being symbolically swallowed by

a monster; and, in this connection, those readers familiar with Mircea Eliade's *Myths, Dreams, and Mysteries* will undoubtedly recall especially the following paragraph:

> Let us take note of the ambivalent part played by the marine monster. There can be no doubt that the fish that swallows Jonah and the other mythical heroes symbolizes death; its belly represents Hell. In medieval visions, Hell is frequently imagined in the form of an enormous marine monster, which perhaps had its prototype in the biblical Leviathan. To be swallowed by it is therefore equivalent to dying, to the descent into Hell–the experience which all the primitive rites of initiation we have been discussing clearly leave one to infer. But on the other hand, descent into the belly of a monster also signifies the re-entry into a pre-formal, embryonic state of being. As we have already said, the darkness that reigns in the interior of the monster corresponds to the cosmic Night, to the Chaos before the creation. In other words, we are dealing here with a double symbolism: that of death, namely the conclusion of a temporal existence, and consequently of the end of time, and the symbolism of return to the germinal mode of being, which precedes all forms and every temporal existence. Upon the cosmological plane, this double symbolism refers to the *Urzeit* and the *Endzeit*. (pp. 222, 223)

In the kaleidoscopic symbolic universe of *Germinal*, is not Le Voreux among many other things a modern resurrection of this same marine monster of the old myths? Zola not only metaphorically transforms Le Voreux into a giant devouring beast; he locates the greater part of it beneath the Torrent–"that subterranean sea . . . a sea with its storms and shipwrecks" (V, 353; Sig., 369). The miners swallowed by Le Voreux descend, as we know, into what is portrayed metaphorically as an underworld reminiscent of medieval and classical visions of hell. That the act of entering this hell is, in Zola's mind, the equivalent to dying there can be no doubt whatsoever, not only because he characterizes the miners as shades, but also because in Part VII he introduces, we recall, one scene of dying in the depths of the mine after another, reaching a climax in Catherine's death and Etienne's near death: "Everything was fading away, the darkness itself had vanished, he was nowhere, beyond space, beyond time" (V, 394; Sig., 417). Only after this harrowing experience is Etienne saved by the rescue party and conducted by it from this realm of death back into the realm of the living. But on the other hand, we may apply to the miners in *Germinal* Eliade's observation that "descent into the belly of a monster also signifies the re-entry into a pre-formal, embryonic state of being." This is clearly evident in the recurrent metaphor equating the miners with seeds germinating in the earth and in the final metaphoric transformation, on the last page, of the mine and, more generally, the earth under the field of growing wheat into a womb–a womb in which the black avenging army of the future, the brave new world of Zola's and Etienne's millenarian dreams, is growing. The darkness which Catherine and Etienne are plunged into in the mine monster's belly is not only the darkness of death; it also corresponds, we can be quite sure, to the cosmic Night, the Chaos before the creation, of which Eliade speaks—the same Night, the same primordial Chaos that reigns in the depths of Tartarus, reincarnated in *Germinal* by Tartaret. By means of the ordeal through which the Montsou miners—and, symbolically, the whole modern industrial proletariat for which they stand—are forced to go in *Germinal*, they are thus initiated into precisely that "germinal mode of being," which, as Eliade says, "precedes all forms and every temporal existence." As in the old myths, we have to do, on the cosmological plane, with the *Urzeit* and the *Endzeit.* [22]

But this ordeal, this rite of passage from one state, or mode, into another state, or mode, is not undergone solely by Zola's coal miners and the emergent social class they represent. Whatever our own class origins may be, we cannot read *Germinal* without participating in the same rite vicariously. And like those primitive boys who have been led through their rites of passage into manhood, we find afterwards that something in us has also irreversibly changed. If and when the new world of Zola's humanitarian dream arrives, we will be more ready than we might have been without *Germinal* to enter it.

6

Life Continuing and Recommencing

As the concluding remarks of the preceding chapter might lead one to suspect, Zola was also profoundly influenced in *Germinal* by his conception of life as an eternally self-renewing force.

Anyone at all familiar with Zola's writings will agree with me, I think, that this conception is one of the most central in his philosophical and religious thought. No more than any of his other ideas, however, did it ever give birth in his mind to a stable, thoroughly reasoned, logically consistent system. Up to the end, it remained, like most of his other philosophical and religious ideas, primarily in the realm of poetic and mystical insight, intuition, revelation.

To refer to it as some critics, most notably Guy Robert and Lawrence Harvey, have, as Zola's "myth of eternal return" is perhaps somewhat misleading.[1] For this makes us think of Nietzsche. Robert even goes so far as to suggest an analogy with Nietzsche.[2] Yet nothing in Zola permits us to conclude that he ever believed, like Nietzsche and his Greek sources, that the image of eternity is the perfect circle. Nowhere does Zola posit, like Nietzsche, the eternal recurrence of precisely the same events at gigantic intervals. Nowhere does he ask, along with Nietzsche: "And this slow spider, which crawls in the moonlight, and this moonlight itself, and you and I in the gateway . . . must not all of us have been there before? And return . . . must we not eternally return?"[3] The sort of reasoning whereby Nietzsche supports this vision is also almost totally foreign to Zola: that, granted a finite number of power quanta as the basic constituents of the world, only a finite number of configurations is possible; that, if the Christian belief in creation is wrong, as it probably is, there is no beginning of the past, nor has a stable end state been attained by now; that, therefore, the only alternative is that the configurations must repeat themselves after enormous periods of time. The notion of the finitude of power quanta can nowhere be found in Zola. Nor is there any indication that Zola ever seriously considered the possibility that the world had had no beginning.[4]

He is, however, much closer in spirit to many other versions of the myth of eternal return as defined and studied by such scholars as Mircea Eliade. As we have already begun to see in the preceding chapter, Zola revives images

traditionally associated with this myth. I am thinking of those that he uses
to mark or suggest the passage from cosmos to chaos to a new cosmos:
descents into the bellies of monsters, cosmic dawns, germination images.
Furthermore, there are apparent vestiges in his writings of the primitive conception according to which the cosmos and man are ceaselessly regenerated
by all sorts of means, the past nullified, and evils and sins thus eliminated.
Obsessed, as we have seen in the preceding chapter, with the idea of world
destruction and renewal, he repeatedly destroys and re-creates the world and
man in his fiction, tending, like archaic thinkers, to magnify crises in the lives
of individuals—for example, a serious illness—or (as in the example discussed
in the last pages of the preceding chapter) momentous social changes into
rehearsals of archetypal scenarios of world destruction and renewal.

An essential element of any cure among many primitive peoples—the
most archaic tribes of India, for instance—is the recitation of the cosmogonic
myth. The ill person is ritually projected back into that original moment of
creation—*illo tempore*—which preceded the fall and resultant corruption
of the world. As Eliade comments, "It is through the actualization of the
cosmic Creation, exemplary model of all life, that it is hoped to restore
the physical health and spiritual integrity of the patient."[5] Zola, whether he
was ever fully conscious of it or not, was apparently susceptible to much the
same magico-religious reasoning. "It seems to me that there is an intimate bond
between myself as I get better and the earth which is being reborn," he jotted
down in his plan for "Printemps: Journal d'un convalescent" (1866?),
undoubtedly inspired by his reminiscences of the grave malady that he had
had at the age of eighteen. "I am like man at the beginning of the world.
I am new and naive thanks to my illness" (IX, 912). Serge Mouret's recovery
from an equally severe illness, in *La Faute de l'abbé Mouret* (1875), similarly
entails a repetition of the cosmogonic act. Like the fictional narrator of "Printemps" and their real-life archaic predecessors, Serge returns to the beginning
of all things, witnesses the emergence of light out of darkness, becomes a new
Adam joined with a new Eve (Albine) in a new Eden (Paradou) and is thereby
fully restored to health.

With Etienne, in *Germinal*, we pass, as we have seen in the last chapter,
through the cosmic ruin symbolized by the destruction of Le Voreux; we
return, through the magic of ritualistic symbols, to the darkness of primeval
chaos; we emerge into an auroral vision of a new golden age; we hear under
the burgeoning wheat "the muffled sound of the new world pushing its way
up through the soil" (VI, 1239). In the denouement of *La Débâcle* (1892), we
find still another repetition of the process of world regeneration, once again
associated with a momentous change in the life of a society. Recalling the
universal conflagration of the Apocalypse, the lurid light of Paris burning
after the fall of the Second Empire and the eradication of the Commune

merges symbolically with the fiery glow of a sunset transformed, in the imagination of the soldier Jean Macquart, into a cosmic dawn.[6] "Oh, what a way to go," Jean exclaims as he contemplates his dead friend and former comrad-in-arms, Maurice Levasseur, "with a whole world crashing down around you!" (VI, 1121). And the novel ends with a prophetic anticipation of "a whole world to rebuild" (VI, 1121).

In *Les Trois Villes* (1894-98), the decline of Christianity and the birth of "the new religion of science" are transformed, in their turn, into a drama of universal destruction and renewal. The tragically heroic Cardinal Boccanera, loyal to the end, cries out from the depths of his ruined palace: "O mighty God, sovereign Master, I am at your command. Make me, if it be thy will, the pontiff of the destruction, of the death of the world!" (VII, 972). As perceived from a Vatican window, the spectacle of Rome by night, with its traditional lamps and the recently installed electric lights along the Corso and other major arteries, is magnified into a vision of cosmic metamorphosis:

A few scattered constellations, some brilliant stars tracing mysterious and noble figures were trying in vain to struggle and disengage themselves. They were drowned, blotted out by the confused chaos of this dust of an old star, which must have broken up there, leaving there the remnants of its glory, henceforth reduced to nothing more than a kind of phosphorescent sand. (VII, 914)

Describing the final loss of faith of the trilogy's hero, Abbé Pierre Froment, in Catholicism, Zola tells us: "Pierre could feel within himself the supreme collapse. That really was the end. . . . nothing was left of the old world" (VII, 1002).

Zola's final series of novels, *Les Quatre Evangiles* (1899-1903), contains similar dramas of cosmic destruction and reconstruction.

There is something very primitive about all this. Like our distant ancestors, Zola was obscurely compelled to assimilate history to myth, to force historical events to conform to mythical cosmogonic archetypes, to re-create the world afresh symbolically at every instant. It must also be noted, in passing, that he was also haunted by the myth of the recurrent cycle of the four cosmic ages (golden, silver, etc.).[7] Bowed over Maurice's corpse, Jean reflects:

He had gone from life, hungering for justice, in the supreme throes of the great, somber dream that had possessed him, that grandiose, monstrous conception of the old society destroyed, Paris burned, the field plowed up once again so that from the renewed and purified soil might spring the idyll of a new golden age. (VI, 1121)

That Zola shared essentially the same dream there can be no doubt, for, in the same passage, he declares:

And yet, beyond this fiery furnace still roaring about him, Hope, the eternal, was being reborn in the depths of the vast, tranquil sky. It was the certain rejuvenation of an everlasting Nature, of an imperishable Humanity, the renewal promised to him who keeps on working and does not despair, the tree that throws out a new and vigorous shoot to replace the rotten branch that had to be chopped off because its blighted sap was causing the young leaves to wither and turn yellow. (VI, 1121, 1122)

Echoing this dream once again, a chorus in one of the opera librettos Zola composed in his old age, *Violaine la Chevelue* (1897?), exclaims at a climactic moment: "Miracle, miracle! The Age of Gold has come back!" (XV, 633).

But if there is much in Zola, including *Germinal,* that reminds us of archaic versions of the myth of eternal return and the mentality that went along with it, there is also much that sets Zola apart from them. As we have just seen, we can find traces in his thought of ancient concepts positing recurrent ages, including the notion of an initial golden age, and we can discover him repeatedly re-creating the world through the assimilation of historical events to cosmogonic myths, thereby returning to and perpetuating the mythical instant, *illud tempus,* which existed before history, at the beginning of time. But the myth of eternal return must always contend in his writings with the much more powerful influence of other conceptions of nature and history which clash with it. As we noted in the last chapter, he remains in some respects still attached to the apocalyptic tradition, with its essentially linear view of history. Furthermore, both the view of time as a ceaseless series of recommencements, a perpetual rehearsal of timeless archetypes, and the apocalyptic vision of a final End Time, when history will cease, must contend in his thought with more modern conceptions of history. Living as he did in the age when modern historicism was still in full expansion, Zola was profoundly impregnated by the modern historical mentality. As we have already begun to see, he tended to look upon history as a series of new forms and unprecedented events and liked to think—and perhaps even believed in his more optimistic moods—that history was subject to a law of progress.[8]

There were moments when, just as much as any primitive man, he wanted to escape from, revolt against, devaluate, even nullify concrete, historical time—and it is precisely to this impulse that Eliade, as we know, ascribes the strong appeal of the myth of eternal return.[9] One of the reasons why Zola loved bucolic nature was that for him (as for many other moderns) it not only provided an escape from urban life, but also from history. Nature was, for him, a refuge where, as Hegel had said, nothing *new* ever happens. We may note in this respect, for example, the exaltation of immobility and of aloofness to the troubles of man's agitated, erratic existence which is an essential ingredient of Zola's romantic cult of trees:

I love big trees. They are fully alive, you can be sure of that, and they watch us passing by from the lofty heights of their majestic calm. What must they be thinking, these deans of the forest, who have contemplated our struggles and fevers for hundreds of years? They say, "We are wise, and men are mad. We have the power, we live up here in the sky, in the grave, immobile attitude which befits gods. . . . God has put in us his entire thought, which consists of calmness and strength. These men make us laugh when they claim to be the supreme achievement, the last word, of the Creator. We are his supreme achievement, we big trees, who live in the clouds and inhale in great drafts the free, pure air in our sacred immobility." (X, 575, 576)

But in contrast to archaic man, for whom only mythical archetypes possessed meaning and reality and for whom historical objects and events could acquire significance and reality only insofar as they incarnated or imitated these transcendent models, Zola generally regarded history as real and meaningful. A thoroughgoing historical relativist at heart, he was usually intrigued by change and the endless spectacle of novelties it produced. For him, innovation, far from being the sacrilege that it was for primitive thinkers, was decidedly a virtue.[10] He loved the fracas, the disorder, of a world in the process of becoming and joyously plunged into this disorder. Just the thought of trying to turn the clock back to an earlier stage of civilization, of trying to escape one's time, of refusing to be of it, horrified him. "My whole excuse," he declared at the very outset of his career, "is in the time I live in" (XIV, 1221). He rejected all absolutes, including any absolute ideal of beauty, ascribing to each age, each society, its own particular beauty (X, 545) and deploring the Parnassians' nostalgia for the distant past and imitation of ancient models (X, 741-44)—not to mention the endless reproduction of Greek and Roman gods and heroes that was still going on in the academic art studios of his day.

I am not interested in beauty or perfection. I don't care a damn about the great centuries. All that matters to me is life, struggle, feverish activity. I am completely at ease in our generation. It seems to me that no artist could ask for a better milieu, a better epoch. There are no more masters, no more schools. We are in a state of utter anarchy, and each of us is a rebel who thinks for himself, who creates and fights for himself. . . . what wide horizons! How intensely we can feel trembling within us the truths of tomorrow! (X, 27)

Few other modern writers offer us a better illustration of Eliade's remark: ". . . the modern man can be creative only insofar as he is historical; in other words, all creation is forbidden him except that which has its source in his own freedom; and, consequently, everything is denied him except the freedom to make history by making himself."[11] Whereas archaic man trembled at the thought of straying from the old archetypes, the old sacred, transhistorical models, Zola was a joyful iconoclast. He exalted everything that was most individual in an artist's temperament. He insisted on absolute liberty for the artist. When he did use models from the past, he did so of his own free will and never hesitated to modify them according to his own very modern needs. He was excited, however, by the thought that his age was creating the archetypes that would dominate the society of the future, and he dreamed of being one of its lawgivers.[12]

At the source of his own personal "myth" of life's eternal recommence-ment, we can discern his persistent fascination, going back to his boyhood in Aix (IX, 348), with life as a subject of meditation. We can also perceive at the root of this myth his acute awareness from an early age on of the multiple kinds of renewal or repetition with or without variations that the empirical and historical observation of life reveals: biological reproduction, the annual resurgence of the life of plants, the recurrent patterns observable in individual human lives, the decompositions and recompositions in human history, the successive periods of natural history, in each of which the face of the earth has been renewed. Furthermore, he tended to make the old analogy between the endlessly repeated round of the seasons and the stages through which individuals progress in each generation. "I have had my four seasons," remarks the narrator of "Les Quatre Journées de Jean Gourdon," "and now the time has come . . . for my dear Marie to recommence the eternal joys and the eternal pains" (IX, 485). In the grips of the same personal myth, Zola also, like many earlier writers, sets up parallels between the recurrent round of the seasons and the successive stages in the lives of social collectivities. We may see this, for example, in *La Terre,* where the rhythmic succession of events (which stretches out for a period of ten years) is governed by the alternation of the four seasons and their respective labors: sowing and plowing, haymaking, and harvest.

For Zola, furthermore, the notion of life's perpetual recommencement was always inseparable from the notion of life's persistence. As he saw it, one life never gives way to another life; life simply changes forms, passing from one reproduction or metamorphosis to another. We always have to do with the same life. For example, he has Jean, thinking of his daughter, Marie, reflect in the conclusion of "Les Quatre Journées de Jean Gourdon": "I am the frozen winter, but I can feel stirring within me the coming spring. How right my uncle Lazare was when he said, 'We never die'!" (IX, 485). In the denouement of *La Débâcle,* with its grandiose vision of world destruction and renewal, Zola insists: "In the midst of all these ransacked buildings, these torn-up pavements, all this suffering and ruin, you could still hear life going on . . ." (VI, 1121). Over and over again elsewhere, he expresses the same faith, stressing along with "the eternal recommencement of life" (XV, 672), the eternity of life. It is implicit in, among other things, all those juxtaposi-tions that he makes between images of death and images of birth and renewal: Albine's funeral and the birth of Désiré's calf, in *La Faute de l'abbé Mouret*;

Mama Coupeau's wake and the children's circle games going on outside in the courtyard, in *L'Assommoir*; Jeanne's burial and the radiant spring morning and warbling finch, in *Une Page d'amour*; Fouan's interment and the wheat sowers, in *La Terre*. Summing it all up in *Vérité*, the novel he wrote just before he died, he tells us that Marc, finding Mme Duparque's corpse, "felt something like a breath pass by, eternal life being reborn in this dead person" (VIII, 1402).

The same myth of life's eternal renewal also lies, certainly, at the root of another of Zola's major cults, his cult of spring, with which it is repeatedly associated in his writings—that "eternal poem that heaven never grows tired of reprinting and that men never grow tired of rereading" (X, 411).

Furthermore, unlike the archaic myth of eternal return, Zola's personal myth of life's eternal recommencement by no means excludes linear conceptions of history. On the contrary, he would, apparently, have been unable to conceive of the possibility of progress without life's capacity to discard old forms, to nullify the effects of senescence, to adopt new forms, to wipe the slate clean and start afresh. As we have seen, he liked to think that the world was still in the process of creation and that this was effectuated in large part by great natural catastrophes which, by destroying the older races, made it possible for life to renew itself in more perfect forms. There can be no doubt, moreover, but that he looked upon the ability of organisms to reproduce themselves and upon the laws of heredity as he understood them, according to Lucas, as progressive factors. Lucas had emphasized the ability of life to create offspring with original traits,[13] and, for Zola, this was a source of enormous optimism. It meant not only that families could renew themselves, free themselves from the hereditary ills caused by the sins of ancestors (Zola's equivalent to original sin), but that sooner or later a superior race might be created. As Clotilde puts it while nursing her infant in the final pages of *Le Docteur Pascal*:

> Life was not afraid to create one more living being. . . . It kept on working at its task, propagating itself . . . going on. . . . It had to keep on creating, even at the risk of creating monsters, because despite the maimed and the mad there was always the hope that someday it would create a new, healthier, wiser race. Oh, life! Life! Life! Forever continuing and recommencing! Forever rushing on like a mighty torrent toward its unknown objective! (VI, 1400)

Linking his apocalypticism with the same line of reasoning, Zola even goes so far as to dream, via the same persona, that the New Messiah for whom the world was waiting might be produced by the same process (VI, 1401). He was also undoubtedly thinking along the same channels when he wrote in his preliminary notes for the same novel: ". . . heredity makes the world, and if we could intervene, understand it in order to make use of it, we could make the world."[14] It was, in short, precisely through the successive rebeginnings of life, with all the unprecedented forms that this made possible, that progress could be achieved and the goal of history ultimately attained.

No discussion of Zola's personal myth of life's eternal recommencement would be complete, moreover, that did not stress its persistence and importance in Zola's thought and writings. It may be traced back to "Religion" (1861?), where it appears as a major part of the divine revelation set forth in the last seven verses:

> One wave succeeds another; the swallow's nest
> With each new spring sees open in its down
> New eggs, frail hope of a new mother.
>
> A rose fades; a bud opens;
> The wind loses its fragance, then expires in the air;
> A new song always succeeds the song that must end;
> Everything follows the great law: appears, loves, and fades away. (XV, 925)

"Life continues, recommences," Zola wrote in his preparatory notes for *Le Docteur Pascal*, "this is the idea behind the series."[15] The better we know *Les Rougon-Macquart*, the more evident this appears. The idea of life's perpetual renewal of itself, inseparably linked, as I have pointed out, with the notion of life's persistence, is, indeed, what, more than anything else, holds most of the other major themes of this enormous, twenty-volumed work together. The massive, soaring, complex thematic structure of the series would be much less coherent without it. It provides an important common factor to volumes as different as, for example, *La Faute de l'abbé Mouret, Germinal,* and *La Terre*. It is what enables Zola to depict, on the one hand, the emergence of a new society out of the ruins of an old society and, on the other hand, the round of the seasons, couples making love, or the birth of a calf—all instances of life's continuing and recommencing. Without this central theme, moreover, Zola would probably not have placed as much emphasis as he does in *Les Rougon-Macquart* on the theme of heredity, with its overriding concern with the continuation and recommencement of life on the biological level.

Even after he had finished *Les Rougon-Macquart,* the same theme still fascinated Zola, both on the biological level and the historical level. Developed primarily on the latter, it is an essential part of the fundamental thematic structure of his last major works, *Les Trois Villes* and *Les Quatre Evangiles,* which complete the epic tale of world destruction and renewal begun in *Les Rougon-Macquart.*

Nowhere, moreover, does Zola affirm more insistently his faith in life's persistence and capacity to renew itself than in his very last short story, composed in 1899, only three years before he died, "Angeline ou La Maison hantée." The "ghost" of this story about a presumably haunted house turns out to be only a girl with the same name as another girl, distantly related to her, who had died in the house many years before. The story ends with the words:

> Oh, the dear ghost, the new child which was being reborn out of the dead child! Death was vanquished. My old friend, the poet V***, was absolutely right, nothing is ever lost, everything recommences, beauty as well as love. The voices of their mothers beckon these little girls of today, these amorous women of tomorrow, and they live again under the sun and among the flowers. It was from the reawakening of the child that the house was haunted, the house which today has become young and happy again, in the finally rediscovered joy of eternal life. (IX, 1162)

Obviously, this personal myth, this poetic vision of life's stubborn endurance and never failing capacity for self-renewal on every level, from the most primitive cell to the whole cosmos, possessed immense value for Zola. Including the notion of the repeated occurrences of nature, it provided him, as we have already noted, with a refuge from history whenever he needed one. Comprising the conception of each generation's living on in the next, the life of the parent continuing in the child, it assured him of the impermanence of disease, failure, corruption, gave him hope for a better tomorrow, helped him live in a disastrous time. Like the ancient myth of eternal return, from which it had retained numerous elements, this personal myth provided, what is more, the basis of a whole ritual of purification and regeneration. In particular, exposure to spring, the season par excellence of life's renewal, always has in Zola's works much the same beneficent effects as the ritual return of archaic man to that sacred primordial instant, *illud tempus*, when the foundation of the world occurred. Zola's evocations of spring assimilate it to the Garden of Eden or the original golden age. The return of spring is thus, for him, the return of Paradise. "The countryside is spotless and .clean," he says in a newspaper article,

> as a new piece of work, fresh from the workshop, should be. The sky has been scrubbed clean with great quantities of water. There is not a single stain anywhere on the immense blue ceiling. All the filth of winter has been swept away . . . a paradise . . . a kind of universal quivering with hope and joy. Everything is young. Everything is ready for life. (X, 411)

The fictional narrator of "Printemps" is restored to health after his near fatal illness thanks largely to the curative action of spring. "Now spring will complete his cure," his doctor remarks at the beginning of the story, and in the following pages this recovery effectuated by spring is recounted step by step. Submitting to the perfumed caresses of spring, breathing in the springtime air, with its sharp, exciting odor of the earth "in childbirth," he feels his body becoming more supple; he is drawn from his bed into the garden outside his house, he is filled with "a furious desire to live again"; and little by little he enters with spring into the battle of life against death and partakes along with everything else in nature in the triumph of life. In *La Confession de Claude,* exposure to vernal nature restores to a prostitute, at least momentarily, her virginity (I, 70). In *L'Argent,* Madame Caroline, its aging heroine, the mistress of the corrupt financier Saccard, has only to step into the street outside her house on a sunny April day to regain her youth and, with it, her capacity for love, for hope, for happiness despite all the depressing events to which she has been subjected in the course of the story. "From this moment on, overwhelmed, she had to surrender herself to the irresistible forces of continual rejuvenation. . . . she had just been in the depths of despair, and now hope was reborn in her once again" (VI, 657).

Zola's vision of the eternal recommencement of life was also manifestly linked in his mind with his conception of his poetic role as that of a regenerator of society—a conception which went back to the beginning of his career and which there is no reason to suppose he ever abandoned.

Above all, however, this vision, this myth, must have helped him in his incessant struggle to cope with his terrible necrophobia. The comforting words that he ascribes to Jean Gourdon's uncle Lazare (whose very name implies the notion of resurrection) Zola had often, we can be quite certain, repeated to himself:

> Man, my child, was made in the image of the earth. And, like our common mother, we are eternal: the green leaf is reborn every year out of the withered leaf; I am reborn in you, and you will be reborn in your children. I'm telling you this so that old age won't frighten you, so that you'll be able to die in peace, like all this verdure, which will grow again out of its own seeds next spring. (IX, 471)

Because of life's power to rejuvenate itself, to pass itself on from aging forms into new, fresh forms, death—or so, at least, Zola very evidently wanted to persuade himself—had indeed, as he proclaimed exultantly in "Angeline ou La Maison hantée," been "vanquished."

Furthermore, it is precisely here, no doubt, that we have the main reason for the central place that Zola gave the theme of "life continuing, recommencing" in *Les Rougon-Macquart,* not to mention several of his lesser works. As I have noted in Chapter 3, his supreme motive in writing was to defeat death, at least symbolically, by achieving literary immortality. In his effort to create works that would endure, Zola was, therefore, in a way fighting for his life. His fiction, as he saw it, was—to use a phrase he repeatedly employed—his own flesh and blood. It was only fitting that a dominant theme of these works intended not only to help regenerate society but also to provide a means for his own survival should be an affirmation of life's ability to triumph over the destructive power of time.

The theme of "life continuing, recommencing," with all it meant to Zola, is just as central in *Germinal* as in *Les Rougon-Macquart* considered as an artistic whole. To be sure, Zola, as I have noted in Chapter 1, specifies in his preliminary outline of the novel that it is to be about the revolt of the proletariat, the conflict between capital and labor, and goes on to observe that that will be what will give the book its importance. As I have also pointed out in Chapter 1, nearly all the main elements of the plot can, in fact, be "derived" from this socioeconomic theme. But the better we know the novel, the more apparent it becomes that the revolt of the proletariat, with all the social changes that it was bringing with it, was primarily, in Zola's mind, only another instance of the capacity of eternal life to regenerate itself, thus overcoming the forces of senescence, sickness, and death. (I am speaking here of the optimistic Zola, the dreamer, the would-be bringer of a new secular faith.) As we have seen in Chapter 4, there is much in *Germinal* that permits us to interpret it as an account of still another episode of the continuing genesis of the world as Zola had conceived of it in "La Géologie et l'histoire." As we have seen in Chapter 5, we can also, quite legitimately, see in *Germinal* a reflection of Zola's humanitarian vision of the upheavals which had preceded and would doubtless continue to precede the advent of fraternal, egalitarian society. Yet each of these larger, more cosmogonic scenarios can, in turn, be regarded as a manifestation of life persisting, recommencing.[16]

The novel's title, *Germinal,* whatever its other connotations may be, also suggests the same theme. So also, of course, does all the imagery in the novel which we may associate with the title interpreted in this way: seeds, germination, spring, the round of the seasons, the earth as womb or Great Mother, and so on.

As in "Les Quatre Journées de Jean Gourdon," for example, or *La Terre,* the action of the story is linked to the progression of the seasons. Here again, we have the impression of an attempt on Zola's part to assimilate history to nature, to submit history to nature's endlessly recurrent patterns. The events recounted in *Germinal* take place in little more than a year. Parts I and II are situated in early March 1866. Part III carries us forward from early March to the end of November 1866. Part IV includes all of December 1866 and the beginning of January 1867. Part V occurs on a day early in January 1867. Part VI commences with the beginning of February and ends just before the coming springlike weather, in the same month. Part VII begins where Part VI leaves off, during those first February days—"Even the weather had turned fine, and there was a bright shining sun, one of those early February suns whose warmth tinges the lilac bushes with green" (V, 340; Sig., 354)—and ends on a tepid, fresh April day, when the sun casts a golden light over the fields of growing wheat. Zola's decision to begin the story in early March and to terminate it in April is particularly significant; for it does as much as anything else in the novel to suggest the extent to which he looked on the historical events it relates as, like the movement of the year from winter to spring, a manifestation of life's power to survive and renew itself.

This poetic identification of the rise and revolt of the proletariat with the ideas of recommencement, regeneration, resurrection, is further reinforced by the movement from darkness to light suggested by Zola's having the novel begin before dawn and end under a brilliant rising sun. As we have noted in Chapter 2, he associated darkness with death. He also, quite naturally, associated the sun and its light with life, strength, and health.[17] The sky under which Etienne approaches Montsou for the first time is, Zola insists, a "lifeless sky" (V, 23; Sig., 5), a "dead sky" (V, 30; Sig., 13); and, drowned in absolute darkness, Montsou itself at that moment is a dead land in which the first human beings Etienne can make out are only "moving shadows" (V, 24; Sig., 6). But as the novel concludes, after the miners' uprising, "the life of the earth," Zola tells us, we recall, is "rising with the sun" (V, 396; Sig., 419).

Seed imagery, suggesting the persistence and recommencement of life on the vegetable level, is particularly prevalent in *Germinal*, as the title might lead one to suspect. The image of germination occurs as early as Part I, Chapter v, where, commenting on the miners' reaction to Négrel's threat to have them paid for the timbering separately, Zola remarks that "rebellion was taking root in this cramped space more than eighteen hundred feet underground" (V, 66; Sig., 50). As Etienne stands looking down over the black coal country at the end of Part I, flying black dust is falling on the plain, "sowing the earth" (V, 74; Sig., 59). In Part III, Chapter i, spring brings with it fresh images of germination. Describing the advent of Etienne's first spring in Montsou, Zola observes: ". . . a whole world was germinating, springing from the earth, while he, down below, was groaning with wretchedness and exhaustian" (V, 124; Sig., 112). In Part III, Chapter iii, the same image, expanded once again, even more clearly recognizable by now as an anticipation of the novel's concluding vision, reoccurs, ascribed for the first time to Etienne:

> But now the miner was waking up down there; he was germinating in the earth just like a real seed, and one day you'd see what would spring up in these fields: men would spring up—yes, an army of men who would reestablish justice. (V, 144; Sig., 135)

Throughout the remainder of the novel, Zola can repeatedly be found developing these same thematic elements, charging them with the explosive force with which they will be recapitulated in the final pages.

Moreover, we cannot read *Germinal* without being impressed also by the insistence with which Zola in this work, too, as in many others, communicates to us his vision of "life continuing, recommencing" through juxtapositions of images of destruction and death with images of fecundity and life. Réquillart, the dead mine, is also a place of burgeoning life—and not only human life (the copulating couples), but plant life as well.

Heaps of broken carts and stacks of half-rotted timber were everywhere, and some kind of hardy vegetation was reclaiming this piece of land, spreading out in a thick growth and springing up as young, but already sturdy trees. (V, 114; Sig., 102)

The blood spots that reveal to La Maheude the arrival of Catherine's puberty are, as we have seen in Chapter 3, symbolically linked with the death of Maheu, shot by the troops. The chapter relating the massacre of Maheu and thirteen others (Part VI, Chapter v) is immediately followed by a chapter including a lyrical description of a weather change heralding the approach of spring (Part VII, Chapter i). Later on, just after the description of the firedamp explosion that kills Zacharie, we glimpse La Maheude, terrified by the flames, clutch to her breast the wailing Estelle—a baby, the symbol par excellence of life "continuing, recommencing." Nor must we fail to recall how, as I have pointed out in other contexts, the mine is symbolically presented first as a place of death, a veritable hell, only to be transformed in the novel's conclusion into a womb.

Moreover, at the very heart of *Germinal,* there is the vision of Tartaret, the burning mine, and, directly over it, Côte-Verte

like a miracle of eternal spring . . . with its perpetually green grass, its beech trees with their endlessly renewed leaves, and its fields in which as many as three crops a year would ripen. It was a natural hothouse, heated by the fire in the buried depths. (V, 244; Sig., 245)

As I have said in Chapter 4, Tartarus (the archetype of Tartaret) is a symbol of the revolutionary forces that eternally exist deep within the earth. The placement of Côte-Verte over Tartaret thus symbolizes the life-sustaining, regenerative power of the sort of revolutionary activity in which the Montsou miners are engaged. But at the same time, it should be noted that Tartarus is represented in Homer and Virgil as a place similar in some ways to the Christian hell—a place of death. So we may also see here, in addition, still another attempt on Zola's part to express the theme of the persistence and eternal renewal of life and, with it, the corollary notion of death as an indispensable part of this process.[18]

Furthermore, is not the whole novel and particularly the final chapter a reflection of the cult of spring which was, as we have seen, always closely associated in Zola's mind with this theme, or personal myth? As we have seen, the last paragraph would seem to be a variation in some respects of the paragraph in "Les Quatre Journées de Jean Gourdon" where Uncle Lazare sets forth his version of the lesson that spring teaches us. But the final chapter of *Germinal* would also appear to echo another of Zola's short stories celebrating spring, "Printemps: Journal d'un convalescent." Like the convalescent narrator of "Printemps," Etienne, just out of the hospital and still weak from his incarceration in the flooded mine, responds to the beneficent action of spring. In both "Printemps" and *Germinal,* we are immersed in an outpouring of light; the whole world is made young and pure again; and we are filled once again with joy and hope.

> The sun was rising gloriously on the horizon, and the whole countryside was joyously awakening. From east to west the immense plain was flooded with gold. The living warmth was rising, spreading, in a surge of youth pulsating with the rustling sounds of the earth, the song of the birds, the murmur of the streams and the woods. It was good to be alive; the old world wanted to experience still another spring. (V, 402, 403; Sig., 425)

After the hell of winter, we have once again returned to the paradise of spring. As in "Printemps," moreover, we can hear, deep down in the entrails of the earth, "the doleful murmurings of those tiny beings who were struggling painfully to bring her back to health" (IX, 909):

> And beneath his feet the heavy, stubborn hammering of the picks was still going on. His comrades were all there—he could hear them follow his every strike. Wasn't that La Maheude under the beet field, her back breaking, her harsh breathing rising in time with the rumble of the ventilator? To the left, to the right, farther along, he thought he could recognize the others, under the wheat fields, the hedges, the young trees. (V, 405; Sig., 428)

As in "Printemps"—not to mention "Les Quatre Journées de Jean Gourdon," *La Terre, L'Argent,* and many of Zola's other writings—images of spring are identified in *Germinal,* especially in this concluding chapter, with images of parturition. The soil across which Etienne strides on his way to join Pluchart in Paris is, like a mother, giving birth. As we venture forth with Etienne from the darkness of the pit where he has bid farewell to La Maheude and other former comrades into this renascent world, this new golden age, we become more than ever aware of the great extent to which our collective salvation is bound up with the self-purging, self-regenerating powers of eternal life. We can say of the sick society portrayed in *Germinal* what the convalescent's doctor says in "Printemps": "Now spring will complete the cure."

7

"An Unprecedented Anarchy"

No other great novelist that I can think of is more radically incoherent on the philosophical or religious level than Zola. Although the frequent recurrence of a large number of ideas provides his writings with a certain consistency, not even the semblance of a logical system binds them together. The enormous efforts that he made—especially, it would seem in his last years—to arrive at some overall logical order did not get him very far.[1] Obsessed by a multitude of disparate dreams, intuitions, hypotheses, doctrines, torn, as he had himself foreseen at the age of twenty that he would be (*Corr.*, I, 170), between doubt and faith, hope and despair, he never attained to a comprehensive philosophy or religion that he could permanently embrace.

Undoubtedly there were moments when he was persuaded that he had found such a philosophy or religion or at least the basis for it or the key to it. There is no reason to suspect that when, for example, he recorded in "Religion" the divine revelation that Eros is the supreme principle of creation he was not convinced that he had penetrated to the core of things. But such moments never, it would appear, lasted very long. As I have noted in Chapter 3, he is constantly coming up with new philosophies and new religious faiths. He repeatedly formulates his thoughts in forms reminiscent of the Catholic Credos, but never recites the same creed twice. Moreover, it is precisely with respect to the most central questions that he provides us with the most divergent answers. It is impossible to pin him down to any firm definition of God.[2] He entertains wildly conflicting ideas concerning the nature of man, man's relationship with God,[3] the problem of evil,[4] death,[5] history, and progress.[6]

Even toward the end of his career, Zola's philosophical and religious thought was just as unsettled and pervaded by tensions and contradictions as ever before. In December 1893, only five months after the publication of *Le Docteur Pascal*, with its ringing manifesto of his religion of life, he composed *Lazare*, with its bitter rejection of life, its intense longing for utter extinction. In August 1898, the same month that he began *Fécondité*, with its deification of life and love—"divine desire"—he disconsolately wrote his friend Fernand Desmoulin, "I have never believed in anything but work . . ." (XIV, 1506). As for *Les Quatre Evangiles*, it is, despite Zola's efforts to make it logically coherent, full of glaring contradictions. The final flowering of his old ambition to be the new prophet whom the world was waiting for, it submits to us not just one new religion, but, rather, a series of largely disparate new faiths, each with a different supreme value, each with a different New Messiah, each with a different vision of the shape of things to come.[7]

Obviously, all Zola's life, that unified, harmonious vision, that "one entire Truth which alone can cure my sick soul" (IX, 182), eluded his grasp. At the heart of his philosophical and religious thought, we find only a vast cacophony.

This cacophony invades all his major fictional series, including *Les Rougon-Macquart.* When we consider this imposing assemblage of twenty novels as a single work (which is the way Zola wanted us to regard it), we can find no more philosophical or religious harmony than we can in the whole corpus of Zola's writings. For example, the optimistic vision of the world conveyed to us by *Au Bonheur des Dames* and the pessimistic vision of the world conveyed to us by *La Bête humaine* are impossible to reconcile logically. Or one might cite among many other possible examples of the contradictory elements inherent in *Les Rougon-Macquart* the clashing soteriological doctrines implicit in it. *La Faute de l'abbé Mouret* suggests that happiness is to be achieved through the mystical union with the supreme forces of creation that results from the act of love. *Le Rêve,* on the other hand, advances the theory that man can be saved by entertaining the right illusions, that is to say, by the power of the imagination to alter the world, which is nothing but an illusion of the senses, "in such a way that the environment, the so-called grace come from God, will come from man to improve man."[8] Yet in *Le Docteur Pascal,* the philosophical conclusion of *Les Rougon-Macquart,* Zola places all his trust in the saving powers of reason, science, work, and life (VI, 1190).

Any attempt to perceive a logically consistent philosophical or religious core in *Les Rougon-Macquart* will, moreover, find no support in Zola's working notes or numerous letters and articles dealing with the series or with his fiction in general. The Taine-like philosophy that dominates the "Notes générales sur la marche de l'œuvre" and "Notes générales sur la nature de l'œuvre" that he jotted down while first planning the series in 1868 and 1869 is not at all identical with the Claude Bernard- or Littré-like positivism professed in *Le Roman expérimental* (1880).[9] Neither of these different positivistic philosophies goes together with the unanimism with which Zola identifies himself in his letter of July 22, 1885, to Jules Lemaitre—not to mention Zola's effort in his working notes for *Le Docteur Pascal* to base the series retroactively on Renan's *Credo* as summarized by Melchior de Vogüé.

As for Zola's individual novels, some, obviously, reflect the contradictions, fissures, and confusions in Zola's philosophical and religious thought more completely and faithfully than others, and *Germinal* would appear to be an excellent, perhaps even the best, example. It certainly does so much more completely and faithfully than, for instance, *La Terre,* which is dominated by only one of Zola's competing visions of nature, the vision summarized in the great hymn to the Great Mother in the final pages, or *La Bête humaine*, with its unadulterated pessimism. Even *L'Assommoir*, with its mingled pessimism and optimism, its incoherent mixture of Zola's more or less competing cults of life, nature, love, science, progress, force, and work, or *La Joie de vivre*, with its sharp, unresolved conflict between the quasi-Schopenhauerian elements in Zola's thought and his cult of life, cannot, I suspect, altogether compete with *Germinal* in this regard.

Unlike nearly all of Zola's other creative works, including those novels I have just mentioned, *Germinal* would seem not only to reflect all the major competing philosophical and religious tendencies in Zola's thought but to ascribe to each of them much the same weight it has in Zola's thought in general, that is to say, a weight approximately equal to that of each of the others. The metaphysically skeptical factualist and positivist, the curiously incoherent pessimist, and the even more incoherent optimist would all appear to be equally represented in *Germinal,* just as, in my opinion, they are in Zola's thought considered as a whole.

For this very reason, moreover, *Germinal* would seem to me to testify more strongly than many if not all of Zola's other novels (I will not even mention his short stories, plays, and librettos) to the absoluteness of his failure to work out for himself some faith that he could permanently and consistently embrace, to create a solid, coherent fictional world,[10] or even to impose just any logical order on his thought simply for the sake of order.

I have no idea what others may think of *Germinal*'s ability to tolerate, even, in some cases, invite, so many clashing philosophical or religious interpretations. Insofar as I know, this has never received the critical attention that it deserves. Even its full magnitude has never, to the best of my knowledge, been noted by any other commentator. Critics have generally contented themselves with one reading. None that I know of has attempted more than three.[11] Even Zola's philosophical and religious thought in general has not aroused the same widespread attention as some of his other aspects. Although excellent studies, some in considerable depth, have been published on certain important elements of it, we have as yet no satisfactory attempt to present it in its entirety. There are, I suppose, good reasons for this. Since the present revival of critical interest in Zola began, in the fifties, critics have, as a group, been more concerned with his mythopoeic dimensions and structural qualities. The school of thought—represented in France by, among others, Lanson—which tended to regard literature as a vulgarization of philosophy has throughout this same period been out of fashion. Furthermore, many critics have tended not to take Zola very seriously as an intellectual, rather unjustly, I suspect. Moreover, even those about whom this is not necessarily true may be all too easily tempted to dismiss the philosophical and religious contradictions that can be read into *Germinal,* despite their number and violence, as simply further confirmation of the truism that most creative artists are not systematic philosophers or theologians.

In my own personal opinion, however, the philosophical and religious contradictions that we can observe or at least legitimately suspect in *Germinal* must very definitely be included among those factors that make it the exceedingly powerful novel that it is. I am glad that these contradictions are there or at least may very possibly be there, that Zola did not decide while planning *Germinal* to include in it only ideas that would not logically clash, to make it the vehicle of a single consistent vision. Each reader is free to perceive in it a world view congenial to his own. Furthermore, what it lost in systematicness, in unity, it gained in fidelity to Zola's own personality. Indeed, I can think of no other individual novel of Zola's that comes so close to attaining one of his major artistic ideals—to give himself to us, as he once said, "whole, in all my violence and in all my gentleness, such as God made me" (X, 38).

There is also—at least for me—something unutterably poignant in these contradictions. I cannot contemplate them without thinking of the immense, but futile, spiritual and intellectual struggle that produced them, and I find this struggle, which they evoke, every bit as moving as the epic battle for social justice that the novel relates.

Moreover, insofar as Zola was able, in writing *Germinal,* to express the whole range of his mature philosophical and religious thought, with its violent discordancies and lack of any fixed center, he came closer to attaining another, almost equally important artistic aim: that of embodying in his own works the mind of his age, of "being of his own time."

The main outlines of the history of French philosophical and religious thought during Zola's lifetime are well known: the breakdown of the eclectic philosophy of Cousin; the predominance of positivism from around 1850 on; the critical reaction provoked during those same years by that very predominance; the skepticism and pessimism that culminated in the philosophical dilettantism and vogue for Schopenhauer and von Hartmann in the 1880s; the Catholic renaissance and idealistic revival from around 1880 or earlier. What, however, has been less widely remarked is the strong elements of discord and division discernible throughout this entire period both in its philosophical and religious speculations as a whole and in the outlook of many of the individual thinkers behind them.

As D. G. Charlton has emphasized, "The progress of philosophy in the nineteenth century is not so much a succession of pitched battles in which one side or another is triumphant and banishes its opponents from the field, as a debate prolonged throughout the century."[12] As much as ever before, Paris during Zola's lifetime was a seething melting pot of ideas. Everything conspired to make the philosophical and religious setting in which Zola wrote one of rich complexity, controversy, confusion, ambiguity: the widespread rejection of Christianity; the accelerating pace of the scientific revolution; the collapse of eclecticism; the decline of faith in the vast, soaring metaphysical systems and religious-substitutes of the first half of the century; the impact of a host of foreign philosophers, scholars, and writers—Kant, Hegel, Schelling, Fichte, Herder, Creuzer, Strauss, Schopenhauer, von Hartmann, Marx, Nietzsche, J. S. Mill, Spencer, Coleridge, Shelley, Carlyle, Tennyson, Browning, Ruskin, and numerous others; not to mention the influence of a multitude of native thinkers, critics, poets, and novelists propounding a great variety of doctrines, many of which were incompatible—Saint-Simon, Fourier, Cabet, Enfantin, Leroux, Proudhon, Lamennais, Michelet, Quinet, Comte, Hugo, Sainte-Beuve, Lamartine, Vigny, Littré, Bernard, Renan, Taine, Leconte de Lisle, Baudelaire, Flaubert, Cournot, Lequier, Renouvier, Vacherot, Ravaisson, Simon, Paul Janet, Lachelier, Fouillée, Boutroux, Bergson, Bourget, Barrès, Brunetière, Anatole France . . .

During the period when positivism was dominant, opposition to positivism was neither dormant nor ineffective; the readers of the Second Empire were solicited by opponents of positivism quite as forceful and alert as the positivist writers whom they attacked. Indeed, Ravaisson, one of the most perspicacious contemporary observers of French philosophy in the 1850s and 1860s, concluded in 1867 that the general tendency of thought at this time was toward idealism.[13] Paul Janet, writing the following year, was equally hopeful, even going so far as to claim that "the spiritualist school is still the most active, the most fecund, I might even say the most progressive of contemporary schools."[14] Meanwhile, initiated by Cournot, Lequier, and Renouvier, neo-criticism had already become a formidable force. In short, the "age of positivism" is also the age of neo-criticism and a revitalized spiritualist philosophy.[15]

Furthermore, during the next fifty years or so, the years of the critical reaction and so-called idealistic revival, positivism not only survived, but was in many ways even more militant than under the Second Empire. Ribot, Dumas, Pierre Janet, and others carried the positivistic outlook into psychology; Richet into physiology; Le Dantec into biology; Espinas, Izoulet, Durkheim, and followers like Levy-Bruhl into sociology; Charles Lalo into aesthetics; Henri Berr and Lacombe into the philosophy of history. Among professional philosophers, it persisted in the generation after Taine, Renan, and Littré in such men as Abel Rey, Goblot, Cresson, Jules de Gaultier.

Although pessimism was particularly widespread in the 1880s, strong pessimistic currents—it need hardly be pointed out—ran through the literature and thought of the whole period.

Throughout Zola's lifetime, moreover, the tradition that had produced in such rich profusion the great optimistic metaphysical systems and secular faiths of the first fifty years or so of the century—the cults of science, social religions, metaphysical religions, occult and neo-pagan religions, cults of history and progress—was far from exhausted. Hugo's prophetic voice kept ringing out at the center of French society until 1885, the year *Germinal* was published. Michelet's visionary *L'Oiseau, L'Insecte, La Mer,* and *La Montagne* came out between 1856 and 1867. *L'Amour* was published in 1858. The spirit of the great social prophets of the first half of the century lived on in the republican and socialist thought of the second half. Littré, Berthelot, Le Dantec, and many others helped perpetuate the worship of science and progress. As late as 1888, Theophilanthropy, a secular religious cult founded in 1798, still had, as Julien Vinson notes, more than 85,000 adherents.[16] Led by Laromiguière and Laffitte, Comte's Religion of Humanity was still practiced by a faithful following in the 1890s. Humanitarianism in general remained throughout the whole period (to quote Guérard) "the spiritual backbone of the French nation."[17] Stirred by the passions of the Dreyfus affair, it demonstrated once again its strong secular appeal as the century approached its close. As Paul-Hyacinthe Loyson was to confess in 1910, "It was through the Affair that the men of our generation communicated for the first time in Humanity. For us, Humanity was and remains a religion."[18]

Moreover, the extreme intellectual divisions of Zola's period were by no means confined to explicit oppositions between positivists and anti-positivists, optimists and pessimists, spiritualists and materialists, believers and doubters. Not only the young dilettants described by Bourget in the 1880s, but also most other individual intellectuals, including Taine, Renan, and the other intellectual leaders of Zola's generation, were violently torn between conflicting attitudes and ideas. It was the great age of the "divided mind." When Renan, comparing himself to the legendary hircocervus, half goat, half stag, of the medieval scholastics, wrote, "Each of my halves was forever trying to demolish the other,"[19] he could have been speaking not only of himself, but also of a multitude of his most thoughtful contemporaries.

Among the leading positivists, only a few, notably Bernard, remained consistently faithful to pure philosophical positivism. Even Littré, as Renan remarked, "spent his whole life forbidding himself to think about higher problems while never ceasing to do so."[20] Taine's philosophy appears in the final analysis as a logically unacceptable fusion of J. S. Mill's positivism with Spinozism and German idealism. Renan's positivism was subverted by his search for a religion of science. Others—one may think of Louise Ackermann, for example—combined positivism with pessimism. Many of the leading opponents of positivism, on the other hand, remained attached to positivism in one way or another. This is true of Ravaisson and his fellow idealist Vacherot, whose principal work, *La Métaphysique et la science,* is subtitled *Principes de métaphysique positive.* It is also true even of the Symbolist writers, whose emotional anti-positivism clashes with the philosophical positivism of their religious and metaphysical views and who probably occupy, as A. G. Lehmann has suggested, an intermediate position between "two contrasting moments of aesthetic history, the contemporary and the positivist."[21]

But if the clash between positivism and idealism or spiritualism was reflected in the thought of many individual thinkers, so also were many other oppositions in the philosophical and religious ideas of the age. Michelet, who had an enormous impact on Zola's generation during its early, most formative stage,[22] was torn between the religion of humanity, history, progress, and France, and the religion of nature, love, and woman. Nor could he reconcile his fatalistic view of nature with his need to believe in liberty. Taine not only vainly attempted, as we have said, to marry positivism and idealism; he shifted between an intellectual, rationalized idealism, on the one hand, and, on the other, a romanticism of the heart, intuiting an immense goodness at the core of things, sympathizing with Michelet's erotic pantheism, exalting bucolic nature, thinking in vegetative images, animating boulders and mountains, expressing a mystical friendship for giant oaks. Renan, for his part, was torn not only between positivism and, as we have noted, his longing for a new religion, but also, as anyone at all familiar with him knows, between a host of contradictory nonpositivistic philosophical and religious ideas. If at certain moments he championed a religion of humanity and science, at others he was drawn toward a religion of the ideal, a creed surpassing humanity itself, or he fell from faith into a nearly total skepticism. He conceived of God as a progressively created final cause, the object of "the divine work of progress."[23] But he also asserted that God is "eternal and immutable, without progress or becoming."[24] At times, Renan claimed that philology would discover general laws as evident and sure as the laws of natural science. At other times, he held that the reality of human life is far too complex and multifaceted to be reducible to neat systems and laws. He affirmed that progress is determined and inevitable, but also asserted that man has free will. He generally assumed that Nature is good, yet could also support the view that Nature is morally neutral or even picture it as evil.

In *Essais de psychologie contemporaine,* published in 1883, the year before Zola began *Germinal,* Paul Bourget wrote of the vast confusion that characterized his more thoughtful contemporaries in general. He noted how difficult, if not impossible, it was to inhale the Parisian atmosphere of the day—that atmosphere "supercharged with contrary electricities, where many different, detailed bits of information dart about like a population of invisible atoms"[25] —and maintain any systematic unity in one's own ideas. "We are living in a time of religious and metaphysical collapse," he stated, "when all the old doctrines lie scattered about on the ground. . . . An unprecedented anarchy is now the rule among all those who think." He went on to note how he and his contemporaries, in contrast to eighteenth-century skeptics, had even reached the point of calling into question their own doubts.[26] In 1886, only a year after the publication of *Germinal,* Charles Fuster, struck by much the same phenomena as Bourget, summed them all up very well when he wrote:

> Contemporary life is a long torrent of lava. You will not find anything precise in
> our ideas, because we entertain all ideas. Current thought—I mean the thought
> of those people who think (there are precious few)—fed by doctrines which are
> too opposed to survive together, has been invaded by an inexpressible chaos. In
> this singular malaise of a thought that has become too refined, too open to all
> the most contradictory impressions, there is no faith exempt from doubt, no doubt
> ... that does not have its moments of faith.[27]

Not only most of the individual ideas, but also most of the philosophical
and religious tensions, fissures, and contradictions that can be read into individual Zola novels like *Germinal* as well as into Zola's combined works viewed as
a whole are, of course, not only Zola's but those of this whole age—this age
when the intellectual and spiritual upheaval provoked by the rise of modern
civilization was surely at its peak.

Finally, I must point out that much of what seems to me most admirable
in the artistic form of *Germinal* lies precisely in how Zola appears to have
consciously or unconsciously coped in it with the artistic problems resulting
from his philosophical and religious contradictions.[28]

I have in mind, first of all, the truly masterful way in which he would seem
to have managed in *Germinal*, as in *L'Assommoir, La Joie de vivre,* and several
of his other novels, to translate his violent philosophical and religious ambiguity
into the very form and substance of his fiction, thus producing, as we know, a
veritable feast of ambiguity—an even richer feast indeed, as I have tried to
show among other things in this book, than some of us may have at first
suspected.[29]

Does *Germinal* belittle or exalt, undermine or reinforce the humanitarian
dream of "the great final kiss"? Is *Germinal* a deterministic novel, and, if so,
what kind of determinism does it express—scientific determinism, Tainian
determinism, pantheistic determinism? Does *Germinal* hold out to us the
hope of significant social improvement, or does it not suggest, rather, the tragic
futility of the nineteenth-century faith in progress? Is Nature as Zola portrays
it in the novel good or bad? Does the novel deify Earth or not? Is the novel
pantheistic or not? If it is pantheistic, which of the different kinds of pantheism
discernible elsewhere in Zola does it reflect? Must we interpret the novel's
emphasis on the sordid, painful side of existence as an expression of Zola's
pessimism? Or could it not be motivated by, among other things, his desire,
as he put it in his notes for *Le Docteur Pascal,* "to show courageously what
things are really like, so that I could say that despite everything life is great
and good because we live it with so much eagerness"?[30] Is not the novel's
repeated insistence on the smallness and frailty of man just another possible
expression of Zola's pessimism? Or could it not originate in the rejection of
anthropocentrism which marks his essentially optimistic "new faith" based
on geology? Is the time of the novel geological time? Or is it some other kind
of time—the circular time of the myth of eternal renewal or a time more in

accordance with romantic humanitarianism? What is the symbolic meaning, if any, of Etienne and Négrel's fraternal embrace? Does the title *Germinal* reflect the positivistic historian or sociologist in Zola or the optimistic, visionary prophet?[31] To what extent are the optimistic visionary elements of the novel serious prophetic visions, not just mere reveries? Does the novel's structure mirror Zola's philosophical positivism or his scientism—that is to say, his tendency, so typical of his age, to try to "derive" a metaphysics or religion from science?[32] As this book may, among other things, have helped some readers to see more clearly, one cannot try to answer these questions—or any of the dozens of similar questions which must inevitably occur to anyone contemplating *Germinal* in the light of Zola's philosophical and religious thought—without realizing how wonderfully ambiguous this novel is on the philosophical and religious level.

But I also have in mind the way Zola has managed consciously or unconsciously in *Germinal,* despite its lack of any solid, coherent vision of reality, to achieve an overwhelming realism—partly through the use of illusionistic tricks involving every sort of violence (violent actions, violent contrasts, Expressionistic color, etc.),[33] partly through an intense emphasis on, and fidelity to, that side of reality which our predominantly sensate culture tends to mistake for the whole of reality, and partly through his preoccupation with themes that have to do with those aspects of our modern collective experience that most vitally concern us and therefore seem most real.

I also have in mind how effectively the firm, harmonious artistic structure of *Germinal* offsets—and in a way compensates for—its philosophical and religious ambiguity. As elsewhere in Zola's fiction, his love of stability and order, frustrated on the higher intellectual plane, asserts itself with a vengeance on the aesthetic level—in the rigorous, almost mathematical logic with which nearly everything in this massive, complex work is organized around its central theme; in its tight, geometrical compartmentation; in its powerfully stylized, architectonic use of color; in its strong symmetries, achieved primarily through correspondences of form, emphasis, or arrangement set up between contrasting elements. Even some of the most contradictory elements of the ambiguous and, I might add, largely protean, miragelike world view that, as we have seen, the novel appears to reflect when contemplated in the context of Zola's overall philosophical and religious thought themselves become parts of the harmonious artistic design. The positivistic and visionary elements set off each other in aesthetically pleasing contrapuntal relationships. The optimist counterbalances the pessimist; the doubter, the man of faith; the scientific iconoclast, the advocate of scientist new religions; the serious reformer, the spinner of escapist reveries; the geologist-prophet, the romantic humanitarian; the perpetuator of ancient myths and rites, the radically modern intellectual.

Lastly, I am thinking of the thematic value of *Germinal*'s philosophical and religious ambiguity insofar as it may indeed be interpreted as symptomatic of Zola's confused, unstable (and no doubt always partly unconscious) vision of reality. For some of us, it heightens the impression of being plunged into a world racked by cosmic catastrophe, a world wholly caught up in the process of destruction and renewal. It suggests the immensity, the all-pervasive nature of a process which transforms man's fundamental principles and symbols as well as his external environment. Looking outward through, as it were, Zola's eye, we see this process going on on the socioeconomic level—the Montsou strike, the rise of the proletariat, the war between labor and capital. Reversing our gaze, peering into Zola's eye itself, we glimpse signs of the spiritual and intellectual chaos engendered by the same process.

Notes

Chapter 1: The Factualistic, Positivistic Basis

1 For a definition of philosophical positivism as opposed to other kinds of positivism—"social," "religious," and "Comptian"—and to the "positivist *état d'esprit*," see D. G. Charlton, *Positivist Thought in France During the Second Empire, 1852-1870* (Oxford: Oxford University Press, 1959), pp. 5-11. As Charlton reminds us, "philosophical positivism" is a theory of knowledge. "It holds, in its simplest form, that, excepting knowledge of logical and mathematical systems—all of them without any necessary connection with our observable world—science provides the model of the only kind of knowledge we can attain. All that we can know of reality is what we can observe or can legitimately deduce from what we observe. That is to say, we can only know phenomena and the laws of relation and succession of phenomena, and it follows that everything we can claim to know must be capable of empirical verification. Positivism thus denies the validity of such alleged means of knowing as have been termed *a priori,* and it equally denies that we can have any knowledge about religious and metaphysical questions since these are by definition largely concerned with a realm alleged to lie behind phenomena, in a world that can never be observed" (p. 6). Although Zola frequently insisted that he was a positivist, he did not distinguish between the various kinds of "positivism" any more than did most of his contemporaries, and the word, consequently, has, as he uses it, the same ambiguity as it does in much other nineteenth-century writing. Whether he was ever an absolutely pure philosophical positivist is debatable. A careful study of his works will show, however, that, from an early point on, he had a tendency toward philosophical positivism, a tendency culminating in his association of his own literary naturalism with the philosophies of Claude Bernard and Littré, in *Le Roman expérimental* (1880), *Les Romanciers naturalistes* (1881), and *Documents littéraires* (1881). When I speak of Zola's "philosophical positivism," I have in mind this tendency and those passages or elements of his writings which manifest it most strongly, as opposed to the abundant evidence which his works also contain of contrasting proclivities. For instance, as every student of Zola knows, he was almost constantly torn between philosophical positivism *à la* Bernard or Littré, and scientism—the use of science as a foundation for, or path to, metaphysical or religious speculation or knowledge—*à la* Taine or Renan.

2 Among the many expressions of Zola's skepticism, none is more revealing than his youthful poem "Doute" and its variant, "Religion," reprinted in Henri Mitterand's edition of Zola's *Œuvres complètes* (Paris: Cercle du Livre Précieux, 1966-69), XV, 921-25, 934-36. (Unless otherwise indicated, subsequent references to Zola's writings will be to this edition. Translations are mine.) See also Zola's 1865 essay "Les Moralistes français" (X, 105-13), and, of course, *Les Trois Villes.* On July 29, 1894, Paul Alexis,

reviewing *Lourdes,* saw in it a book "bathed in tears like a prayer" and went on to confirm
what many of Zola's readers had probably already suspected, that Abbé Pierre Froment,
its troubled hero, is none other than Zola himself–"a Zola tortured by doubt" (*"Naturalisme pas mort": Lettres inédites de Paul Alexis à Emile Zola, 1871-1900,* ed. B. H.
Bakker [Toronto: University of Toronto Press, 1971], pp. 417, 418). Having, like countless
other members of his generation, rejected Christianity, Zola had suffered the same trau-
matic consequences as many of them had–the pressing unanswered metaphysical questions,
the diminished trust in the power of human reason unaided by empirical observation, the
disorientation, the anguish. Repeatedly in his writings, including many dating back to
the 1860s, when his mature style and aesthetic theories were beginning to take shape, we
find him directly associating his love of cold, hard, empirical fact, brute reality, the world
of direct sense experience, with his acute metaphysical and religious doubt. For example,
in *Le Salut Public* of December 14, 1865, he speaks of that "naked, living reality" which
"this life of suffering, of doubt . . . makes you deeply love" (X, 74), and, in *La Confession
de Claude* (1865), he wrote, "The brutal truth has a strange charm for those tormented
by the problem of life" (I, 43). Over and over again, he also contrasts the infallibility of
science with the unreliability of philosophy and/or religion. For example, in *Le Figaro*
of October 21, 1879, he replies to a critic: "I agree that we should not attempt to examine
these questions on philosophical grounds, which have no solidity, but let us do so on
scientific grounds . . . for then we will be dealing in certainties" (X, 1334). In *Le Figaro* of
September 5, 1881, he remarks: "It is easy to see why people occasionally despair in times
like these. How often even the staunchest among us, losing sight of land, let themselves
become discouraged in the midst of the storm and blaspheme against their beliefs! And
that is why we must base every form of human activity on science. Science is the only
certainty" (XIV, 654). "It is said that religion is eternal," he says elsewhere, "but, surely,
science also is eternal and even more so . . . for each of its conquests is forever, the truths
that it finds remain, and it is science that puts dogma on the rack to make it agree with it,
rather than *vice versa*" (XIV, 839).

3 "If I had asked Balzac to define a novel for me, he would certainly have replied:
'A novel is a treatise of moral anatomy, a compilation of human facts, an experimental
philosophy of the passions. Its objective is to depict with the help of some verisimilar
action, men and nature with absolute truthfulness' " (X, 281, 282). "Since imagination is
no longer the dominant quality of the novelist, what has come to take its place? One must
always have one dominant quality or another. Today, the dominant quality of the novelist
is his sense of reality. . . . When you portray life, you must above all see it as it is and
give us an exact impression of it" (X, 1286, 1287). "One of our naturalist novelists wants
to write a novel about the theatrical world. He starts out with this general idea, without
having as yet a single fact or a single character. His first task will be to gather in his notes
everything that he can find out about the world that he wants to paint. . . . Once this
documentation is complete, his novel, as I have said, will create itself. All the novelist
will have to do is to distribute logically the facts. The dramatic plot, the story he needs
to draw up his chapter plans, will grow out of his observations" (X, 1286).

4 Richard H. Zakarian, *Zola's "Germinal": A Critical Study of Its Primary Sources*
(Geneva: Droz, 1972), p. 49.

5 "How great that feeling of uncertainty is may be seen most of all in the search for
little, hard facts (a kind of *'fait-alisme,'* which is now ruling in France)–a kind of insanity
which has never been seen before on earth; and not only science, but also a great deal of

the art that is being turned out at the present moment stems from this need" (*Werke* [Leipzig: C. G. Naumann, 1903-19], XIV, 183).

6 "Mes notes sur Anzin," Bibliothèque Nationale (Paris), MS. Nouvelles acquisitions françaises 10308, fols. 208-316. See Ida-Marie Frandon, *Autour de "Germinal"– La Mine et les mineurs* (Geneva: Droz, 1955); Louis-Laurent Simonin, *La Vie souterraine, ou les mines et les mineurs* (Paris: Hachette, 1867); and Zacharian.

7 Simonin, pp. 115, 130, and fig. 54 (reproduced in V, 67).

8 B. N. MS. Nouv. acq. fr. 10308, fol. 279.

9 Zacharian, p. 182.

10 B. N. MS. Nouv. acq. fr. 10308, fols. 3, 97-106.

11 "You cannot know a people if you are not perfectly conversant with its religious beliefs. . . . I am convinced that the archaeologist and the scholar, the historian and the artist must know the gods to know men. Tell me whom you worship, and I will tell you who you are" (X, 569). The importance that Zola gave to the religious aspect of his subject in *Germinal* may be seen in his rough outline where, after inventing the main features of the plot, he adds: "Naturally, I shall add several groups of workers in order to have all the specialities, trammers, timbermen, children, women, and all that distributed among all the typical characters. Don't forget the doctor. The priest, with the role of religion" (B. N. MS. Nouv. acq. fr. 10307, fols. 419, 420).

12 Almost from the outset of his career, Zola, like many of his contemporaries, tended to regard the artist as a living camera lens. For example, in *L'Evénement* of May 4, 1866, he wrote: "There are, in my opinion, two elements in any work of art: the element of reality, which is nature, and the element of individuality, which is man. . . . if temperament did not exist, all pictures would necessarily be simple photographs" (XII, 797). In *Le Roman expérimental,* he approvingly cites Claude Bernard's remark: "The observer simply notes the phenomena before his eyes. . . . He should be the photographer of phenomena; his observations should represent nature exactly as it is" (X, 1178).

13 The passage in question from Boëns-Boissau's book is cited by Frandon, p. 93.

14 V, 200, 201. The English translation is from the Signet Classics edition of *Germinal,* tr. Stanley and Eleanor Hochman (New York: New American Library, 1970), pp. 195, 196. (This edition will hereafter be designated by the abbreviation Sig.) Compare Zacharian, pp. 160-62.

15 B. N. MS. Nouv. acq. fr. 10308, fol. 219.

16 Whether Zola actually took some of these theories as seriously as he seemed to in his fiction has, however, been questioned by F. W. J. Hemmings, *Emile Zola,* 2nd ed. (London: Oxford University Press, 1966), pp. 57, 58.

17 *Les Rougon-Macquart,* ed. Henri Mitterand and Armand Lanoux, Bibliothèque de la Pléiade (Paris: Gallimard, 1960-67), V, 1724.

18 Although (as we shall see in Chapter 4) Zola's first hero among the great nineteenth-century naturalists was probably Cuvier, Zola ended up, like many other members of his generation, as an admirer of Darwin, whose *Origin of the Species* (1859) first came out in French in 1862. In *Le Roman expérimental* (1880), the novelist suggests to those other literary naturalists who felt that they must have some philosophy or other that the best one might be transformism (X, 1199). He was undoubtedly thinking here of Darwin, not Lamarck. He also cites Darwin favorably in later writings. See, for example, XIV, 568, 569, 606. *Au Bonheur des Dames,* completed in 1883, just two years before *Germinal,* is a Darwinian novel. *La Débâcle* (1892) embraces a Darwinian vision of warfare. In my opinion, the extent to which *Germinal* may be considered an expression of Zola's Darwinism can probably never be precisely determined. Concerning Darwin's popularity in France, see D. G. Charlton, *Secular Religions in France: 1815-1870* (London: Oxford University Press, 1963), p. 195. Looking back on his youth, Anatole France recalled: "at that time, Darwin's books were our Bible." Sully Prudhomme wrote of the "ineffable grandeur of transformism." Brunetière based his approach to literature on Haeckel and Darwin. Cf. the section on Zola's Darwinism in Alain de Lattre's *Le Réalisme selon Zola: Archéologie d'une intelligence* (Paris: Presses Universitaires de France, 1975), pp. 152-59. See also Robert J. Niess, "Zola et le capitalisme: Le Darwinisme social," *Cahiers Naturalistes,* No. 54 (1980), 57-67.

19 Professor of the History of Civilizations at the Ecole d'Anthropologie in Paris between 1885 and 1902, Letourneau was first President (1886) then Secrétaire Général (1887-1902) of the Société d'Anthropologie de Paris. He is today perhaps best known for his belief that sociology should be based on ethnography.

20 Charles Letourneau, *Physiologie des passions* (Paris: Gemer-Baillière, 1868), pp. 3, 219, 220. See also Zola's notes on Letourneau, *Les Rougon-Macquart,* Pléiade ed., V, 1677-91.

21 "And let me add that I firmly believe that I have given their due to all the organs, the brain along with all the others. My characters think as much as they should think, as much as people think in everyday life" (letter to Jules Lemaitre concerning *Germinal,* March 14, 1885, XIV, 1439).

22 "I shall study the ambitions and appetites of a family . . ." (*Les Rougon-Macquart,* Pléiade ed., V, 1738, 1739).

23 Marcel Girard, "L'Univers de *Germinal,*" *Revue des Sciences Humaines,* fasc. 69 (1953), p. 68.

24 "The same determinism must govern the stones of our roads and the human brain" (X, 1182). See also X, 1176, 1186, 1190.

25 For a good analysis of Taine's determinism, see Charlton's *Positivist Thought,* pp. 141-47, and *Secular Religions,* pp. 60, 61. For Zola's adhesion to Taine's philosophy, see, for example, X, 563-65.

26 Of the *Rougon-Macquart* characters in general, Zola wrote in his original notes for the series: "On the one hand, I shall show the hidden springs, the strings that animate the human puppet; on the other hand, I shall recount the deeds of this puppet. Having bared the heart and the brain, I shall easily demonstrate how and why the heart and the brain

have acted in certain determined ways and could not behave in any other fashion" (preliminary notes, *Les Rougon-Macquart,* Pléiade ed., V, 1756). He explicitly denies free will in his preface to the 2nd ed. of *Thérèse Raquin* (I, 519) and in *Le Roman expérimental* (X, 1190). See also his notes for *Le Rêve,* B. N. MS. Nouv. acq. fr. 10324, fol. 188: "What will become of free will here? I shall still deny it."

27 With respect to the novel's bourgeois characters in particular, Zola expressly tells himself in his preparatory notes that he must not portray them as deliberate villains. They too, he insists, are only products of a large, impersonal socioeconomic system. The disasters related in the book, he emphasizes, are not willed by them, but determined by the times, the overall state of things. (B. N. MS. Nouv. acq. fr. 10307, fol. 423.)

28 ". . . une humanitairerie se noyant dans un rêve d'amour universel." Apparently Musset was the first to use the word "humanitairerie." See Jean Dubois, *Le Vocabulaire politique et social en France de 1869 à 1872 à travers les œuvres des écrivains, les revues et les journaux* (Paris: Larousse, 1962), pp. 71, 169, 317. See also Musset's *Poésies complètes,* ed. Maurice Allem, Bibliothèque de la Pléiade (Paris: Gallimard, 1957), pp. 783, 784, n. 23. For another example of Zola's condemnation of romantic utopianism, which, it might be noted, was quite typical of French intellectuals after the failure of the Revolution of 1848 to realize the romantic utopian ideal, see II, 133.

29 See X, 1188, 1384-88. Note, however, that Zola's insistence that politics be based on science was motivated not only by his belief that this was the only way to achieve social progress but also by the same intense longing for certainty, for infallibility, that was behind his literary and artistic naturalism. ". . . Science is the only certainty. Make it the foundation of politics as well as literature if you need something to believe in. You will be standing on a rock that nothing can budge" (XIV, 654).

30 See, for example, X, 281-83, 1297, not to mention *Le Roman expérimental.* As his original prospectus for the *Rougon-Macquart* series, prepared for Lacroix, makes abundantly clear, he originally conceived of each novel as a "dramatic action" based on two complementary "studies" (*Les Rougon-Macquart,* Pléiade ed., V, 1755-58). In his "Notes générales sur la nature de l'œuvre," he tells himself that each volume should be "mathematically" deduced from a single "generative fact," preferably a scientific hypothesis (p. 1742).

31 B. N. MS. Nouv. acq. fr. 10307, fol. 402.

32 For an analysis of the logic whereby Zola "deduces" the plot of *Germinal* from its underlying scholarly studies, see Philip Walker, "The *Ebauche* of *Germinal,*" *PMLA,* 80 (Dec. 1965), especially pp. 571-75, 578-80.

33 B. N. MS. Nouv. acq. fr. 10307, fol. 411.

34 Paul Alexis, *Emile Zola: Notes d'un ami* (Paris: Charpentier, 1882), p. 108.

35 Philip Walker, "Zola et la lutte avec l'Ange," *Cahiers Naturalistes,* No. 42 (1971), pp. 81-92.

36 For an analysis of the roles played by science and imagination in the formation of a number of other Zola novels, *Thérèse Raquin, La Fortune des Rougon, La Curée, Le*

Ventre de Paris, La Conquête de Plassans, La Faute de l'abbé Mouret, and *Son Excellence Eugène Rougon,* see Fernand Doucet, *L'Esthétique de Zola et son application à la critique* (The Hague: De Nederlandsche Boek- en Steendruckerij, 1923), pp. 172-75. Doucet's conclusion, that each of Zola's works is the development of an idea originating not in his scientific observations, but in his poetic imagination, is however, obviously too categorical. It is a pity that Doucet did not include either *Germinal* or any of the other novels that I have just mentioned in his discussion of this topic.

Chapter 2: The Black Poem

1 "How can one explain Musset's strangely powerful hold on my generation? There are few young men who, after having read him, have not been permanently affected by his sweet charm. And yet Musset has taught us neither how to live nor how to die; he fell down after every step; in his agony, he was never able to do anything more than get up on his knees, to cry like a child. Nevertheless, we loved him; we loved him passionately, like a mistress who would fecundate our hearts by crushing them. It is because he gave voice to our century's despair" (IX, 423).

2 *Journal: Mémoires de la vie littéraire* (Paris: Flammarion-Fasquelle, 1935-36), VI, 127.

3 *Correspondance,* ed. B. H. Bakker (Montréal: Les Presses de l'Université de Montréal, 1978-   ), I, 170. (This edition will hereafter be referred to as *Corr.* Translations are mine.)

4 See Mitterand's notes for *La Joie de vivre* in *Les Rougon-Macquart,* Pléiade ed., III, 1751. See also ibid., p. 1742, and Edmond Toulouse, *Enquête médico-psychologique sur les rapports de la supériorité intellectuelle avec la névropathie: Emile Zola* (Paris: Flammarion, 1896), pp. 251, 252.

5 B. N. MS. Nouv. acq. fr. 10311, fols. 164, 165, 219.

6 *The Divine Comedy, I, Hell,* tr. Louis Biancolli (New York: Washington Square Press, 1966), pp. 18, 19. There can be no doubt that Zola harbored an urge to emulate Dante, whom he had much admired in his youth. *La Comédie amoureuse,* in three parts, transports us into the hell, purgatory, and paradise of love. *L'Assommoir* and *Germinal* are both modern *Infernos.* Among other notable reminiscences of Dante's masterpiece in *Germinal,* one must surely include: (1) the nine levels on which the hellish Guillaume Vein, where Maheu's crew works—"in hell," as the miners say (V, 47; Sig., 31)—is mined; (2) the Torrent, which corresponds to the Acheron; (3) the episode of the doomed lovers Etienne and Catherine clinging to each other in the depths of the flooded Le Voreux, a possible echo of the immortal episode of Paolo and Francesca, in Canto V—to which Zola twice admiringly alludes in his early correspondence (*Corr.,* I, 130, 140).

7 In *"L'Assommoir* et la pensée religieuse de Zola," *Cahiers Naturalistes,* No. 52 (1978), p. 71, I have tried to show how this incident is part of what would seem to be an attempt by Zola in this novel to attack the Christian doctrine of divine providence.

8 Cited by Irving Putter, *The Pessimism of Leconte de Lisle: The Work and the Time* (Berkeley: University of California Press, 1961), p. 363.

9 See also XIV, 712: "Always the human animal remains deep down there, under the skin of civilized man, ready to bite whenever his appetite overwhelms him."

10 See, for example, Zola's letter to Baille, Aug. 10, 1860 (*Corr.*, I, 221-28), "Paolo" (XV, 898-913), or "Un Coup de vent" (IX, 871-93). Mimi, the heroine of "Un Coup de vent," is an "Eve before the fall," a "radiant child of Heaven," whose soul has not yet been sullied by "the mire of this world" (IX, 886). For Zola's early religious beliefs, religious education, and participation in parish life, see X, 881, IX, 409, and *Corr.*, I, 223-27. It is not known exactly when or how his estrangement from much of what is most essential in Christianity began; but by the time he first seriously set out to be a writer, at the age of nineteen, he was already in a period of transition between his Catholic starting point and the break with Christianity in general that is one of the chief characteristics of his mature thought. As late as August 1860 he could still proclaim that "if to be a Christian means being a disciple of Christ, I proudly take that name; his precepts are mine, his god is mine" (*Corr.*, I, 227). From this point on, however, he never again refers to himself as a Christian. By the end of 1864, if not earlier, his loss of faith in Christianity was complete. "I do not know what the beliefs of our children will be," he wrote in December 1864, "but as for ourselves, we will bequeath to them a sky swept clean of all phantoms" (X, 325).

11 "They were sinking into a damp darkness when, in a sudden flash of light, he had a vision of men moving around in a cave. Then they were falling into nothingness again" (V, 44; Sig., 28). "Little by little, the darkness was thickening; the rain was now falling slowly, continuously, covering the nothingness below with its monotonous streaming" (V, 120; Sig., 108).

12 Girard, p. 63.

13 "Yes, I have loved life, black as I have painted it" (XII, 664).

14 In a letter to Rod, Zola wrote that his whole purpose in including Mme Hennebeau's banal adultery in the novel was to make possible this passage where Hennebeau gives vent to his human suffering in the face of all the social suffering in Montsou. "I thought it was necessary, " the novelist added, "to show over and above the eternal injustice of the classes, the eternal suffering of the passions" (XIV, 1440).

15 David Baguley, "The Function of Zola's Souvarine," *Modern Language Review*, 66 (1971), 786-97.

16 Jules Lemaitre, "Emile Zola," *Les Contemporains*, Ière série (Paris: Boivin, 1903, p. 281.

17 The affinities between Zola and Schopenhauer have been explored in depth by Benjamin Hudson in his unpublished doctoral dissertation, "Zola and Schopenhauer: The Affinity of Some Aspects of Their Thought as Reflected in the *Rougon-Macquart* Series," University of Michigan 1959. Hudson convincingly proves his contention that "consciously or unconsciously, Zola expressed ideas and convictions which link him to

a definite philosophical current, a current other than positivism. When these ideas are assembled into a recognizable pattern, they bear a marked resemblance to many of the major tenets of the philosophical system of Arthur 'Schopenhauer" (p. 3). Several of Hudson's underlying assumptions, however, would, I believe, be rejected today by most Zola specialists: that Zola's main goal in life was to achieve wealth and fame; that *Thérèse Raquin, Madeleine Férat,* and the *Rougon-Macquart* series constitued "a calculated and deliberate hiatus in his career, a financially rewarding interlude which he discarded after the completion of *Le Docteur Pascal*"; that he changed from the romanticism of his youth to realism and scientistic optimism "not because of any real conviction or basic change in his philosophical thinking, but because he had the rare faculty of recognizing the currents of the times, which were running against such literature" (p. 4); that his definitive philosophy, with its "glowing pantheism" (p. 2), did not emerge until late in his career; and that this "glowing pantheism" (p. 2), had "little effect or influence on the majority of the *Rougon-Macquart* novels" (p. 2). The facts simply do not support these allegations. My own conception of Zola is that, like many of his contemporaries, he was a "divided soul," a jumble of contradictions, a battleground of conflicting ideas. I have also been led to conclude that there was less evolution in Zola's thought than Hudson and some other scholars have supposed, that the major ideas and attitudes contending for predominance in Zola's mind remained for the most part the same throughout his adult career, and that he never arrived at a definitive philosophy. All this should become more evident by the final chapter. Nevertheless, what Hudson has to say about Zola's Schopenhauerian qualities makes this a most valuable thesis.

18 Lemaitre, p. 284.

Chapter 3: Pan

1 See in particular the Preface of *La Confession de Claude* (I, 9).

2 For example, see his letter of circa Feb. 10, 1861, to Baille: "I am perfectly aware that I am daydreaming, that I will never obtain what I want; but there is a *perhaps* and that's the branch I cling to. I hang on to the idea of possibility, and take off from there to whip up long romances where everything is for the best. . . . Then, when my dream has evaporated, I sometimes doubt that it was a dream, I am convinced that I really was the hero of this poem. I can think of nothing more to ask from the Heaven which has endowed me with an imagination lively enough to deceive myself in this way" (*Corr.,* I, 266). Or see his essay, first published in *Le Salut Public* of July 7, 1865, on Pelletan's *La Mère,* in which he confesses how he takes refuge in Michelet's quasi-religious mystique of woman whenever he needs "a beautiful lie" to console him for the pain inflicted by reality (X, 92); or his letter of Nov. 29, 1899, to Octave Mirbeau, concerning *Les Quatre Evangiles*: "All of that is very utopian, but what would you have me do? For the past forty years I have been dissecting; I think I have a right to dream a little bit in my old age" (VIII, 516). This last assertion, it must be noted, is, however, somewhat misleading. Not only *Les Quatre Evangiles,* but much of Zola's earlier work, including *Les Rougon-Macquart,* is full of his dreams—either indisputable dreams (e.g., *Le Rêve*) or ideas which, in his more skeptical, positivistic, or pessimistic moods, he qualified as "dreams." For example, in the final chapter of *La Terre,* he treats the vision it contains of the Great

Mother–the vision behind this entire great novel–as "this vague, confused dream [rêvasserie]" (V, 1142). In *Le Docteur Pascal*, the "philosophical conclusion" of the *Rougon-Macquart* series, he has Clotilde, who represents the voice of doubt, reflect regarding the vitalistic religious beliefs ascribed to Pascal, ". . . he had dreamed the most beautiful of dreams" (VI, 1395)–thus characterizing the concluding vision of *Les Rougon-Macquart* as a figment of the imagination.

3 For example, the dream ascribed to Claude in *La Confession de Claude*: "I had this dream that each soul goes to the great whole, that in death humanity is only a single immense breath, a single spirit. On earth, we are all separate, we don't know anything about each other, we suffer from our inability to reunite; beyond the grave, there is complete penetration, the marriage of everyone with everyone, one single, universal love. I looked at the sky. It seemed to me that I could see there . . . the soul of the world, the eternal being made up of all beings" (I, 109). (Cf. "Souvenir VI, Les Cimetières": ". . . it's a corner of universal life, where the souls of the dead pass into tree trunks, where there is nothing any more but a vast kiss, a vast embrace of what was yesterday with what will be tomorrow" [IX, 422]; or the last sentence of *Travail*: "And Luc expired, entered into the torrent of universal love, universal life" [VIII, 969].) Or recall Pascal's credo or the concluding visions of *La Terre, La Débâcle, Paris,* not to mention the penultimate sentence of *Le Rêve*: "Everything is only a dream" (V, 1318).

4 I have in mind here the eclectic, still largely Christian faith–reminiscent in some ways of Lamartine and Musset–that is most fully and systematically expressed in Zola's letter of Aug. 10, 1860, to Baille (*Corr.*, I, 221-28). But see also "Paolo," especially the long concluding prayer to God and the Holy Virgin (XV, 911-13), and Zola's letter of June 25, 1860, to Paul Cézanne, which contains a summary of the philosophical and religious ideas behind this poem (*Corr.*, I, 194-95).

5 These ideas and the various philosophies, creeds, visions of reality, etc., that Zola fashioned out of them are set forth explicitly in numerous passages here and there throughout Zola's writings, most notably the following: Zola's letters of Dec. 29, 1859, and Jan. 14, 1860, to Baille (*Corr.*, I, 117, 128-30); Zola's letter of June 25, 1860, to Cézanne (*Corr.*, I, 194-95); Zola's letters of June 2 and Aug. 10, 1860, to Baille (*Corr.*, I, 169-70, 221-28); the Prologue to *La Genèse,* c. 1860 (XV, 937); "Religion," c. 1861 (XV, 924-25); "Du progrès dans les sciences et dans la poésie," *Le Journal Populaire de Lille,* April 16, 1864 (X, 313); *La Confession de Claude,* 1865 (I, 109); "La Géologie et l'histoire," *Le Salut Public,* Oct. 14, 1865 (X, 100-01); "Correspondance littéraire," *Le Salut Public,* Nov. 20, 1866 (X, 684); "Les Quatre Journées de Jean Gourdon," 1866 (IX, 456); "Printemps: Journal d'un convalescent," 1866? (IX, 903-14); "Causerie," *La Tribune,* June 28, 1868 (XIII, 112-17); "Le Forgeron," 1868 (IX, 396-97); *La Faute de l'abbé Mouret,* 1875 (III, 170-75); "La Démocratie," *Le Figaro,* Sept. 5, 1881 (XIV, 650-55); Zola's letter to Jules Lemaitre, March 1885 (XIV, 1439); Zola's letter to Gustave Geffroy, July 22, 1885 (XIV, 1443); *L'Œuvre,* 1886 (V, 566-67); the "Ebauche" of *La Terre,* 1887 (*Les Rougon-Macquart,* Pléiade ed., IV, 1509-13); preparatory notes for *Le Rêve,* 1888 (B. N. MS. Nouv. acq. fr. 10324, fols. 186, 190-94); preparatory notes for *Le Docteur Pascal,* 1893 (*Les Rougon-Macquart,* Pléiade ed., V, 1600-02); *Le Docteur Pascal,* 1893 (VI, 1190); address, Banquet of the Association Générale des Etudiants, May 18, 1893 (XII, 681-83); *Paris,* 1898 (VII, 1560-62); *Fécondité,* 1899 (VIII, 92-93, 499-500); Zola's letter to Fernand Desmoulin, Aug. 13, 1898 (XIV, 1506); *Travail,* 1901 (VIII, 669, 954-55); *Vérité,* 1903 (VIII, 1146-47).

6 The word *religion* or *religious,* like *philosophy* or *beauty,* is, of course, almost impossible to define, being used in a confusing variety of different ways by different thinkers. Following Charlton's example (*Secular Religions,* p. 214), I am tempted to accept as the minimum definition Nathan Söderblom's conclusion that "there is no real religion without a distinction between holy and profane," that "the only sure test is holiness," the holy being that which "inspires awe" ("Holiness," *Encyclopaedia of Religion and Ethics,* ed. James Hastings [New York: Charles Scribner's Sons, 1928], VI, 731). But since the answer to what is holy will, as Charlton reminds us, clearly vary with each man's temperament, I also find myself in agreement with his suggestion that we "ought therefore to say, adopting a distinction of Gabriel Marcel's, that in the last resort the definition of 'religion' poses not a solvable 'problem' but a 'mystery' in which each of us is permanently involved, that can only be personally decided" (*Secular Religions,* p. 214).

7 See, for example, "Nantas": "Little by little he had fabricated for himself a *religion* of force, seeing nothing but force in the world . . ." (IX, 717). Or *Paris*: "A *religion* of science, that is the appointed, certain, inevitable denouement of the long march of humanity toward knowledge" (VII, 1560, 1561). Or *Le Docteur Pascal*: "I believe that the pursuit of truth through science is the *divine* ideal that man should set himself" (VI, 1190).

8 For example, see his letter of Aug. 10, 1860, to Baille (*Corr.,* I, 221-28); "Paolo" (XV, 898-913); "Religion" (XV, 921-25); the Prologue to *La Genèse* (XV, 937); "Du progrès dans les sciences et dans la poésie," a kind of manifesto in which he proclaims that his chief literary ambition would be to show, in the skies swept clean of all the old myths, "the god Infinite and the immutable laws that flow from his being and rule the worlds" (X, 313); his review of Nourrisson's *Spinoza et le naturalisme contemporain* in *Le Salut Public* of Nov. 20, 1866 (X, 684-85); "La Géologie et l'histoire" (X, 99-101); the "Causerie" that he composed in Gloton on June 25, 1868 (XIII, 115); "La République et la littérature" (X, 1395); "Lettre à la jeunesse" (X, 1219); *Le Docteur Pascal* (VI, 1246); *Paris* (VII, 1560-61); *Travail* (VIII, 954-55).

9 "Lettre à la jeunesse": "We do not deny God; we are trying to ascend again to him through returning to the analysis of the world" (X, 1219); "La République et la littérature": "The naturalist writer feels that he does not have to come to a conclusion as to the question of God's existence. There is a creative force, and that is it. Without participating in discussions about that force, without presuming as yet to make any pronouncement as to its specific nature, he takes up once again the analytical study of nature, beginning at the beginning. His job is the same as that of our chemists and physicists. All he does is collect and classify documents without trying to relate them to any common measure, without concluding with some form of idealism. If you like, it is an inquiry into the nature of the ideal, of God himself, instead of being, as in the classical and romantic schools, a dissertation on some dogma or other, a rhetorical amplification based on extrahuman axioms" (X, 1395).

10 See, for example, the Prologue to *La Genèse* (XV, 937).

11 See, for example, "Religion" (XV, 921-25, especially pp. 924-25) or the ending of *La Confession de Claude*: "All night long I had before my eyes the darkness of space pierced by the yellow rays of the stars; I had tried in vain to sound the depths of the

somber abyss, frightened by its immense calm, its unsoundable nothingness. This calm, this nothingness, were filled with light; the shades trembled and slowly retreated, revealing their mysteries; the terror of the dark gave way to the hope of the first glow of dawn. The whole sky slowly became ablaze; it was decked with rosy tints, sweet as smiles; it opened up, dispersing the pale rays of light, letting me see God. . . . And I, in my solitude, confronted by this rending of the night, this slow, majestic birth of day, became aware of a fresh, invincible strength in my heart, an immense hope" (I, 111-12). Or see "Printemps: Journal d'un convalescent" (IX, 903-14); "Les Quatre Journées de Jean Gourdon" (IX, 451-85, especially p. 457); the "Causerie" written in Gloton on June 25, 1868 (XIII, 115); *La Faute de l'abbé Mouret,* especially the first page of Part II, Ch. xvi (III, 175); or Ch. vi of *L'Œuvre* (V, 567).

12 "I believe that the future of humanity lies in the progress of reason through science. I believe that the pursuit of truth through science is the divine ideal that man should propose to himself. I believe that all is illusion and vanity, outside of the treasure of those truths which have been slowly acquired and which will never again be lost. I believe that the sum total of these truths, forever mounting, will ultimately bestow upon man incalculable power and serenity, if not happiness. . . . Yes, I believe in the ultimate triumph of life" (VI, 1190). For other examples, see the "naturalist creed" in "Le Naturalisme," *Le Figaro,* Jan. 17, 1881 (XIV, 511), and the creed recited by Zola in "La Démocratie," *Le Figaro,* Sept. 5, 1881 (XIV, 655).

13 "We must love others as they love us; the same flame brings us all together; our love as lovers and spouses cannot endure unless everyone is happy. Divine love, since nothing can live except by thee, help us to finish our work, kindle our hearts, make all the couples of the City love each other and give birth, in that universal loving-kindness which should unite us all" (VIII, 849).

14 "It had become an accepted custom on the first day of summer for every family to set a table just outside the entrance of its house and to dine outside, in the street, in the plain view of every passer-by. It was like a fraternal communion of the entire City; people broke bread and drank wine publicly; the tables finally joined together, forming a single table, changing the town into one immense banquet hall, transforming the inhabitants into a single family. . . . Along the avenues, in front of the entrances of the festive dwellings, the common meal went on. . . . The Passover of this fraternal people was going to terminate under the stars, in one immense communion, elbow to elbow, on the same tablecloth, among the same overblown roses. The whole town became one giant feast, the families mingled, merged into one single family, and all lungs were animated by the same breath, all hearts beat with the same love. From the great, pure sky, there fell a delicious peace, a sovereign peace, the harmony of the worlds and of men" (VIII, 932, 940, 941).

15 "All revealed truth is a lie; experimental truth alone is valid, whole, eternal. Hence the prime necessity of opposing the Catholic catechism with the scientific catechism, the world and man explained by science, seen once again as they really are, with all their true vitality, their march toward a perpetual, ever more perfect future" (VIII, 1146-47).

16 B. N. MS. Nouv. acq. fr. 10301, fol. 8.

17 Cf. Lepelletier, *Emile Zola: Sa vie, son œuvre* (Paris: Mercure de France, 1908), p. 441.

18 See Marcel Cressot's "Zola et Michelet. Essai sur la genèse de deux romans de jeunesse: *La Confession de Claude, Madeleine Férat,*" *Revue d'Histoire Littéraire de la France,* 35 (July-Sept. 1928), 382-89, David Baguley's *"Fécondité" d'Emile Zola: Roman à thèse, évangile, mythe* (Toronto: University of Toronto Press, 1973), pp. 53, 54, and Allan Pasco's "Love *à la* Michelet in Zola's *La Faute de l'abbé Mouret,*" *Nineteenth-Century French Studies,* 7 (Spring-Summer 1979), 232-44. See also, among other writings by Zola himself treating of Michelet, the "Causerie" composed in Gloton on June 25, 1868 (XIII, 112-17). Although much work remains to be done on the subject of Michelet's influence on Zola, it is already apparent that it is at least as great as Hugo's, Musset's, or Taine's.

19 Cf. the following lament, from Zola's preliminary notes for *Les Trois Villes:* "Faith alone fecundates, but faith is impossible . . ." (cited by René Ternois, *Zola et son temps: "Lourdes"–"Rome"–"Paris"* [Paris: Les Belles Lettres, 1961], p. 291).

20 Concerning "Paolo," Zola wrote Cézanne on June 25, 1860: "In 'Paolo' I had two objectives: exalt Platonic love, make it more attractive than carnal love; then show that, in this century of doubt, pure love can serve as a faith, give the lover belief in a god, in an immortal soul" (*Corr.,* I, 194). "Un Coup de vent," composed in late 1860 (see Mitterand's note, IX, 1164) is also obviously an attempt on the part of the young Zola to promulgate certain ideas central to his quasi-religious cult of love, which was then rapidly evolving. Note that as early as December 1859, when he was still eighteen, he was contemplating a series of what amounted to evangelical works in the form of short stories: "I am going to undertake a volume of short stories . . . I shall show that for lovers there is a god and that neither hell, nor men, nor priests with their evil doctrines can destroy a pure love" (*Corr.,* I, 117).

21 See Geffroy's review of *Germinal, La Justice,* July 14, 1885 (cited in *Les Rougon-Macquart,* Pléiade ed., III, 1864). Among recent critics who have stressed the pantheistic aspects of the novel, one thinks above all of Pierre-Henri Simon. See Simon's introduction to *Germinal* (V, 13-20).

22 E.g., the famous "symphonie des fromages" in *Le Ventre de Paris* (II, 756-61) or the transformation of floral scents into voices of musical instruments in the account of Albine's death in *La Faute de l'abbé Mouret* (III, 261-62).

23 Cf. the Preface to *Nouveaux Contes à Ninon:* "I want to couch humanity on a white page, all beings, all things; a work which would be the immense ark" (IX, 351).

24 "Paolo": "And my soul devines / A powerful Creator in these divine concerts" (XV, 912). "Du progrès dans les sciences et dans la poésie": "It should be noted that the scientist and the poet still have the same point of departure even today. Both find themselves face to face with the world; both have as their task to discover its secret mechanism and try to provide in their works an idea of universal harmony" (X, 312). *Travail:* "From the great, pure sky, there descended a delicious, a sovereign peace, the harmony of the worlds and of men" (VIII, 941). *L'Ouragan:* "The birds sing; the insects sing; the giant tree sings; all the forest and all the earth sing: the concert of eternal life sings, unites us, and carries us away" (XV, 654).

25 Prosper Lucas, *Traité philosophique et physiologique de l'hérédité naturelle dans les états de santé et de maladie du système nerveux* (Paris: Baillière, 1847-50), I, xii. *Les Rougon-Macquart,* Pléiade ed., V, 1693.

26 *Les Rougon-Macquart,* Pléiade ed., V, 1601.

27 Is not this conception implicit in, for example, the following remark from *Vérité*: "Everyone had an imperious need to become part of all others; and personal action, the individuality which was so necessary, the liberty of every being, could be compared to the distinct play of the various organs, all under the domination of the universal being" (VIII, 1148)?

28 For an indication of Zola's youthful attitude toward spiritualism, see, for example, his letter of March 25, 1860, to Cézanne (*Corr.,* I, 140-41).

29 "I must assume above all a philosophical tendency, not to parade it, but to impart unity to my books. The best would be perhaps materialism; I mean the belief in forces which I will never need to explain" (*Les Rougon-Macquart,* Pléiade ed., V, 1744). Note that neither here nor elsewhere does Zola's "materialism" exclude, any more than that of the Stoics, a belief in the indwelling divine.

30 *La Confession de Claude*: "I dreamt this dream that each soul goes to the great whole" (I, 109). "La Géologie et l'histoire": "Instead of affirming that the sky and the earth were created just for our use, we should think, rather, that they were created for the use of the great Whole . . ." (X, 100). First detailed plan for *La Terre*: ". . . but how petty all that is in the great whole. Our sufferings count almost for nothing in a cosmic cataclysm" (cited by Guy Robert, *"La Terre" d'Emile Zola: Etude historique et critique* [Paris: Les Belles Lettres, 1952], p. 218).

31 See also Zola's article "L'Amour des bêtes," *Le Figaro,* March 24, 1896 (XIV, 736-42) and the discourse that he delivered at the 1896 annual meeting of the French Society for the Protection of Animals (XIV, 841-42).

32 Letter to Baille, Aug. 10, 1860: "His temple is the universe" (*Corr.,* I, 225).

33 See, for example, his "Causerie" in *La Tribune* of June 21, 1868: "Ah! How far away Paris is! All human strife is forgotten. I do not know any more if there are masters and valets. I feel myself live with profound joy in the immense liberty of the sky, in the great fraternity of the trees and water" (XIII, 108); or the following passage from *Fécondité*: "After the burning Paris pavement, seared by the bitter battles of the day, by the sterile, whorish rut of evening, under the conflagration of the electric lamps, what blessed peace and quiet: this vast silence, this soft, heavenly blue light, this endless unfolding of plains bathed in refreshing shadow . . ." (VIII, 81).

34 In *La Faute de l'abbé Mouret,* for example, the holy of holies of the garden of Paradou is occupied by the great Tree of Fecundity, like an altar. As Serge and Albine approach it, a hush falls over the garden—"a great, trembling silence, a religious expectation" (III, 170). In *L'Ouragan,* Jeanine and Richard hear, as they approach a similar tree on a wild ocean island, a "divine music" (XV, 654). For Zola's conception of great forest trees as a higher, more godlike order of beings, see his review of Fulgence Marion's *Les Merveilles de la végétation* in *L'Evénement* of Aug. 5, 1866 (X, 575, 576). For a general study of the immensely rich meanings and associations that trees acquire in Zola—especially the young Zola, "the young transplant"—see J. B. Sanders' sensitive, perceptive essay "Emile Zola: Le Transplanté et l'arbre," in *Fiction, Form, Experience: The French Novel from Naturalism to the Present,* ed. Grant E. Kaiser (Montréal: Editions France-Québec,

1976), pp. 53-66. Those interested in elucidating Zola's tree imagery may also find helpful the passage concerning the image of the Tree in Mircea Eliade's *Myths, Dreams, and Mysteries: The Encounter between Contemporary Faiths and Archaic Realities*, tr. Philip Mairet (New York: Harper and Row, 1967), pp. 19, 20. Eliade points out among other things that the appearance of this image in dreams would appear to indicate "that the drama which is being enacted in the unconscious—one that concerns the integrity of psycho-mental activity, and therefore of the person's whole existence—is on the way to finding a positive solution" (p. 19).

[35] For a helpful discussion of French pantheism between 1815 and 1870, a period including Zola's most formative years, see Charlton's *Secular Religions*, pp. 117-25. See also Philip Walker, "The Survival of Romantic Pantheism in Zola's Religious Thought," *Symposium*, 23 (Fall-Winter 1969), 354-65.

[36] "At the summit, absolute unity, the unified general formula, which is God; and then the chain of beings and things which descend from it and whose every link is strongly welded to those which precede and follow it"—*Le Salut Public*, Nov. 20, 1866 (X, 684). (Zola then goes on to point out that "the philosophers known as 'positivists' are all more or less the spiritual offspring of Spinoza . . . Littré, Michelet, Ernest Renan, H. Taine"!)

[37] "The poets of the beginning of the century, in resuscitating ancient pantheism, inevitably gave rise to a school of landscape painting loving the countryside for itself, finding in it enough interest and enough life to make it possible to interpret it in its banality, without trying to invest it with additional nobility. The classical landscape is dead, killed by life and *truth*"—"Les Paysagistes," *L'Evénement Illustré*, June 1, 1868 (XII, 875).

[38] ". . . but how petty all this is in the great whole. . . . God doesn't care a fig about us!" (cited by Robert, *"La Terre" d'Emile Zola*, p. 218).

[39] ". . . life . . . the soul of the world"—notes for *Le Docteur Pascal* (*Les Rougon-Macquart*, Pléiade ed., 1600, 1601). Cf. the list of alternate titles for *L'Œuvre*, including *La Vie universelle, L'Ame épandue, L'Ame des choses* (*Les Rougon-Macquart*, Pléiade ed., I, 1338).

[40] "We are going toward the future, a phase of the creature . . ."—"La Géologie et l'histoire" (X, 100).

[41] ". . . life, which is only a movement"—notes for *Le Docteur Pascal* (*Les Rougon-Macquart*, Pléiade ed., V, 1601). "Life can only be defined as this communicated movement which it receives and passes on"—address, banquet of the Association Générale des Etudiants, May 18, 1893 (XII, 682).

[42] See Philip Walker, "The Mirror, the Window, and the Eye in Zola's Fiction," *Yale French Studies*, No. 42 (1969), p. 67.

[43] "So is it true then" asks Denise, in *Au Bonheur des Dames*, "that death is necessary to fertilize the world . . . ?" (IV, 997); and the answer provided by the plot is very much in the affirmative. In *Vérité*, Zola more explicitly affirms: ". . . death went on ceaselessly

performing her unknown task, mowed down men as if to fertilize the field where other men would grow" (VIII, 1470).

44 *Les Rougon-Macquart,* Pléiade ed., IV, 1513.

45 Recall, for example, that almost surrealistic passage in *La Fortune des Rougon* where Zola imagines that the emaciated hands of the dead buried in the cemetery where Miette and Silvère meet grow up in the form of plants through the ground in order to seize the young lovers and force them into each other's arms. When the stems are broken, they exude a potent, fecundating, life-giving fluid which the coffins buried in the ground slowly secrete and whose sharp, penetrating odor makes the young couple drunk with desire (II, 187). Cf. the sweatlike vivifying liquid pouring from the bark of the Tree of Life in *La Faute de l'abbé Mouret,* which, as Hemmings has noted, is essentially a phallic symbol ("Emile Zola et la religion," *Europe,* 46ᵉ année, Nos. 468-69 [April-May 1968], p. 134); or the following passage from *Fécondité*: "The sap of the earth mounted, procreated in the shadows, redolent with an odor of vital intoxication. It was the streaming of seeds, carried along ceaselessly by the worlds. It was the thrill produced by the coupling of thousands of living beings, the universal spasm of fecundation, the necessary, continuous conception of life forever producing more life" (VIII, 92).

46 See, for example, "Les Quatre Journées de Jean Gourdon" (IX, 456).

47 See especially Uncle Lazare's summary of the lesson of spring (IX, 456).

48 *Le Docteur Pascal*: "Health to be found in the universal task, in the power which fecundates and gives birth. The work was good when love resulted in the production of a child" (VI, 1400). Preface for *Le Roman d'un inverti*: "Man and woman have certainly been placed here below solely to have children, and they kill life the moment when they do not do more than is necessary to have them" (XII, 702). *Fécondité*: "The only reason a living being is born is to create, transmit, propagate life" (VIII, 36). Cf. Toulouse: "He regards prolonged virginity as reprehensible. . . . Likewise, he cannot understand unconsummated love, because in his opinion, the perpetuation of the species is the object of lovemaking" (p. 249).

49 Richard Grant, *Zola's "Son Excellence Eugène Rougon": An Historical and Critical Study* (Durham, N. C.: Duke University Press, 1960), pp. 125, 126.

50 *Les Rougon-Macquart,* Pléiade ed., V, 1586.

51 *Les Rougon-Macquart,* Pléiade ed., V, 1600, 1601.

52 *Profession de foi du dix-neuvième siècle* (Paris: Pagnerre, 1852), p. 410 (cited by Charlton, *Secular Religions,* p. 199). Between 1868 and 1870, Zola worked on the staff of *La Tribune* in association with Pelletan, one of its founders.

53 Its earliest expression in Zola's writings is in a letter addressed to Baille and dated March 9, 1859: "Jesus forgot to include in his teachings one happy beatitude, those who can work" (*Corr.,* I, 109). See also one of Zola's earliest short stories, "Le Sang," where, after pointing out Christ's failure to redeem the world ("Look, the earth is as evil as it ever was. Jesus has died, and the land is no more verdant than yesterday. Come on now!

It was just one more murder"), Zola has the heroes of this story turn to productive labor for their salvation (IX, 74, 75).

54 This is, I suspect, implicit in Médéric's response to Sidoine's question at the end of "Les Aventures . . ." as to where wisdom is to be found: "Go get yourself a spade" (IX, 184). But see also Zola's address of May 18, 1893, to the Association Générale des Etudiants: "As soon as we accept this task [the work that life gives us] it seems to me that even those among us who are most tormented will find peace of mind. I know that there are souls who are tormented by the thought of the infinite, who suffer from the mystery of it all, and it is those I am speaking to in a brotherly way, in advising them to keep themselves busy with some enormous labor. . . . No doubt, that will not solve any metaphysical problem . . . but isn't that already something—to achieve good physical and mental health and escape the danger that resides in dreams . . . ?" (XII, 682).

55 For example, see, besides the last sentence of the passage quoted above, note 54, from Zola's address of May 18, 1893, to the AGE and other remarks concerning the benefits of work in the same text, Zola's short story "Le Forgeron" (IX, 393-97), whose narrator (none other than Zola himself) is cured from a nervous breakdown by the sight of a blacksmith at work. ("It was there, in the smithy, that I recovered forever from my malady of sloth and doubt"—p. 397.) See also Zola's letter to Delpech, May 29, 1898 (XIV, 1497, 1498) and *Travail* (VIII, 668, 669).

56 "Adult work is the work of culture: everyday tasks are conducted under the guiding principles of the culture's assumptions about transcendence and are subservient to the prevailing moods of immortality. Each steel girder installed, each mile driven by a taxi, each product order typed and approved contributes to a culture's collective effort to cope with individual mortality through lasting enterprises, structures and sequences. Adult work is always tied in with a larger spiritual principle—whether that principle is the Protestant ethic, the deification of capital, or the revolutionary vision" (R. J. Lifton, "The Struggle for Cultural Rebirth," *Harper's Magazine*, April 1973, p. 90).

57 For example, he asserts in *Fécondité*: "A newborn infant is a piece of work" (VIII, 499). Note also the association of ideas in the following alternative titles for *L'Œuvre: L'Œuvre de chair; L'Œuvre humaine; L'Œuvre vivante; Le Travail: Parturition; Fécondation (The Work of Flesh; Human Work; Living Work; Labor; Parturition; Fecundation) (Les Rougon-Macquart, Pléiade ed., IV, 1338).

58 For example, see the description of the advent of May in Part I of *La Faute de l'abbé Mouret*: "At this early morning hour, when everything was caught up in the full labor of growth, the warm air was full of humming sounds; everywhere a long silent straining upward, the thrill of life dislodging rocks. But the priest was oblivious to the ardor of this laborious birth" (III, 32). Or see the next-to-the-last page of *La Terre* (V, 1142); or the assertions that life and work are identical in Zola's address to the AGE of May 18, 1893 (XII, 682) and *Travail* (VIII, 668).

59 For example, he wrote in *Au Bonheur des Dames*, concerning Octave Mouret: "Truly, there must be something wrong with those . . . who refused to put their shoulders to the wheel, in a time of such great industry, when the whole century was forging ahead. And he poked fun at the faint of heart, those who had no stomach for the task, the pessimists . . . who could do nothing better than take on the airs of whimpering poets or frowning skeptics in the midst of *the immense building yard* of our age" (IV, 759). The

conception of nineteenth-century society as a workshop is implicit in the final paragraphs of "Le Forgeron" (IX, 397). Zola's "Causerie" in *La Tribune* of Sept. 20, 1868, presents contemporary civilization as a place of labor, a giant concert of hammering sounds, an immense forge full of flames and smoke, fabricating a symbolic plow (X, 762, 763).

60 For example, see his address of May 18, 1893, to the AGE; or see *Travail* (VIII, 669).

61 *Les Rougon-Macquart*, Pléiade ed., V, 1601.

62 Address to the AGE, May 18, 1893: "One cannot define life except by this communicated movement that it receives and passes on and that, in the last analysis, is nothing but work" (XII, 682).

63 ". . . dear beasts issued from my heart and imagination, all of you with whom I have peopled my books. You are part of my family; I can once again see you galloping behind the thousand human beings that I have brought into the world, and that gives me pleasure, and I am happy to have reserved a place for you in the immense ark. . . . I am grateful to the whole pullulating farmyard of Désirée. . . . I am grateful to the family pets of my good Pauline . . . I am grateful to my two mine heroes, my two martyred horses, Trompette and Bataille . . . and to the little white rabbit, Pologne. . . . I am grateful to all those male and female beasts that labored and suffered in *La Terre* . . . my lamentable, tragic horses in *La Débâcle* . . . and all those others that it would take too long to mention . . ."–*Le Figaro*, May 30, 1896 (XIV, 794-96).

64 See Girard, p. 67.

65 I am thinking in particular of the final paragraph of the novel, especially the fifth and sixth sentences: ". . . the teeming earth [*la terre* qui enfantait]. Life was springing from her nourishing flank . . ." (V, 405; Sig., 428).

66 See Philip Walker, "Zola's Art of Characterization in *Germinal*: A Note for Further Research," *L'Esprit Créateur*, 4 (Summer 1964), 65, 66.

67 Stanley and Eleanor Hochman's otherwise excellent translation of the sentence cited here–"Des croyances endormies se réveillaient dans ces âmes éperdues, ils invoquaient la terre . . ." (V, 381)–would, in my opinion, have been even better if they had begun it with "Forgotten beliefs" instead of "Forgotten superstitions" (Sig., 401). Zola does not actually qualify the beliefs in question as superstitions. It is true, however, that the following sentence–"One old man was stammering forgotten prayers and turning his thumbs out to appease the evil spirits of the mine"–could be interpreted as an indication that we have indeed to do with superstitions. But see my discussion of the essential ambiguity of Zola's thought and style in Chapter 6.

68 *Les Rougon-Macquart*, Pléiade ed., III, 1822.

69 Cf. Zola's use of the word "soul" ("âme") elsewhere in his adult writings. For example, Zola declares in his preface to the second edition of *Thérèse Raquin* that its characters are human beasts, nothing more, and goes on to state emphatically that his conception of them completely excludes the notion of a soul ("L'âme est parfaitement absente, j'en conviens aisément, puisque je l'ai voulu ainsi"–I, 520); yet, in Chapter xviii,

he writes of his two guilty lovers: "They shuddered with the same shudder. . . . They possessed henceforth a single body and a single *soul* with which to enjoy life and to suffer" (I, 592). See also VII, 997 (*Rome*) and VIII, 500 (*Fécondité*) and 908 (*Travail*).

70 See his article "Dépopulation" first published in *Le Figaro,* May 23, 1896 (XIV, 785, 786). The original title was "Le Déchet." In this article, Zola says that he had been thinking about writing it for ten years or so (XIV, 785).

71 See Mitterand's note 23, XIV, 857.

72 For an interpretation of Catherine and Etienne's relationship in the light of Zola's cult of Eros, see Chantal Bertrand-Jennings, *L'Eros et la femme chez Zola* (Paris: Klincksieck, 1977), Ch. iv, especially pp. 109-13.

73 Elsewhere I have suggested that this may symbolize the ideal social order that could result from social cooperation ("Prophetic Myths in Zola," p. 450). Cf. André Wurmser's interpretation, in his preface to the Gallimard ed. of *Germinal* (Paris, 1978), p. 46. According to Wurmser, Etienne and Négrel's embrace symbolizes the social order that will arise not from class cooperation, but from a social transformation abolishing class divisions and hence class antagonisms. I am not sure that Wurmser and I disagree quite as much as he supposes. I never meant to imply that the ideal social order would, in Zola's mind, even at the moment he wrote *Germinal,* perpetuate class divisions. I had in mind the fact that during this period he still seems to have entertained hopes that the fortunate members of society could be induced (by such works as *Germinal* among other things) to make the reforms that would institute a just society. See, for example, his letter of Dec. 1885 to an unnamed newspaper editor (XIV, 1449). *Germinal,* it seemed to me, appeared to suggest that the process of reform would involve a working together of the bourgeoisie and the proletariat toward the common good (the rescue operation in which all factions in the novel take part). Faced by the catastrophic evils which have been brought about by social injustice and which threaten to destroy the whole of society (the mine disaster), the different classes would in the process of trying to cope with these evils cast aside class differences, motivated by a sense of their common humanity. (Recall also that in *Travail,* Luc and Jordan, the reformers of Beauclair, are from the bourgeoisie.) However, after giving the matter further thought, I now suspect that we have to do here, as elsewhere in *Germinal,* with a symbolism which is largely ambiguous, multifaceted, susceptible to divergent interpretations. (See the last chapter of this book.) What is to prevent us, for instance, from perceiving in the same fraternal accolade an Anarchist symbol if we wish— an anticipation of the better world that, according to Bakunin, could result only from the complete *destruction* of the old world (symbolized by Souvarine's destruction of Le Voreux)?

74 Erich Auerbach, *Mimesis: The Representation of Reality in Western Literature,* tr. Willard R. Trask (Princeton: Princeton University Press, 1953), pp. 506-15.

75 Cf. Roger Ripoll, *Réalité et mythe chez Zola* (Paris: Librairie Honoré Champion, 1981), II, 748-50. Contemplating *Germinal* in a very different context, Ripoll, for his part, finds it impossible to agree with this interpretation. Given his point of view, Ripoll's own interpretation of the novel strikes me as perfectly possible. It certainly is one of the most brilliant and intriguing. However, it does not, in my opinion, invalidate most of those with which it conflicts, including those suggested in this and other chapters of this book. It merely adds still another interpretation to the many, largely clashing interpretations

which this extraordinarily ambiguous novel appears fated to sustain. But it should be pointed out that the notion, entertained by Zola, that work is not a curse, but a blessing, does not exclude, as Ripoll apparently assumes it does, the notion that work may also be a source of suffering and violence—any more than Zola's exaltation of love as a supreme value prevented him in *Vérité* from regarding it as a source of division and conflict.

Chapter 4: The Geological Gospel

[1] The unfinished poem referred to by P. Alexis in *Emile Zola*, pp. 53, 54, as *La Genèse* and *La Chaîne des êtres*, are obviously the same poem, or, more precisely, two stages of the same projected, but never completed, poem. As Mitterand suggests (XV, 937), *L'Œuvre de Dieu*, mentioned in the list of lost Zola manuscripts which he published in *Cahiers Naturalistes*, No. 39 (1970), pp. 84-90, is perhaps still another title for the same work. The list of scholastic prizes awarded Zola between 1853 and 1857 has been published by Lepelletier, p. 50. In the aforementioned letter, Zola says that the idea for the poem in question had been turning round and round in his head for more than three years (*Corr.*, I, 182).

[2] Although Zola's debt to Darwin has been widely acknowledged (see, for example, de Lattre's *Le Réalisme selon Zola*, pp. 152-59), the impact of Cuvier on Zola has, in my opinion, been greatly underestimated. It must be recalled that Darwin's *Origin of the Species* (1859) did not appear in French translation until 1862, when Zola was already twenty-two. Throughout his childhood and youth, various forms of scientific catastrophism were still quite popular in France and other Western countries. See Reijer Hooykaas, "Catastrophism in Geology: Its Scientific Character in Relation to Actualism and Uniformitarianism," in *Philosophy of Geohistory: 1785-1970*, ed. Claude C. Albritton, Jr., Vol. XIII of *Benchmark Papers in Geology* (Stroudsburg, Penn.: Dowden, Hutchinson and Ross, 1975), pp. 310-56. Among nonspecialists, even such an eminent historian as Victor Duruy, deeply versed in natural history, still espoused a radically catastrophistic theory as late as 1865, as we can see from his popular *Introduction générale à l'histoire de France*, published that same year. We know from the list of lost Zola manuscripts (*Cahiers Naturalistes*, No. 39 [1970], p. 84) that, while preparing *L'Œuvre de Dieu*, Zola took notes on Cuvier as well as Zimmermann and Flourens. An indication that Zola still held Cuvier in high esteem even after 1862, when Darwin was introduced to French readers, may be perceived in Zola's admiring characterization of Flaubert, in *La Tribune* of Nov. 28, 1869, as "A poet changed into a naturalist, Homer turned into Cuvier . . ." (X, 917).

[3] See the section entitled "Kant and Cosmic Evolution" in Chapter vi of Stephen Toulmin and June Goodfield's *The Discovery of Time* (Chicago: The University of Chicago Press, 1965), pp. 129-35.

[4] According to Alexis, writing in 1882, twenty-two years later, the three parts of the poem would have been entitled, however, "La Naissance du monde," "L'Humanité," and "L'Homme de l'avenir." Part III, instead of showing mankind becoming extinct and being replaced by a higher species, would have shown "Man raising himself higher and higher on the scale of beings . . . Man becoming God" (*Emile Zola*, pp. 53, 54). Whether we have to do here with a later version of Part III, influenced perhaps by some form of transformism or Hugh Miller-like theory of progress, or simply a description based on

the mature novelist's inaccurate recollection of a long-abandoned project, we shall probably never know.

5 See Philip Walker, *Emile Zola* (London: Routledge & Kegan Paul, 1968), p. 5. Cf. the conclusion of Michel Serres's brilliant, highly personal study of Zola, *Feux et signaux de brume* (Paris: Bernard Grasset, 1975): "It was *La Genèse,* in its entirety . . ." (p. 379). Note also in this connection the following clearly autobiographical remarks from *L'Œuvre* (ostensibly concerning Sandoz): "He had started by toying with the idea of a gigantic undertaking and had projected an 'Origins of the Universe' in three phases: the creation, established according to scientific research; the story of how the human race came to play its part in the sequence of living beings; the future, in which beings succeed beings, completing the creation of the world through the ceaseless activity of living matter. He had cooled off, however, when he began to realize the hazardous nature of the hypotheses of this third phase, *and was now trying to find a more limited, a more human setting for this ambitious plan"* (*The Masterpiece,* tr. Thomas Walton [Ann Arbor: The University of Michigan Press, 1968], p. 48). Could *Les Rougon-Macquart* and its sequels, *Les Trois Villes* and *Les Quatre Evangiles,* have provided just the more limited, more human setting the poet was looking for?

6 See, for example, Charles G. Gillispie's *Genesis and Geology: A Study in the Relations of Scientific Thought, Natural Theology, and Social Opinion in Great Britain, 1790-1850* (Cambridge, Mass.: Harvard University Press, 1951). As Gillispie points out, such pioneer scientists as Cuvier and Buckland had set the example. For instance, in "Vindiciae Geologicae; or, the Connection of Geology with Religion Explained," the first of a series of lectures delivered in 1819, Buckland had asserted: ". . . as any investigation of Natural Philosophy which shall not terminate in the Great First Cause will be justly deemed unsatisfactory, I feel no apology to be necessary for opening these Lectures with an illustration of the religious application of Geological science" (cited by Gillispie, *Genesis and Geology,* p. 104). The assumption underlying the first eight verses of *La Genèse,* that the universe is one of law and the law itself an expression of the Deity's mind, was, of course, one of the basic propositions of natural theology. It had, moreover, been widely popularized by such eminent geologists as Robert Chambers, whose *Vestiges of the Natural History of Creation* had, as Gillispie informs us (p. 153), gone through eleven editions by 1860.

7 "In our own day, the thought of Teilhard de Chardin proposes a vision of the world analogous to Zola's" (X, 183, note 34).

8 Zola's affinities here with Madame Ackermann strike me as especially close. Not only do both "La Géologie et l'histoire" and *La Nature à l'homme* betray a pantheistic bent. Not only do both express a fervent belief in progress. Both dismiss the notion that man is the realization of the ideal toward which Nature has been advancing through countless forms from time immemorial. Both look forward to the creation of a superman. For both, man is only, as Madame Ackermann puts it, ". . . the rough, imperfect sketch / Of the masterpiece which I [Nature] have dreamed of . . ." (*Œuvres–Ma Vie; Premières Poésies; Poésies philosophiques* [Paris: Lemerre, 1885], pp. 112-13). See the section entitled "Louise Ackermann and Pantheism" in Charlton's *Positivist Thought,* pp. 177-79.

9 Cited by Charlton, *Positivist Thought,* p. 225.

10 Zola may be thinking here of Cuvier's opinion according to which the last great catastrophe occurred between 5,000 and 6,000 years ago. For Cuvier, however, mankind must have been created sometime between the last catastrophe and the one preceding it (*Essay on the Theory of the Earth*, tr. Robert Jameson, 3rd ed. [Edinburgh: William Blackwood, 1817], pp. 171, 172).

11 In the sentence from Duruy that Zola is citing, "and God rested" is in quotation marks (*Introduction générale à l'histoire de France* [Paris: Hachette, 1865], p. 41)—an obvious allusion to Genesis 2.2: "And on the seventh day God ended his work which he had made; and he rested on the seventh day from all his work which he had made." This forms together with Genesis 1.2 ("and darkness was upon the face of the deep. And the Spirit of God moved upon the face of the waters"), quoted by Duruy on p. 8, a biblical frame for his summary of the geological formation of France, Chs. ii-vi (pp. 8-42). There is no indication, however, that Duruy takes these verses or any other part of the biblical account of creation literally. In fact, in contrast to Zola, he seems carefully to avoid linking his recital of the "facts" of natural history with any religious or metaphysical cosmology. He seems to accept the existence of the Creator of natural theology, but that is all. After briefly summarizing the theories of Cuvier and d'Orbigny, the majority of the English geologists of the period, Lamark, Geoffroy Saint-Hilaire, and Agassiz, he concludes: "But let us leave behind us . . . this insoluble problem, for we are completely ignorant as to the origin [of the world] and we shall never know the secret which God has reserved for himself alone" (p. 53).

12 We must not see here necessarily an indication of any evolutionism, or transformism, on Zola's part. He could still write a year later, in a tradition far closer to Cuvier than Darwin: "And tomorrow, as the world goes on creating itself, there will come a cataclysm which will destroy the present order of the globe and crush the life out of humanity, in order to clear the ground and hand the world over to more perfect beings" ("Volcans et tremblements de terre," *L'Evénement*, Oct. 12, 1866, X, 655.) Cf. also Agassiz' theory, cited by Duruy, according to which the creative force intervenes every time a new species appears, but also according to which the new species are contained in those that precede them, just as the adult animal is contained in the embryo (*Introduction générale à l'histoire de France*, p. 52).

13 *Les Rougon-Macquart*, Pléiade ed., V, 1600.

14 "Notes générales sur la marche de l'œuvre," *Les Rougon-Macquart*, Pléiade ed., V, 1739.

15 In an interesting recent study, "Rude Sublime: The Taste for Nature: Colossi During the Late Eighteenth and Early Nineteenth Centuries" (*Gazette des Beaux Arts*, 6th Ser., 87 [April 1976], 113-26), Barbara Stafford treats of this taste in connection with the preromantic and romantic taste for caverns, grottos, boulders, etc. See in particular p. 120: "Mining, geology, and mineralogy exerted a magical attraction on the pre-Romantics. The descent into the mine became a common feature in travel literature. William Daniell's *Salt Mine* shows men creating, quite literally, constantly shifting forms as they quarry their environment. The Plutonic realm of the Saltzburg salt mines was frequently evoked. Ker Porter in his *Travelling Sketches in Russia and Sweden* (1813) ventured into an iron mine where he admired the many forms while 'suspended between the upper and the nether world and looked towards the distant sky, or downwards into regions of a lurid

night. . . .' " Cf. also H. A. M. Snelders, "Romanticism and *Naturphilosophie* and the Inorganic Natural Sciences, 1797-1840," *Studies in Romanticism,* 9 (Summer 1970), 194: "Mining and disciplines like geology and mineralogy exerted on the Romantic scientist an almost magical attraction; many of the Romantics (e.g., Novalis, Steffens, von Humboldt, Baader, and Schubert) studied at the famous Mining School at Freiberg." Simonin's *La Vie souterraine, ou les mines et les mineurs* (1867), one of Zola's chief sources for *Germinal,* reflects something of this same fascination, much of which can be ascribed in particular to the influence of the great pioneering geologist and mineralogist A. G. Werner (1750-1817), a miner's son and professor of mineralogy at Freiberg.

16 Cf. Simonin, pp. 166-69: ". . . At Le Brûlé, near Saint-Etienne, there is a coal mine which has been burning since time immemorial. The soil, on the surface, is sterile, calcined; hot vapors escape from it; flowers of sulfur, products of a diverse nature, alum, sal ammoniac are deposited there; one would take it for a part of one of those cursed towns consumed in olden times by terrestrial and celestial flames."

17 Cf., for example, Ker Porter's description in his *Travelling Sketches in Russia and Sweden* (1813) of a copper mine near Sala with its "subterranean plains, washed by rivers that had never known the sun's rays" (cited by Stafford, p. 120). For Zola's source, see Frandon, *Autour de "Germinal,"* pp. 87, 88.

18 For a concise introduction to Vulcanism and Neptunism, or Wernerism, see Toulmin and Goodfield, *The Discovery of Time,* pp. 152-55.

19 E. M. Grant, *Zola's "Germinal": A Critical and Historical Study* (Leicester: Leicester University Press, 1962), p. 171.

20 Cited by Ternois, p. 292.

21 See in particular Ch. vii ("The Earth Acquires a History") of Toulmin and Goodfield's *The Discovery of Time,* pp. 141-70.

22 Philip Walker, "Prophetic Myths in Zola," *PMLA,* 74 (Sept. 1959), 450, 451.

Chapter 5: Romantic Humanitarianism

1 Here as elsewhere in this book, I am using the term "secular religion" in the sense employed by Charlton in his *Secular Religions* (see in particular pp. 3, 4). With respect to the debate as to whether humanitarianism can or cannot be legitimately defined as a religion, see Albert-Léon Guérard's *French Prophets of Yesterday: A Study of Religious Thought under the Second Empire* (New York: D. Appleton, 1920), still a valuable study, especially the footnote on p. 120. For a more recent discussion, see Paul Bénichou, *Le Temps des prophètes: Doctrines de l'âge romantique* (Paris: Gallimard, 1977), Ch. xii, "L'Hérésie romantique," pp. 423-25, and "Dernières remarques," pp. 568, 569. Regarding the close association between Zola and humanitarianism in the minds of many of his contemporaries especially during the Dreyfus Affair as well as the religious character that this movement still retained even at this late point in the century, see Guérard, pp. 275, 276: "A dozen years ago . . . it was in the name of Humanitarianism that Zola led his

great crusade for truth and justice. It was our privilege to attend many a tumultuous meeting in those days; with quiet courage the speakers–scholars, scientists, ministers, anarchists, for all were welcome to their share of honour and dangers–were facing obloquy, ostracism, and even death; no elaborate High Mass in an ancient cathedral, no revivalist meeting of the most successful evangelist, has ever given us a deeper feeling of what religion should be." In the same passage, Guérard recalls the Humanitarian Church which a former priest, Victor Charbonnel, organized at that time and which counted Zola along with Hugo, Michelet, and Anatole France among its Fathers. Note also that Zola himself calls one of the several "new faiths" he imagines in his works "the religion of humanity" (VIII, 849).

2 For example, see the fourth paragraph of Zola's letter of June 2, 1860, to Baille. (In my opinion, the thirteen lines beginning with the sentence "Our century is a century of transition; leaving behind us an abominable past, we are marching toward an unknown future" constitute a major germinal text in Zola's writings.) For other examples, see X, 23-28, 56, 57, 147-48, 753, 927, 932, 1093, XIII, 47, XIV, 1532, XV, 843, 844. See also Zola's letter of May 22, 1901, to Maurice Le Blond: ". . . what particularly cheers me is the hope that the younger generation has awakened to these ideas about humanity and love. In the deep distress that the present moment has caused me, you who bring with you a future characterized by a better, more abundant life are my only joy. I like to think that you will hasten the advent of this golden age of which you speak, which lies ahead of us and which will consist of beauty and justice" (*Correspondance II*, ed. Maurice Le Blond [Paris: François Bernouard, 1929], pp. 880, 881).

3 See, for example, X, 310-14, 753, XIV, 395, XV, 843, 844, *Corr.*, I, 129.

4 "I had this dream that each soul goes to the great whole, that in death humanity is only a single immense breath, a single spirit. . . . I looked up at the sky. It seemed to me that I could see there . . . the soul of the world, the eternal being made up of all beings" (I, 109). "Forward! Forward! The centuries press us on and we want to advance so that we can lose ourselves in the great whole, in free, happy humanity" (X, 761).

5 For other examples, see V, 566, X, 546, 753, 947, 1093, XI, 283 ff, XIII, 47, XIV, 653. There can be little doubt that Zola's cult of his century in some ways took the place of his youthful cult of the Virgin Mary. In his letter of June 2, 1860, to Baille, he not only compares their century to a mother big with child, but also exhorts his contemporaries to fall down on their knees before it–"so beautiful, so holy" (*Corr.*, I, 170). Echoing the *Ave Maria,* he spoke, in *Le Salut Public* of Oct. 5, 1865, of "our century, which will be great among all centuries, for it is in it that the strong societies of tomorrow are being born" (X, 57).

6 In *La Débâcle,* he likens France "crucified" at Sedan to Christ on the Cross (VI, 1118). In his plans for what would have been his fourth "Gospel," "Justice," he rapturously evokes "France, messiah, redemptor, savior" and prophesies that when France has finally, in great pain and torment–"her painful calvary"–established truth and justice on her own soil, the whole worldwide fabric of ignorance and oppression will be rent asunder and the evil old systems everywhere will come crashing down (VIII, 1517).

7 See, in addition to the most obvious examples in the concluding chapter of *Paris* (VII, 1556, 1566, 1567), the "Causerie" that Zola published in *Le Corsaire* of Dec. 3, 1872 (X, 977, 978).

8 Cf. Zola's "Causerie" in *La Tribune,* June 28, 1868, where he cites with obvious sympathy Michelet's belief that we will all love each other like brothers when we really get to know each other and "that the world will be engulfed in an immense kiss when science has demonstrated the close kinship between things and beings" (XIII, 116, 117). For other examples of Zola's humanitarian conceptions of the future, see, in addition to the final pages of *Paris* and, of course, the various utopias depicted in *Les Quatre Evangiles,* his letter of July 18, 1861, to Baille (*Corr.,* I, 305-06), "Du progrès dans les sciences et dans la poésie" (X, 310-14), and *L'Œuvre* (V, 566).

9 Cf. Guérard, p. 275.

10 See also VII, 997, X, 771, 927, 974, 977, XIII, 201, and the list of possible titles for *L'Œuvre* reproduced by Mitterand in the Pléiade ed. of *Les Rougon-Macquart,* IV, 1338: *Faire un enfant, faire un monde, Enfantement, Accouchement, Conception, Fécondation, Les Couches saignantes, Les Créateurs de monde, La Force créatrice, Le Siècle en couche, Les Couches du siècle . . .*

11 Cf. the following verses from *Rodolpho*: "Our Father, it is time. Oh! Grant that another Jesus / May expire on the cross and deliver us from chaos. / Our bodies, vile rags, contain only dead souls. / Come, or I will believe that you no longer exist!" (XV, 886). Note also Zola's identification of Christ with socialism in his response to a questionnaire submitted to him by a journalist, B. Guinaudeau, in the spring of 1892: "After all was not Christ a revolutionary and a socialist?" (cited by Ternois, pp. 164, 165).

12 "The poet's role is sacred. . . . He must devote himself to progress. If God will only give me the strength I need, I am ready" (*Corr.,* I, 206). "Poet, be true to your mission! You are one of those inspired spirits who must divine and preach the future" (X, 763). "The only thing I can be proud of is that I took cognizance of my mediocrity as a poet and plunged courageously into the task of the century, with the rude tool of prose" (cited by Alexis, *Emile Zola,* p. 232). It is perhaps significant in this respect that when, in the summer of 1860, Zola, then only twenty, agreed to serve as a model for a poor artist friend, Chaillan, the pose they selected was that of the son of Zeus and Antiope, Amphion, who, by the music of a magical lyre given him by Hermes, walled the city of Thebes (*Corr.,* I, 213-14). Luc, the messianic hero of *Travail* and one of Zola's many fictional alter egos, is another Amphion: "The town builder that he had in him was filled with joy at each new building . . . enlarging the town that had just been born. Was that not his mission? Was not everything and everyone going to arise and form groups at the sound of his voice? He felt within himself the power to command the very stones of the field, to make them float up, fall into line, produce private dwellings, public edifices, where he would lodge, along with their human occupants, fraternity, truth, justice" (VIII, 699). One is reminded of Clotilde's desire for her son, with its mixture of Christian and Orphic qualities: "He will take up the experiment where it left off, rebuild the walls, bring certainty to his groping fellows, build the city of justice . . ." (VI, 1401). Anatole France, to his eternal credit, was the first to perceive this Amphion-like aspect of Zola's fiction: "His work is only comparable in grandeur to that of Tolstoy. They are two vast ideal cities reared by the lyre, at the two extremities of European thought" (Zola's funeral oration, reproduced in *Vers les temps meilleurs: Trente ans de vie sociale, I, Introduction générale,* ed. Claude Aveline [Paris: Emile-Paul Frères, c. 1949], pp. 117, 118).

13 For a definition of the humanitarian epic, see pp. ix, x, of Gustave Rudler's Avant-Propos to Herbert Hunt's *The Epic in Nineteenth-Century France: A Study in Heroic and Humanitarian Poetry from "Les Martyres" to "Les Siècles morts"* (Oxford: Basil Blackwell, 1941). Note in this connection Sainte-Beuve's remark in *Le Globe* of Oct. 11, 1830: "The mission, the appointed task of art, today is the human epic" (cited by Bénichou, p. 385).

14 For a fuller treatment of this subject, see Philip Walker, "Zola: Poet of an Age of Transition," *L'Esprit Créateur*, 11 (Winter 1971), 3-10.

15 We must also take into account here the widespread disillusionment with romantic humanitarianism that had followed the excesses of June 1848 and the fall of the Second Republic, whose leaders—Lamartine, Hugo, Louis Blanc, Ledru-Rollin, et al.—had been motivated by romantic humanitarian ideals. Still adhering as he did to the basic humanitarian values and still, despite himself, charmed by romantic humanitarian reveries, Zola shared the resentment of those many other humanitarians of his day who felt that the romantics had not only deceived them, but also let them down. Promoting a new, scientific, positivistic humanitarianism, he was obviously obliged, furthermore, to combat the romantic form which, as the Commune of 1871 showed, was still a powerful rival.

16 "I greatly fear that I have, for my part, soaked too long in the romantic mixture. I was born too soon. If I am occasionally angry with romanticism, it is because I hate it for all the false literary education that it gave me. I am part of it, and that infuriates me" (X, 1323).

17 See in particular *La Fortune des Rougon*, Ch. iv, the paragraph beginning "It was natural that someone endowed with this kind of mind, both ardent and repressed, should have become very excited by republican ideas" (II, 132, 133).

18 It could be maintained that the concept of love at the heart of the Christian religion, *agape*, is still very much alive in Zola, despite Zola's rejection of Christianity. When, in *Germinal, Paris*, and elsewhere, he attacks Christian charity, what he really means by this, as the context makes clear, is "a people made up of the rich supporting a people made up of the poor, this terrain of almsgiving on which the social edifice, despite all the furious commotions by which it has been beset, has managed to survive for the past eighteen centuries without toppling" (XII, 659). As for true Christian charity—the "total charity" advocated by Tolstoy, for example—he regarded it as identical with what he meant by the word "justice" (XII, 659, 660). In *La Joie de vivre, Le Docteur Pascal*, and certain other novels, he exalts what he calls in his notes for *Le Docteur Pascal*, "The new charity"—that is to say, that "altruism," that "love for others," which comes to those, he says, who have "a passionate devotion to life" (*Les Rougon-Macquart*, Pléiade ed., V, 1593).

19 *Les Rougon-Macquart*, Pléiade ed., V, 1740.

20 *Les Rougon-Macquart*, Pléiade ed., V, 1775.

21 For example, we have seen in the preceding chapter how Zola revives the ancient myth of the Great Mother. See also in this connection Rachelle A. Rosenberg's interesting article "The Slaying of the Dragon: An Archetypal Study of Zola's *Germinal*," *Symposium*,

26 (1972), 349-62, as well as her doctoral dissertation, "Zola's Imagery and the Archetype of the Great Mother" (University of Michigan 1969). Recall also Thomas Mann's
remark in his long essay "Zola and the Golden Age": "This Astarte of the Second Empire
named Nana, is she not both a symbol and a myth? Where did she get her name? It is
a primitive desinence, one of those ancient, voluptuous stammerings of humanity: Nana
was one of the appelations of the Babylonian Ishtar. Did Zola know this? It would be
even more remarkable and characteristic if he did not" (from the French tr. by Louise
Servicien, in *Présence de Zola* [Paris: Fasquelle, 1953], p. 11).

22 Cf. Patrick Brady, "Structuration archétypologique de *Germinal*," *Cahiers Internationaux de Symbolisme*, Nos. 24-25 (1973), pp. 87-97.

Chapter 6: Life Continuing and Recommencing

1 Lawrence Harvey, "The Cycle Myth in *La Terre* of Zola," *Philological Quarterly*,
38 (Jan. 1959), 89; Robert, *"La Terre" d'Emile Zola*, pp. 384-91.

2 Robert, *"La Terre" d'Emile Zola*, p. 385, n. 23.

3 *The Portable Nietzsche*, tr. and ed. Walter Kaufmann (New York: The Viking Press,
1954), p. 270.

4 See the section entitled "Eternal Recurrence" in A. M. Ludovici's translation of
The Will to Power (Edinburgh: T. N. Foulis, 1910), II, 422-32.

5 Mircea Eliade, *Cosmos and History: The Myth of Eternal Return*, tr. Willard R. Trask
(New York: Harper and Row, 1959), p. 82.

6 Cf. Eliade, *Cosmos and History*, pp. 87, 88, 113, 115, 120, 122-28, 134-37. Jean
reflects Zola's own thoughts in May 1871: "All night long it was like a bloody dawn"
(cited by Henri Mitterand, *Zola journaliste: De l'affaire Manet à l'affaire Dreyfus* [Paris:
Armand Colin, 1962], p. 148).

7 Cf. Eliade, *Cosmos and History*, pp. 124-27, 132, 134-37.

8 X, 80, 545, XII, 608, 830, XIV, 651. See also Zola's notes for *La Terre*, B. N. MS.
Nouv. acq. fr. 10328, fol. 385 ("The to-and-fro motion of progress, ceaselessly never
backwards"); and Zola's notes for *Le Docteur Pascal* reproduced by Mitterand in the
Pléiade ed. of *Les Rougon-Macquart*, V, 1600.

9 Eliade, *Cosmos and History*, pp. 85-92.

10 "I accept all works of art for the same reason, as manifestations of human genius.
They all interest me almost equally; they all possess true beauty: life, life in its thousand
and one expressions, always changing, always new" (XII, 830); "Life! An immense sea,
a limitless expanse, where there is always something new to see, where one is ceaselessly
confronted with new emotions, new lessons" (XII, 608).

11 Eliade, *Cosmos and History*, p. 156.

12 "The moment is breathless, fraught with anxiety: we are waiting for those who will strike the hardest and closest to the mark, whose fists will be powerful enough to shut everyone else's mouth; deep down in every newcomer to the fray there is the vague hope of being the dictator, the tyrant of tomorrow" (X, 27); "Despite myself, I become lost in revery before these models of our architecture. It seems to me that they will remain standing for at least ten centuries and that they will astonish future generations. They are archetypes and as such deserve immortality (XIV, 346).

13 Lucas, *Traité*, I, xxiii.

14 *Les Rougon-Macquart*, Pléiade ed., V, 1601.

15 *Les Rougon-Macquart*, Pléiade ed., V, 1582, 1583.

16 Cf. Naomi Schor: "The concept of a great life-death-life cycle underlies the whole of the *Rougon-Macquart* series. The super fertile cemetery of the aire Saint-Mittre sets up in the very first pages of *La Fortune des Rougon* the basic schema of Zola's historical world view. At first glance this myth of eternal renewal would seem to guarantee man a form of immortality, and, more important, in novels such as *Germinal* and *La Débâcle*, promise the beginning of a new cycle, the return to a golden age. In fact, however, the cycle condemns each generation to repeat the actions of the preceding one. Silvère must die like Macquart, Miette, like the Marie on whose tombstone the lovers sit. The cycle appears to be a metaphor for heredity" ("Zola: From Window to Window," *Yale French Studies*, No. 42 [1969], p. 50). Is it not possible that Miss Schor's interpretation of Zola's myth of eternal renewal, brilliant as far as it goes, too categorically dismisses the other meanings ascribable to this myth, which, like so many other things in Zola, would seem (at least to this reader) ambiguous, protean? Moreover, insofar as the cycle is a metaphor for heredity, must it be a predominantly pessimistic one? See, for example, "Les Quatre Journées de Jean Gourdon" or "Angélique." Note also, in this connection, that Zola appropriates Lucas' theory that life not only imitates and recalls, but also invents and imagines. Pascal Rougon illustrates this latter phenomenon (inneity). There is always the possibility that Pascal through his son, the "Unknown Child" of *Le Docteur Pascal*, may bring about man's salvation. Given the fissures and contradictions in Zola's conception of history, is it really possible, finally, to speak of "the basic schema of Zola's historical world view"?

17 See the section on sun symbolism in Winston Hewitt's valuable study of man and nature in Zola's works, *Through Those Living Pillars* (The Hague: Mouton, 1974), pp. 83-85.

18 Cf. Naomi Schor, *Zola's Crowds* (Baltimore: Johns Hopkins University Press, 1978), pp. 175-76.

Chapter 7: "An Unprecedented Anarchy"

1 A complete study of the various steps whereby Zola sought to unify his ideas, drawn originally from sources as different as Hugo, Musset, Lamartine, Michelet, Sand, Taine,

Cuvier, Letourneau, Lucas, Bernard, and Darwin, would require a volume in itself. Although as yet no such study has been made, the overall direction of Zola's philosophical and religious thought from disorder to order should be apparent already to any careful reader of his works. At the outset of his career, he was clearly more concerned with intellectual or spiritual value than logical coherence. He appropriated from the metaphysical and religious chaos of his time whatever appealed to him. Rightfully mistrustful of systems, he even boasted occasionally of his lack of consistency. "You accuse me of being systematic and you are wrong," he wrote Baille in June 1860; "nothing is less systematic than my spirit" (*Corr.*, I, 171). Yet in subsequent writings he expressed repeatedly his love of harmony, his nostalgia for a unified faith, his desire to be one of the chief creators or imposers of the new order destined, he believed, to emerge out of the present turmoil. "If one were to push me further," he once confessed, "I would have to admit that my sole dream . . . in our present literary anarchy, would be to be the pacifier of ideas and forms, one of those soldiers fighting for order" (XIV, 511). His acceptance of the doctrine that life is essentially movement, which he formulates for himself for the first time in his preparatory notes for *Le Docteur Pascal*, represented in this respect a giant step forward; for it enabled him to tie together more systematically than ever before at least four key concepts in his thought: life, history, heredity, and work. All, he realized, are different aspects of the same movement. If life is movement, history is also movement—the movement of life writ large. Heredity is the movement of life perpetuating itself, renewing itself, passing itself on. As for work, he maintained: "One cannot define life otherwise than by this communicated movement that it receives and passes on and which is, in short, nothing but work, on that great task which will be completed at the end of time" (XII, 682). Finally, in *Les Quatre Evangiles* (1899-1903), he still further unified his philosophical and religious thought by linking his various lifelong cults of love, life, work, truth, etc., together more tightly through the four key notions of fecundity, work, truth, and justice. It is true that we can already find these notions tending to recur together, in a kind of ideological constellation, in his early writings, but in *Les Quatre Evangiles* he elevates them to the rank of major values, not only attaching to them in the process all of his other favorite philosophical or religious ideas, but also relating them to each other in a kind of system: "Fecundity which populates the world, the presently uninhabited parts, and which makes life. Work, which organizes and regulates life (it also makes life). Truth, which is the objective of science and which paves the way for justice. Justice, which reunites humanity, brings it together, reduces it to that single family which will make peace possible and will ultimately bring about the happiness which is our common goal. The four subjects interpenetrate; fecundity requires work, which requires science, which entails justice" (VIII, 512).

2 His early writings reflect an especial susceptibility to the theological ideas of Musset and Lamartine. Echoing Musset's *Espoir en Dieu*, he exclaims in a letter to Cézanne: "Oh! If only Jupiter, Jesus, God, the Great Whole, whatever his name may be, would grant me his power for only one moment!" (*Corr.*, I, 132). In "Paolo," he calls God "the sublime Artist" (XV, 911). In a letter to Baille, he confesses: "God, poetry, these are synonymous words for me" (*Corr.*, I, 223). But it is clear from his early works that he was already attracted in his youth by conceptions of God of the sort we may associate with such other romantics as Michelet or such pseudo positivists as Taine. In "Religion," Zola associates God with love, nature, life, fecundity. In the Prologue to *La Genèse*, he addresses his prayers to "the unique First Force" (XV, 937). In other writings composed in his twenties, he seems to identify God with humanity (I, 109, X, 761) or speaks reverently of "the one, absolute truth which rules all worlds and pushes us all toward the future" (X, 24), or confesses that his poetic objective is to reveal "the God Infinite and

the immutable laws that flow from his being and govern all worlds" (X, 313). Or he defends Spinoza's vision of "the absolute unity, the one, general formula, which is God" at the summit of "the great chain of things and beings which descends from it" (X, 684). Or, as in "La Géologie et l'histoire," he envisages God as a synthesis of the Judeo-Christian celestial creator God and a pantheistic Great Whole identical with a still unfinished, ceaselessly evolving creation. In the article that he wrote in Gloton on June 25, 1868, he combines the notion (here specifically associated with Michelet) of a divine Great Mother with the more "scientific" concept of "the first force which governs the world" (XIII, 115). It was during this same period in the late 1860s when he was drawing up his plans for Les Rougon-Macquart that he also became subject, we recall, to the "scientific" theories of Dr. Prosper Lucas, for whom God, the Macrocosm, Nature, the Cosmic Matrix, Creation, and Universal Life were all the same. In the late 1870s, when Zola's enthusiasm for the pure philosophical positivism of Claude Bernard was at its peak, he grew for a while markedly more cautious in his efforts to define the Deity. He would admit only to the existence of a vague "Creative Force" (X, 1395) whose precise nature science might reveal someday. But in the mid-1880s—the period of Germinal, L'Œuvre, and La Terre—the vision of God as Nature, Earth, Cybel, the Great Mother, tended to dominate his manner of envisaging God once again. Still later, when he was finishing Les Rougon-Macquart, he embraced, at least for a moment, Renan's elaborate metaphysical notion (as summarized by Melchior de Vogüé) of "a kind of inner spring, a nexus [which] pushes everything toward life and toward an ever more developed life . . . a central consciousness of the universe which is progressively taking shape and which can go on becoming forever" (Les Rougon-Macquart, Pléiade ed., V, 1600). It was also then that, rephrasing Vogüé, he most explicitly reaffirmed his belief that Life is God: "the great motor, the soul of the world" (pp. 1600, 1601). In Paris, however, he stresses the identity of God with the cosmos revealed by modern science. In Fécondité, he returns to the notion of God as Eros, Eternal Desire, stating with great conviction: "Desire, the whole soul of the universe is there, the force which supports matter, which makes out of atoms an intelligence, a power, a sovereignty" (VIII, 91). But even this is not Zola's last word as to the nature of God; for, as we recall, it is in his next "Gospel," Travail, that he goes on, with equal conviction, to deify work: "work our savior, the creator and regulator of the world . . . work our king . . . our only master and our only god" (VIII, 954, 955).

3 We have as yet no complete philosophical and religious analysis of Zola's conception of man. However, certain aspects of it should already be apparent to readers of this volume. As we have seen, Zola tends to substitute for the traditional notion of a plurality of individual immortal human souls a single, divine Soul in which individual human beings partake along with everything else in creation. As we have also seen, he rejects the old distinction between body and soul. Aside from this, we have found little consistency in his conceptions either of the individual human being or humanity considered as a whole. From what we have seen in the preceding chapters, it should be evident that he cannot decide, in his attempts to arrive at a new conception of man, whether to exalt man or something higher. At times he tends to represent man as a free agent, as when, in Travail, he defines a man as "an active energy, a will which decides and directs" (VIII, 692); yet at other times, he tends, we may also recall, to regard men as passive instruments of transcendent powers. If, on the one hand, he sometimes equates humanity with God, he also, on the other hand, is tempted at certain moments to envisage humanity as simply another phase of the divine "Creature," or Great Whole. Whereas he sometimes regards man as ultimately the chief beneficiary of progress, he stresses at other times that man is only a means toward a higher end, e.g., the creation of a superman, and attaches profound value to the thought that man can no longer conceive of himself as the center of

the universe. Or, like the author of Job, Zola takes spiritual satisfaction in emphasizing the pitiful smallness, weakness, ephemerality, and all-round vanity of man. It should follow from this evident incapacity on Zola's part to arrive at a fixed, consistent conception of either man or God that he was unable to formulate a consistent doctrine regarding the way or ways in which man can approach, commune with, or know God; and a careful reading of his works will, I believe, show this to be true. Sometimes he adopts an intellectual approach, looking to science to lead us to God. At other times, apparently rejecting this approach (as in *La Faute de l'abbé Mouret* or *Fécondité*), he seems to assume that knowledge of God and contact with God are to be obtained, rather, through other than rational or scientific means—through heeding the dictates of the heart, for example, or listening to nature, or making love.

4 The ideas entertained by Zola regarding the problem of evil are exceedingly diverse: What strikes us as evil is due to the present imperfection of a world which is still in the process of creation (XIV, 652). What seems evil to us is not really so in the eyes of God; indeed, the apparent injustice of nature is the consequence of a logic which is actually a higher form of justice (preliminary notes for *Le Docteur Pascal, Les Rougon-Macquart*, Pléiade ed., V, 1593). Just as frost, hail, thunder, and lightning are necessary perhaps, it is possible that blood and tears are also necessary for the world to function properly (V, 1142, VIII, 1487, XIV, 651; see also *Les Rougon-Macquart,* Pléiade ed., V, 1601). Evil is an accident, an error, of creation (VI, 1394, XIV, 651). If God does not punish evildoers, it is because God is too preoccupied with the overall progress of creation to bother himself with anything so insignificant as the destinies of individual human beings (VI, 1246). The suffering of man counts for very little in the vast, starry mechanism of the cosmos (V, 1142). Whereas men come and go, Earth, the Great Mother, goes on forever, eternally rejuvenated and repurified (V, 1142). Horrible as life is at times, we must love it just the same, not only because it is the supreme power of the universe, but also because it bears within it the promise of a better future—because, indeed, life *is* the future (notes for *L'Argent,* B. N. MS. Nouv. acq. fr. 10268, fol. 287).

5 As we have already begun to see in the preceding chapters, Zola's views on the nature of death had no more consistency than his conception of God or man. If, at times, he thought of death as annihilation (to be desired or feared according to one's mood), at other times he conceived of death as a return of the individual to the Great Whole, the Great Kiss, or marriage of all with all, in which we are united beyond the grave, the ocean, or torrent, of universal life out of which all things come (e.g., I, 109, VIII, 969, IX, 422). At still other times, he regarded death as a mere change of finite forms, a parent's surviving in his children, one generation's surviving in another (e.g., IX, 471, 1162). He compared the burial of a man to the planting of a seed (V, 1137). In "Printemps," he speaks of "the great struggle, the everlasting struggle of life against death" (IX, 909). In his preliminary notes for *La Terre,* however, he asserts that "birth, death, are only stages, words," that the Earth creates only life (*Les Rougon-Macquart,* Pléiade ed., IV, 1513); and in *Fécondité* he writes of that "pantheistic wish" of the fecundated seed "which accepts death only because it is nothing but a renewing, a ferment, of life" (VIII, 75).

6 In addition to the major contradictions in Zola's conception of history which I have treated in preceding chapters, the student of his philosophy of history would have to take into account many other contradictions, or inconsistencies. The better we know Zola, the clearer it becomes that he has no solid view of history, but only an assemblage of competing hypotheses ranging from the deepest pessimism (e.g., IX, 182) to the most exalted optimism (e.g., X, 56, 57). It is true that, except at certain rare moments, he tends to

believe in one kind of progress or another; but he cannot decide whether progress will be fast or slow, attain its goal someday or go on forever (e.g., X, 100, 101), what the main goal of progress is, how progress is being achieved, who or what must be regarded as the principal agent of progress, whether or not progress must be a violent process. With respect to this last question, see, for example, his criticism of the Russian Anarchists' conviction that social progress cannot be attained without a cataclysm in "La République en Russie" (XIV, 565-67). Cf. *Vérité* (VIII, 1375). Note, furthermore, how this conflict in Zola's own thought regarding the necessity of violence is reflected in the inner tensions ascribed to Guillaume Froment in *Paris* or in certain major ambiguities in the historical and prophetic vision presented in *Les Quatre Evangiles.*

7 In particular, recall that each Gospel shows us the ideal society of Zola's humani-tarian dreams arriving in a radically different way. *Fécondité* prophesies that it will take countless centuries of evolution involving the rise and fall of many peoples for this society to be achieved. *Travail,* on the other hand, adopts an extremely apocalyptic scenario; it has, we recall, the (socialist) world of the future born out of a great Universal War, or Final Conflict, in the last years of the "twentieth century." It maintains that all of this will come about not by fecundity, but by a radical reorganization of labor. *Vérité,* however, depicts a millenium initiated by relatively peaceful means, thanks to a French schoolmaster's struggle to assure the victory of truth over falsehood. It is as though Saint John of Patmos had written, instead of only one Book of Revelation, three Books of Revelation, each containing a distinctly different vision of the Second Coming.

8 B. N. MS. Nouv. acq. fr. 10324, fols. 190-94.

9 Even the language of certain portions of the preliminary *Rougon-Macquart* plans has a Tainian flavor: race, moment, milieu, force, logic of deduction, generative fact, mathematically. (*Les Rougon-Macquart,* Pléiade ed., V, 1738-45.)

10 "As for me, it is not the tree, the face, the scene that one describes to me that moves me; it is the man that I find in the work; it is the powerful individuality that has been able to create, alongside the world of God, a personal world that I shall never be able to forget and will recognize everywhere" (X, 45). "Have I breathed life into my characters? Have I begotten a world? Have I brought into existence creatures of flesh and blood, creatures as eternal as man? If the answer is 'yes,' my task is done" (XIV, 800).

11 According to some commentators, notably Henri Barbusse, *Germinal* is an excellent example of Zola's principle that the naturalist novelist should limit himself to the presen-tation of fact, leaving his readers free to arrive at their own conclusions (*Zola* [Paris: Gallimard, 1932], pp. 174-75). Other commentators, starting out with Edmond Deschaumes, Louis Desprez, Huysmans, and, as we have seen, Lemaitre, have conceived of it as a desperately black novel. Still others, including E. M. Grant, Girard, Mitterand, and many other leading contemporary Zola scholars, have seen it either as an optimistic work or as a mixture of optimistic and pessimistic elements. Mitterand has suggested that its message may be the same as the profession of faith in life, humanity, work, and the future which Zola published in *Le Figaro* of Sept. 5, 1881 (*Les Rougon-Macquart,* Pléiade ed., III, 1822). Girard perceives in it a nearly total metaphysical pessimism countered at the very end by an optimistic faith in human solidarity ("L'Univers de *Germinal,*" p. 76). Wurmser finds the underlying vision of the novel astonishingly close to the Marxist version of reality (pp. 16-17). Irving Howe concedes that the "central myth" of *Germinal* is close to the Marxist view of the dynamics of capitalism, but goes on to note that Zola's

attitude toward this myth in the novel would seem to be skeptical (Afterword, *Germinal* [New York: New American Library, 1970], pp. 434-35, 445-46). According to Simon, the novel largely issues from Zola's "Dionysiac pantheism" (V, 18-20). Robert discerns a conflict between the Zola myths of disaster and work-hope, catastrophe and renewal (*Emile Zola: Principes et caractères généraux de son œuvre* [Paris: Les Belles Lettres, 1952], pp. 99-101). Lewis Kamm sees, along with the myth of eternal creation, the message "that man will create in time new and rehumanized relationships between himself and things" (*The Object in Zola's "Rougon-Macquart"* [Madrid: José Porrúa Turanzas, 1978], p. 161). For Ripoll, the universe of *Germinal* is a universe in which there is nothing but conflict, nothing but movement, and the novel, far from terminating with an affirmation of the unity of life, in which every momentary convulsion will ultimately be reabsorbed, announces a future that will manifest itself as a disruptive force; the message implied in the self-contained mythological system of the novel is an affirmation of "the necessity of passing through violence and death to find the path of hope" (*Réalité et mythe chez Zola*, II, 748, 750). Baguley has proposed that the novel's message would seem to commingle the temptation of nihilism and faith in the potentialities of life ("The Function of Zola's Souvarine," pp. 795-97) and has also theorized that cyclical and linear conceptions of history are mixed in the novel's famous conclusion (*"Fécondité" d'Emile Zola*, p. 69). According to Brady, one must include among the possible readings of this novel, which he too regards as ambiguous, those implicit in its structure, astonishingly reminiscent, as he is the first to have pointed out, of primitive fecundity and initiation rites and liberating exploits ("Structuration archétypologique de *Germinal*," pp. 87-97).

12 Charlton, *Positivist Thought*, p. 17. The great extent of my debt to Professor Charlton in this and the following eight paragraphs will be apparent to anyone familiar with his writings, most notably the volume just mentioned and *Secular Religions*. But see also his chapter "Positivism and Its Aftermath," in *The Late Nineteenth Century*, Vol. V of *French Literature and Its Background*, ed. John Cruickshank (London: Oxford University Press, 1969), pp. 1-16, and his chapter "French Thought in the Nineteenth and Twentieth Centuries," in his *France: A Companion to French Studies* (London: Methuen, 1972), pp. 243-90.

13 *Rapport sur la philosophie en France au dix-neuvième siècle*, p. 250, cited by Charlton, *Positivist Thought*, p. 18.

14 "Le Spiritualisme français," pp. 384, 385, cited by Charlton, *Positivist Thought*, p. 19.

15 Charlton, *Positivist Thought*, p. 19.

16 *Les Religions actuelles*, p. 528, cited by Charlton, *Secular Religions*, p. 5.

17 Guérard, p. 275.

18 Guérard, p. 275. As Guérard notes, it was at this time, also, that a former priest, Victor Charbonnel, founded a Church of Humanity in which Berthelot was invited to deliver sermons and Zola himself, along with Michelet, Hugo, and Anatole France, was honored as one of the Fathers (p. 276).

19 Ernest Renan, *Œuvres complètes* (Paris: Calmann-Lévy, 1947-61), II, 760.

[20] Cited by Charlton, *Positivist Thought*, p. 227.

[21] *The Symbolist Aesthetic in France*, p. 316, cited by Charlton, *Positivist Thought*, p. 230.

[22] See Guérard, pp. 140, 141.

[23] Charlton, *Positivist Thought*, p. 112.

[24] Charlton, *Positivist Thought*, p. 115.

[25] Paul Bourget, *Essais de psychologie contemporaine*, 5th ed. (Paris: Lemerre, 1889), p. 74.

[26] Bourget, pp. 198, 199.

[27] Charles Fuster, *Essais de critique*, 2nd ed. (Paris: E. Giraud, 1886), pp. 68, 69.

[28] Regarding the degree to which Zola was aware, as he composed his novels, of the philosophical and religious ideas that he was expressing in them and the means whereby he was doing so, see his letter of May 20, 1884, to Huysmans: "As for me, I try to work as calmly as possible. But I no longer try to understand what I am doing, for the more I write, the more convinced I am that we have absolutely no control over what goes on in our works in gestation" (XIV, 1434).

[29] A thorough study of the different ways in which Zola expresses his philosophical and religious ambiguity in his fiction has yet to be made. It would, however, certainly have to include: (1) his use both in his short stories and in his novels of the serial form, thus making it possible to include in the same composite artistic entity parts each of which could, if he wished, be limited to this or that set of compatible elements of his thought, but which, taken together, would express it in all its richly discordant variety; (2) his tendency to express each of the conflicting elements or separate contradictions in his thought through a separate character, occasionally including two or more such characters in the same novel (e.g., Lazare Chanteau and Pauline Quenu in *La Joie de vivre*, Etienne Lantier, Hennebeau, and Souvarine in *Germinal*, Claude Lantier and Pierre Sandoz in *L'Œuvre*, Pascal Rougon and Clotilde Rougon in *Le Docteur Pascal*, Pierre Froment and Guillaume Froment in *Les Trois Villes*); (3) Zola's tendency in most of his novels almost never to indulge in direct, easily identifiable authorial comment, e.g., à la Balzac; (4) Zola's well-known extensive use of free indirect speech in such a way that it is often impossible to know whether we have to do with just the thoughts of a character, just those of the author, or those of both a character and the author; (5) the presence in Zola's fiction of great numbers of more or less unobtrusive, difficult to identify, metaphorical or diegetic events and objects which may or may not possess symbolic meaning and whose symbolism, if indeed it exists, may be susceptible to two or more conflicting interpretations (e.g., Côte-Verte or the knife which Jeanlin uses to kill Jules and which has the word *Love* engraved on the handle). A complete study of Zola's philosophical and religious ambiguity would also have to take into account the way it is reinforced by Zola's conscious or unconscious exploitation of an ambiguity perhaps always possible in poetry and fiction. I mean that ambiguity which issues from the fact that if poetry and fiction have traditionally been employed as instruments of philosophical or religious communication, they have from time immemorial also been regarded as privileged realms of the escapist

imagination or fancy. Zola tended to assign them both of these contrasting functions. Consequently, we can never really know with which kind of poetry or fiction we have to do in his works. For example, should we conceive of Zola's "Gospels" as authentic gospels or merely compensatory make-believe gospels? That is to say, should we take seriously the "new religions" that they propose or regard them as nothing more than *fictional* religions—the reveries of an aging would-be prophet meant to make up for his failure to find a secular faith capable of satisfying him? But in reading many of Zola's other writings, including *Germinal*, are we not subject to much the same sort of hesitation?

30 *Les Rougon-Macquart*, Pléiade ed., V, 1586. Cf. Zola's remark concerning his alter ego Pascal in the same notes (p. 1586); "If he has left nothing out, no matter how depressing and repulsive it might be, he has done so as a professor displaying the human cadaver and also as a healer who would like to think that the only way he can try to effectuate a cure someday is to know everything he can about the malady."

31 On the one hand, those who prefer to think of *Germinal* as primarily a positivistic historical or sociological study may construe its title as an allusion to the major popular disturbance which occurred during the month of Germinal of the third year of the Revolutionary Calendar—a disturbance comparable in some ways to the Montsou strike. Zola refers to it in his preparatory notes (B. N. MS. Nouv. acq. fr. 10308, fol. 416). On the other hand, those who prefer to think of the novel as a product of Zola's visionary side may cite his letter of October 6, 1889, to Van Santen Kolff: ". . . And one day, just by chance, the word *Germinal* sprang to my lips. I did not like it at first; it seemed too mystical, too symbolic; but it represented what I was looking for, a revolutionary April, a flight of our old, outworn society into spring. If it remains obscure for some readers, it has become for me a ray of sunlight illuminating the entire work" (XIV, 1473).

32 I am thinking of, in particular, the typically Zolian structural relationship between the factualistic, positivistic elements of the novel and its philosophical and religious symbolism. As I have noted in Chapter 1, Zola has tried even harder in *Germinal* than in many of his other novels to provide his fiction with a good, solid, factual, scientific basis. But it is also evident that he has gone on to transform through every poetic device at his command the resultant close imitation of the objective world of common, ordinary experience into a symbolic expression of his metaphysical and religious thought. He has managed to do this, moreover, without sacrificing his documentary, scientific realism. As Henri Mitterand has so precisely put it, "The figure, which is *semiosis*, finds its support in the referential notation, which is *mimesis*" ("Poétique et idéologie: La Dérivation figurale dans *Germinal*," in *Fiction, Form, Experience: The French Novel from Naturalism to the Present*, ed. Grant E. Kaiser [Montréal: Editions France-Québec, 1976], p. 48). Those who might wish to interpret this as a structural expression of Zola's positivism could point out that the elements of the supposedly real events that he narrates are thus mostly based on actual fact and scientific "truth," Zola's own subjective vision of reality being relegated to the merely figurative level, i.e., the level that emerges only in the narration of these events. Those who prefer to see here a reflection of Zola's scientism could cite what Zola, in a more metaphysical or religious mood, called apropos *Germinal* his personal "lie": "We all lie more or less, but what is the mechanism and mentality of our lie? Now—and I may be fooling myself perhaps—I still think that I lie for my part in the direction of truth. I have a hypertrophy for true detail, the leap to the stars from the springboard of exact observation. Truth mounts with a single stroke of its wings all the way up to symbol" (XIV, 1440). We recognize here a strong echo of the Zola who had cried out as a young man, "We are becoming scientists . . . all the social and religious

problems are going to be solved one of these days. We are going to see God, we are going to behold the truth" (X, 56), an anticipation of the Zola who, in his old age, dreamed, in *Paris*, of that day when "the religion of science" would replace Christianity (VII, 1561). Compare, for example, Renan's often-cited remark: "Henceforth, science . . . alone will produce our symbols; only science can solve for man those eternal problems for which his nature imperiously demands the solutions" (*Œuvres complètes*, III, 814). Compare also Taine's almost equally well known remark: "In this use of science and in this conception of things there is a new art, morality, politics, religion, and it is our business today to find them" (*Histoire de la littérature anglaise*, 18th ed. [Paris: Hachette, s.d.], IV, 390).

33 *Germinal* is obviously one of those novels in which Zola has most faithfully followed his advice to Alexis, that to make one's characters "live," one must make them "bleed" (*Corr.*, II, 482). A good example of Zola's illusionism can also be found in his treatment of Madame Maigrat during her husband's death scene, anticipating the principle discovered in the days of the silent film by Pudovkin and Kuleshov in an experiment using close-ups of the actor Mosjukhin: namely, that identical photographs of an actor's face (perhaps quite blank) will, when artfully inserted into different strips of film, appear to the spectator to assume different expressions, which are usually mistakenly attributed to the skill of the actor. In the sequence that I have just referred to, Zola merely repeatedly shows us Madame Maigrat's face, leaving it up to us to bring her alive, to animate her expression. Since Zola's conception of man is as chaotic as everything else in his philosophical and religious vision of reality, his characters, when we look at them very hard, tend to become evanescent and incomprehensible. He obviously had to find techniques for forcing us to ascribe to them a solidity, a reality, that they do not actually have. Among these techniques, we must also include his tendency to give them violently exaggerated physical traits, to describe them with brutal metaphors, and to portray them with lurid, clashing, thickly laid on colors that suggest comparisons to Van Gogh's *Night Café*, for example, or Munch's *The Scream*. Recall, for instance, how repeatedly Zola paints characters in *Germinal* in reds, which tend to change metaphorically into blood. All of this helps impress the characters upon our imagination and forces us to react to them and participate in their creation despite their essential nullity from a philosophical or religious point of view.

Selected Bibliography

I. Zola's Published Works

References to Zola's writings, except for his correspondence between 1858 and 1880, are wherever possible to the edition of the *Œuvres complètes,* in fifteen volumes, prepared under the direction of Henri Mitterand (Paris: Cercle du Livre Précieux, 1966-69). Volume and page references to this edition appear in parentheses in the text. In the case of Zola's correspondence between 1858 and 1880, reference has been made to the excellent but still, unfortunately, incomplete edition of Zola's *Correspondance,* in ten volumes, edited by B. H. Bakker (Montréal: Les Presses de l'Université de Montréal, 1978-   ). This edition is designated in the text by the abbreviation *Corr.* Reference has also been made to the edition of Zola's *Correspondance,* in two volumes, edited by Maurice Le Blond (Paris: François Bernouard, 1928-29); the Bibliothèque de la Pléiade edition of *Les Rougon-Macquart,* in five volumes, prepared under the direction of Armand Lanoux with studies, notes, variants, and appendixes by Henri Mitterand (Paris: Gallimard, 1960-67); and the Bibliothèque de la Pléiade edition of Zola's *Contes et nouvelles,* edited by Roger Ripoll (Paris: Gallimard, 1976). All quotations from *Germinal* are from Stanley and Eleanor Hochman's translation (abbreviated as Sig.), published in the Signet Classics Collection (New York: New American Library, 1970). Quotations from *L'Œuvre* are from Thomas Walton's translation published under the title *The Masterpiece* (Ann Arbor: University of Michigan Press, 1968). (Unless otherwise noted, all other translations from the French in the text are by the author of this volume.)

II. Zola's Manuscripts

With the exception of certain passages from those parts of the *dossier* of *Le Docteur Pascal* which are conserved at the Bodmer Library, Cologny, Switzerland, all quotations from Zola's unpublished writings are from manuscripts at the Bibliothèque Nationale, Paris (B. N. MS. Nouvelles acquisitions françaises 10268-345).

III. Works by Other Authors

This list includes the works cited in the text as well as a selection of other writings particularly relevant to the subject of this study.

Ackermann, Louise. *Œuvres—Ma Vie; Premières poésies; Poésies philosophiques.* Paris: Lemerre, 1885.

Alexis, Paul. *Emile Zola: Notes d'un ami.* Paris: Charpentier, 1882.

_____. *"Naturalisme pas mort": Lettres inédites de Paul Alexis à Emile Zola, 1871-1900.* Ed. B. H. Bakker. Toronto: University of Toronto Press, 1971.

Aubigné, Agrippa d'. *Les Tragiques.* Ed. A. Garnier and J. Plattard. Geneva: Droz, 1932.

Auerbach, Erich. *Mimesis: The Representation of Reality in Western Literature.* Tr. Willard R. Trask. Princeton: Princeton University Press, 1953.

Avebury, Sir John Lubbock. *Prehistoric Times, as Illustrated by Ancient Remains, and the Customs and Manners of Modern Savages.* London: Williams and Norgate, 1865.

Baguley, David. *Bibliographie de la critique sur Emile Zola, 1864-1970.* Toronto: University of Toronto Press, 1976.

_____. *Bibliographie de la critique sur Emile Zola, 1971-1980.* Toronto: University of Toronto Press, 1982.

_____. *"Fécondité" d'Emile Zola: Roman à thèse, évangile, mythe.* Toronto: University of Toronto Press, 1973.

_____. "The Function of Zola's Souvarine." *Modern Language Review,* 66 (1971), 786-97.

Baillie, John. *The Belief in Progress.* London: Oxford University Press, 1950.

Balzac, H. de. *Illusions perdues.* Ed. A. Adam. 2nd ed. Paris: Garnier, 1961.

Barbusse, Henri. *Zola.* Paris: Gallimard, 1932.

Bénichou, Paul. *Le Sacre de l'écrivain, 1750-1830: Essai sur l'avènement d'un pouvoir spirituel laïque dans la France moderne.* Paris: J. Corti, 1973.

_____. *Le Temps des prophètes: Doctrines de l'âge romantique.* Paris: Gallimard, 1977.

Bertrand-Jennings, Chantal. *L'Eros et la femme chez Zola: De la chute au paradis retrouvé.* Paris: Klincksieck, 1977.

_____. "Le Troisième Règne: Zola et la révolution copernicienne en littérature." *Revue d'Histoire Littéraire de la France,* 80e année, No. 3 (May-June 1980), pp. 396-410.

Boëns-Boissau, Dr. H. *Traité pratique des maladies des ouvriers employés dans les exploitations des mines.* Bruxelles: De Mortier fils, 1862.

Bois, Jules. *Les Petites Religions de Paris.* Paris: Chailley, 1894.

Borie, Jean. *Zola et les mythes, ou de la nausée au salut.* Paris: Editions du Seuil, 1971.

Boulier, Jean. *"Les Trois Villes, Lourdes, Rome, Paris." Europe,* 46ᵉ année, Nos. 468-69 (April-May 1968), pp. 135-46.

Bourget, Paul. *Essais de psychologie contemporaine.* 5th ed. Paris: Lemerre, 1889.

Brady, Patrick. "Phenomenon, Initiation, Epiphany: Gates of Ivory within Gates of Horn." *L'Esprit Créateur,* 18 (Summer 1978), 76-81.

_____. "Structuration archétypologique de *Germinal." Cahiers Internationaux de Symbolisme,* Nos. 24-25 (1973), pp. 87-97.

_____. "Vision, Revelation, Prophecy: Zola and the Conformation of Apocalypse." *South Atlantic Bulletin,* 40 (Jan. 1975), 55.

Buckland, William. *Vindiciae Geologicae: or The Connexion of Geology with Religion Explained.* Oxford: Oxford University Press, 1920.

Bury, J. B. *The Idea of Progress: An Inquiry into Its Origin and Growth.* London: Macmillan, 1920.

Case, Frederick Ivor. *La Cité idéale dans "Travail" d'Emile Zola.* Toronto: University of Toronto Press, 1974.

Céard, Henry. "París en América. Mr. Emilio Zola y *Germinal." Sud-América* [Buenos Aires], April 16-18, 1885. See Albert J. Salvan, ed.: "Un document retrouvé. 'M. Emile Zola et *Germinal'* de Henry Céard, retraduit de l'espagnol, présenté et annoté par Albert J. Salvan." *Cahiers Naturalistes,* No. 35 (1968), pp. 42-60.

Cellier, Léon. *L'Epopée humanitaire et les grands mythes romantiques.* 2nd ed. Paris: Société d'Edition d'Enseignement Supérieur, 1971.

Chambers, Robert. *Vestiges of the Natural History of Creation.* 11th ed. London: J. Churchill, 1860.

Chambron, Jacqueline. "Réalisme et épopée chez Zola." *La Pensée,* No. 44 (Sept.-Oct. 1952), pp. 122-33.

Charlton, D. G., ed. *France: A Companion to French Studies.* London: Methuen, 1972.

_____. "Positivism and Its Aftermath." In *The Late Nineteenth Century.* Vol. V of *French Literature and Its Background.* Ed. John Cruickshank. London: Oxford University Press, 1969, pp. 1-16.

_____. *Positivist Thought in France During the Second Empire, 1852-1870.* Oxford: Oxford University Press, 1959.

_____. *Secular Religions in France: 1815-1870.* London: Oxford University Press, 1963.

Cogny, Pierre. "Emile Zola devant le problème de Jésus-Christ, d'après des documents inédits." *Studi Francesi,* No. 23 (1964), pp. 255-64.

Cogny, Pierre, introd. *Fécondité.* By Emile Zola. In *Œuvres complètes.* Ed. Henri Mitterand. 15 vols. Paris: Cercle du Livre Précieux, 1966-69, VIII, 12-23.

_____. *Zola et son temps.* Paris: Larousse, 1976.

_____. "Zola évangéliste." *Europe,* 46ᵉ année, Nos. 468-69 (April-May 1968), pp. 147-51.

Cressot, Marcel. "Zola et Michelet. Essai sur la genèse de deux romans de jeunesse: *La Confession de Claude, Madeleine Férat.*" *Revue d'Histoire Littéraire de la France,* 35 (July-Sept. 1928), 382-89.

Cuvier, Georges. *Essay on the Theory of the Earth.* Tr. Robert Jameson. 3rd ed. Edinburgh: William Blackwood, 1817.

_____. *Discours sur les révolutions de la surface du globe.* 6th French ed. Paris: E. d'Ocagne, 1830.

Dansette, Adrien. *Histoire religieuse de la France contemporaine.* 2 vols. Paris: Flammarion, 1948-51.

Dante Alighieri. *The Divine Comedy. I. Hell.* Tr. Louis Biancolli. New York: Washington Square Press, 1966.

Darwin, Charles. *On the Origin of the Species by Means of Natural Selection, or the Preservation of Favoured Races in the Struggle for Life.* London: J. Murray, 1859.

Dormoy, Emile. *Topographie souterraine du Bassin houiller de Valenciennes.* Paris: Imprimerie Nationale, 1867.

Doucet, Fernand. *L'Esthétique de Zola et son application à la critique.* The Hague: De Nederlandsche Boek- en Steendruckerij, 1923.

Dubois, Jean. *Le Vocabulaire politique et social en France de 1869 à 1872 à travers les œuvres des écrivains, les revues et les journaux.* Paris: Larousse, 1962.

Dumesnil, René. *Le Réalisme et le naturalisme.* Paris: del Duca de Gigord, 1955.

Durand, G. *Les Structures anthropologiques de l'imaginaire: Introduction à l'archétypologie générale.* Paris: Bordas, 1970.

Duruy, Victor. *Introduction générale à l'histoire de France.* Paris: Hachette, 1865.

Eliade, Mircea. *Cosmos and History: The Myth of Eternal Return.* Tr. Willard R. Trask. New York: Harper and Row, 1959.

_____. *Le Mythe de l'éternel retour: Archétypes et répétitions.* Paris: Gallimard, 1949.

_____. *Mythes, rêves et mystères.* Paris: Gallimard, 1961.

_____. *Myths, Dreams, and Mysteries: The Encounter between Contemporary Faiths and Archaic Realities.* Tr. Philip Mairet. New York: Harper and Row, 1967.

Empson, William. *Seven Types of Ambiguity*. 3rd ed. London: Chatto and Windus, 1963.

Fath, Robert. *L'Influence de la science sur la littérature française dans la seconde moitié du XIXᵉ siècle*. Lausanne: Payot, 1901.

Faure, Elie. "Emile Zola." In *Œuvres complètes*. 3 vols. Paris: Jean-Jacques Pauvert, 1964, III, 897, 898.

Flaubert, Gustave. *Correspondance*. 4 vols. Paris: Louis Conard, 1910.

_____. *L'Education sentimentale, histoire d'un jeune homme*. Paris: Michel Lévy, 1869.

Flint, Robert. *History of the Philosophy of History*. Edinburgh: William Blackwood and Sons, 1893.

France, Anatole. *Vers les temps meilleurs: Trente ans de vie sociale, I, Introduction générale*. Ed. Claude Aveline. Paris: Emile-Paul Frères, c. 1949.

Frandon, Ida-Marie. *Autour de "Germinal": La Mine et les mineurs*. Geneva: Droz, 1955.

Franzén, Nils-Olof. *Zola et "La Joie de vivre": La Genèse du roman, les personnages, les idées*. Stockholm: Almqvist & Wicksell, 1958.

Frédol, Alfred. *Le Monde de la mer*. Paris: Hachette, 1865.

Fuster, Charles. *Essais de critique*. 2nd ed. Paris: E. Giraud, 1886.

Gillispie, Charles C. *Genesis and Geology: A Study in the Relations of Scientific Thought, Natural Theology, and Social Opinion in Great Britain, 1790-1850*. Cambridge, Mass.: Harvard University Press, 1951.

Girard, Marcel. "L'Univers de *Germinal*." *Revue des Sciences Humaines*. Fasc. 69 (1953), pp. 59-76.

_____. "Zola visionnaire." *Montjoie*, 1 (1953), 6-9.

Goncourt, Edmond and Jules de. *Journal: Mémoires de la vie littéraire*. 9 vols. Paris: Flammarion-Fasquelle, 1935-36.

Grant, Elliott M. *Zola's "Germinal": A Critical and Historical Study*. Leicester: Leicester University Press, 1962.

Grant, Richard. *Zola's "Son Excellence Eugène Rougon": An Historical and Critical Study*. Durham, N. C.: Duke University Press, 1960.

Greaves, A. A. "Mysticisme et pessimisme dans *La Faute de l'abbé Mouret*." *Cahiers Naturalistes*, No. 36 (1968), pp. 148-55.

_____. "Religion et réalité dans l'œuvre de Zola." *Europe*, 46ᵉ année, Nos. 468-69 (April-May 1968), pp. 122-29.

Guérard, Albert-Léon. *French Prophets of Yesterday: A Study of Religious Thought under the Second Empire.* New York: D. Appleton, 1920.

Guillemin, Henri. "Zola et le sens de son œuvre." *Europe,* 46ᵉ année, Nos. 468-69 (April-May 1968), pp. 169-78.

_____. *Zola: Légende et vérité.* Paris: Julliard, 1960.

Gunn, Giles B., comp. *Literature and Religion.* 1st U. S. ed. New York: Harper and Row, 1971.

Gunn, J. Alexander. *Modern French Philosophy: A Study of the Development since Comte.* New York: Dodd, Mead, 1922.

Harvey, Lawrence E. "The Cycle Myth in *La Terre* of Zola." *Philological Quarterly,* 38 (Jan. 1959), 85-95.

Hemmings, F. W. J. *Emile Zola.* 2nd ed. London: Oxford University Press, 1966.

_____. "Emile Zola et la religion." *Europe,* 46ᵉ année, Nos. 468-69 (April-May 1968), pp. 129-35.

_____. *The Life and Times of Emile Zola.* New York: Charles Scribners, 1977.

Hewitt, Winston R. *Through Those Living Pillars: Man and Nature in the Works of Emile Zola.* The Hague: Mouton, 1974.

Hoffman, Frederick J. *The Imagination's New Beginning: Theology and Modern Literature.* Notre Dame, Ind.: University of Notre Dame Press, 1967.

Homer. *The Iliad.* Tr. Richmond Lattimore. Chicago: University of Chicago Press, 1951.

_____. *The Odyssey.* Tr. Albert Cook. New York: Norton, 1967.

Hooykaas, Reijer. "Catastrophism in Geology: Its Scientific Character in Relation to Actualism and Uniformitarianism." In *Philosophy of Geohistory: 1785-1970.* Ed. Claude C. Albritton, Jr. Vol. XIII of *Benchmark Papers in Geology.* Stroudsburg, Penn.: Dowden, Hutchinson and Ross, 1975, pp. 310-56.

Howe, Irving. Afterword. *Germinal.* By Emile Zola. Tr. Stanley and Eleanor Hochman. A Signet Classic. New York: New American Library, 1970, pp. 429-46.

Hudson, Benjamin Franklin. "Zola and Schopenhauer: The Affinity of Some Aspects of Their Thought as Reflected in the *Rougon-Macquart* Series." Ph.D. diss. University of Michigan 1959. (*DA,* 19 [1959], 3305.)

Hunt, Herbert J. *The Epic in Nineteenth-Century France: A Study in Heroic and Humanitarian Poetry from "Les Martyres" to "Les Siècles morts."* Oxford: Basil Blackwell, 1941.

Janet, Paul. "Le Spiritualisme français au dix-neuvième siècle." *Revue des Deux Mondes,* May 15, 1868, pp. 353-85.

James, E. O. *Creation and Cosmology: A Historical and Comparative Inquiry.* Leiden: E. J. Brill, 1969.

Jung, Carl. "God, the Devil, and the Human Soul." *Atlantic Monthly,* 200 (Nov. 1957), 57-63.

Kafka, Franz. *Metamorphosis.* Tr. A. L. Lloyd. New York: The Vanguard Press, 1946.

Kamm, Lewis. *The Object in Zola's "Rougon-Macquart."* Madrid: José Porrúa Turanzas, 1978.

_____. "People and Things in Zola's *Rougon-Macquart*: Reification Re-humanized." *Philological Quarterly,* 53 (1974), 100-09.

_____. "Zola's Conception of Time in *Les Rougon-Macquart.*" *French Review,* Special Issue 6 (Spring 1974), pp. 63-72.

Kanes, Martin. "*Germinal*: Drama and Dramatic Structure." *Modern Philology,* 61 (Aug. 1963), 12-25.

_____. *Zola's "La Bête humaine": A Study in Literary Creation.* Berkeley: University of California Press, 1962.

Laforgue, Jules. *Complaintes.* Paris: Léon Vanier, 1885.

Lamennais, F. *Esquisse d'une philosophie.* 4 vols. Paris: Pagnerre, 1840-46.

Lanoux, Armand. *Bonjour Monsieur Zola.* Paris: Hachette, 1962.

Lapp, John C. *Zola before the "Rougon-Macquart."* Toronto: University of Toronto Press, 1964.

Lattre, Alain de. *Le Réalisme selon Zola: Archéologie d'une intelligence.* Paris: Presses Universitaires de France, 1975.

Leveleye, E. de. *Le Socialisme contemporain.* 2nd ed. Paris: Germer-Baillière, 1883.

Le Blond, Maurice. *Emile Zola: Son évolution, son influence.* Paris: Editions du Mouvement Socialiste, 1903.

_____. "L'Evangile de Zola." *L'Aurore,* June 4, 1908.

Le Blond-Zola, Denise. *Emile Zola raconté par sa fille.* Paris: Fasquelle, 1931.

Lemaitre, Jules. "Emile Zola." *Les Contemporains.* Ière série. Paris: Boivin, 1903, pp. 249-84.

Lepelletier, Edmond. *Emile Zola: Sa vie, son œuvre.* Paris: Mercure de France, 1908.

Letourneau, Charles. *Physiologie des passions.* Paris: Germer-Baillière, 1868.

Levin, Harry. *The Gates of Horn: A Study of Five French Realists.* New York: Oxford University Press, 1963.

Lifton, Robert J. "The Struggle for Cultural Rebirth." *Harper's Magazine,* April 1973, pp. 84-90.

Lovejoy, Arthur O. *The Great Chain of Being: A Study in the History of an Idea.* Cambridge, Mass.: Harvard University Press, 1936.

Loyson, Paul-Hyacinthe. *Les Droits de l'homme,* Nov. 13, 1910.

Lucas, Prosper. *Traité philosophique et physiologique de l'hérédité naturelle dans les états de santé et de maladie du système nerveux.* 2 vols. Paris: Baillière, 1847-50.

Mann, Thomas. "Zola et l'âge d'or." French Tr. Louise Servicien. In *Présence de Zola* (essays by various hands). Paris: Fasquelle, 1953, pp. 11-12.

Marel, Henri, étude, notes et documents. *Germinal.* By Emile Zola. Ed. Henri Marel. Bordas: Paris, 1973.

Martino, Pierre. *Le Naturalisme français, 1870-1895.* Paris: Armand Colin, 1945.

Matthews, J. H. "The Art of Description in Zola's *Germinal.*" *Symposium,* 16 (1962), 267-74.

_____. *Les Deux Zola.* Geneva: Droz, 1957.

_____. "*Things* in the Naturalist Novel." *French Studies,* 14 (July 1960), 212, 213.

_____. "Zola and the Marxists." *Symposium,* 11 (1957), 262-72.

_____. "Zola's *Le Rêve* as an Experimental Novel." *Modern Language Review,* 52 (April 1957), 187-94.

Maurin, Mario. "Zola's Labyrinths." *Yale French Studies,* 42 (1969), 89-104.

Max, Stefan. *Les Métamorphoses de la grande ville dans "Les Rougon-Macquart."* Paris: Nizet, 1966.

Michelet, Jules. *L'Amour.* Paris: Hachette, 1858.

_____. *La Femme.* 4th ed. Paris: Hachette, 1863.

_____. *La Nature: L'Oiseau, L'Insecte, La Mer, La Montagne.* Paris: Larousse, 1930.

Mitterand, Henri. *Le Discours du roman.* Paris: Presses Universitaires de France, 1980.

Mitterand, Henri, études, notes et variantes. *Les Rougon-Macquart.* By Emile Zola. Ed. Henri Mitterand and Armand Lanoux. Bibliothèque de la Pléiade. 5 vols. Paris: Gallimard, 1960-67.

_____. "Les 'Manuscrits perdus' d'Emile Zola." *Cahiers Naturalistes,* No. 39 (1970), pp. 83-90.

_____. "Poétique et idéologie: La Dérivation figurale dans *Germinal.*" In *Fiction, Form, Experience: The French Novel from Naturalism to the Present.* Ed. Grant E. Kaiser. Montréal: Editions France-Québec, 1976, pp. 44-52.

_____. "Quelques aspects de la création littéraire dans l'œuvre d'Emile Zola." *Cahiers Naturalistes,* Nos. 24-25 (1963), pp. 9-20.

_____. *Zola journaliste: De l'affaire Manet à l'affaire Dreyfus.* Paris: Armand Colin, 1962.

Monod, G. *Les Maîtres de l'histoire—Renan, Taine, Michelet.* Paris: Calmann-Lévy, 1894.

Musset, Alfred de. *Poésies complètes.* Ed. Maurice Allem. Bibliothèque de la Pléiade. Paris: Gallimard, 1957.

Niess, Robert J. "Autobiographical elements in Zola's *La Joie de vivre.*" *PMLA,* 56 (Dec. 1941), 1133-49.

_____. *Zola, Cézanne, and Manet: A Study of "L'Œuvre."* Ann Arbor: The University of Michigan Press, 1968.

_____. "Zola et le capitalisme: Le Darwinisme social," *Cahiers Naturalistes,* No. 54 (1980), pp. 57-67.

_____. "Zola's *Paris* and the Novels of the *Rougon-Macquart* Series." *Nineteenth-Century French Studies,* 4 (Fall-Winter 1975-76), 89-104.

Nietzsche, Friedrich W. *The Portable Nietzsche.* Tr. and ed. Walter Kaufmann. New York: The Viking Press, 1954.

_____. *Werke.* 15 vols. Leipzig: C. G. Naumann, 1903-19.

_____. *The Will to Power.* Tr. Anthony M. Ludovici. 2 vols. Edinburgh: T. N. Foulis, 1910.

Nourrisson, E. *Spinoza et le matérialisme contemporain.* Paris: Didier, 1866.

Paraf, Pierre. "Zola et le mystère." *Europe,* 46ᵉ année, Nos. 468-69 (April-May 1968), pp. 151-56.

Pascal, Roy. "Emile Zola: Use and Abuse." *The Dual Voice: Free Indirect Speech and Its Functioning in the Nineteenth-Century Novel.* Manchester: Manchester University Press, 1977, pp. 112-22.

Pasco, Allan. "Love *à la* Michelet in Zola's *La Faute de l'abbé Mouret.*" *Nineteenth-Century French Studies,* 7 (Spring-Summer 1979), 232-44.

_____. "Myth, Metaphor, and Meaning in *Germinal.*" *French Review,* 46 (March 1973), 739-49.

Pelletan, Eugène. *Profession de foi du dix-neuvième siècle.* Paris: Pagnerre, 1852.

Petrey, Sandy. "Goujet as God and Worker in *L'Assommoir.*" *French Forum,* 1, No. 3 (Sept. 1976), 239-50.

_____. "The Revolutionary Setting of *Germinal.*" *French Review,* 43 (Oct. 1969), 54-63.

Poitou, E. *Les Philosophes français contemporains et leurs systèmes religieux.* 2nd ed. Paris: Charpentier, 1864.

Présence de Zola. Paris: Fasquelle, 1953. (Essays by various hands.)

Putter, Irving. *The Pessimism of Leconte de Lisle: The Work and the Time.* Berkeley: University of California Press, 1961.

Ravaisson, F. *Rapport sur la philosophie en France au dix-neuvième siècle.* 5th ed. Paris: Hachette, 1904.

Renan, Ernest. *Drames philosophiques.* Paris: Calmann-Lévy, 1947-61.

_____. *Œuvres complètes.* 10 vols. Paris: Calmann-Lévy, 1947-61.

_____. *Le Prêtre de Némi.* 9th ed. Paris: Calmann-Lévy, 1886.

Renouvier, Charles. "De la philosophie du dix-neuvième siècle en France." *L'Année Philosophique—Première Année (1867),* 1868, pp. 1-108.

Ripoll, Roger, introd. *Nouveaux contes à Ninon.* By Emile Zola. *Œuvres complètes.* Ed. Henri Mitterand. 15 vols. Paris: Cercle du Livre Précieux, 1966-69, IX, 341-45.

_____, notices, notes et variantes. *Contes et nouvelles.* By Emile Zola. Bibliothèque de la Pléiade. Paris: Gallimard, 1976.

_____. *Réalité et mythe chez Zola.* Thèse présentée devant l'Université de Paris IV le 18 juin 1977. 2 vols. Paris: Librairie Honoré Champion, 1981.

_____. "Zola et le modèle positivist." *Romantisme,* Nos. 21-22 (1978), pp. 125-35.

Robert, Guy. *Emile Zola: Principes et caractères généraux de son œuvre.* Paris: Les Belles Lettres, 1952.

_____. *"La Terre" d'Emile Zola: Etude historique et critique.* Paris: Les Belles Lettres, 1952.

_____. "Trois textes inédits d'Emile Zola." *Revue des Sciences Humaines,* fasc. 51 (1948), pp. 181-207.

Rod, Edouard. *Les Idées morales du temps présent.* Paris: Perrin, 1891.

Rosenberg, Rachelle A. "The Slaying of the Dragon: An Archetypal Study of Zola's *Germinal.*" *Symposium,* 26 (1972), 349-62.

_____. "Zola's Imagery and the Archetype of the Great Mother." Ph.D. diss. University of Michigan 1969. (*DA,* 30 [1970], 3956-A.)

Rosenthal, Erwin. *The Changing Concept of Reality in Art.* New York: G. Willenborn, 1962.

Rostand, Jean. "L'Œuvre de Zola et la pensée scientifique." *Europe,* 46e année, Nos. 468-69 (April-May 1968), pp. 360-69.

Saint-Georges de Bouhélier. *L'Hiver en méditation, ou les Passe-temps de Clarisse.* Paris: Mercure de France, 1896.

Sainte-Beuve, Charles-Augustin. *Correspondance générale.* Ed. Jean Bonnerot. 12 vols. Paris: Stock, 1935-62.

Salvan, Albert J. "Un document retrouvé: 'M. Emile Zola et *Germinal,*' de Henry Céard." *Cahiers Naturalistes,* No. 35 (1968), pp. 42-60.

Sanders, James B. "Emile Zola: Le Transplanté et l'arbre." In *Fiction, Form, Experience: The French Novel from Naturalism to the Present.* Ed. Grant E. Kaiser. Montréal: Editions France-Québec, 1976, pp. 53-66.

Schober, Rita. "*Réalité* und *vérité* bei Balzac und Zola." *Beiträge zur Romanischen Philologie,* 1 (1961), 116-42, and 2 (1963), 127-38.

Schor, Naomi. "Le Cycle et le cercle: Temps, espace et révolution dans quatre romans de Zola." *DAI,* 31 (1970), 1292A (Yale).

_____. "Mythe des origines, origine des mythes: *La Fortune des Rougon.*" *Cahiers Naturalistes,* No. 52 (1978), pp. 124-34.

_____. "Zola: From Window to Window." *Yale French Studies,* No. 42 (1969), pp. 38-51.

_____. *Zola's Crowds.* Baltimore: Johns Hopkins University Press, 1978.

Scott, Nathan A. *The Broken Center: Studies in the Theological Horizon of Modern Literature.* New Haven: Yale University Press, 1966.

_____. *Modern Literature and the Religious Frontier.* New York: Harper, 1958.

_____. *The Wild Prayer of Longing: Poetry and the Sacred.* New Haven: Yale University Press, 1971.

Seillière, Ernest. *Emile Zola.* Paris: Grasset, 1923.

Seltzer, Alvin J. *Chaos in the Novel / The Novel in Chaos.* New York: Schocken Books, 1974.

Serres, Michel. *Feux et signaux de brume: Zola.* Paris: Bernard Grasset, 1975.

Simon, Pierre-Henri. "L'Idéalisme de Zola." *Le Domaine héroïque des lettres françaises, Xe-XIXe siècles.* Paris: Armand Colin, 1963, pp. 384-86.

———, introd. *Germinal.* By Emile Zola. *Œuvres complètes.* Ed. Henri Mitterand. 15 vols. Paris: Cercle du Livre Précieux, 1966-69, V, 13-20.

Simon, Walter. *European Positivism in the Nineteenth Century: An Essay in Intellectual History.* Ithaca, N. Y.: Cornell University Press, 1963.

Simonin, Louis-Laurent. *La Vie souterraine, ou les mines et les mineurs.* Paris: Hachette, 1867.

Snelders, H. A. M. "Romanticism and *Naturphilosophie* and the Inorganic Natural Sciences, 1797-1840." *Studies in Romanticism,* 9 (Summer 1970), 193-215.

Söderblom, Nathan. "Holiness." *Encyclopaedia of Religion and Ethics.* Ed. James Hastings. New York: Charles Scribner's Sons, 1928, VI, 731-41.

Sorokin, Pitirim Aleksandrovich. *The Crisis of Our Age: The Social and Cultural Outlook.* New York: E. P. Dutton, 1942.

Spitzer, Leo. *Classical and Christian Ideas of World Harmony: Prolegomena to an Interpretation of the Word "Stimmung."* Baltimore: The Johns Hopkins Press, 1963.

Stafford, Barbara Maria. "Rude Sublime: The Taste for Nature: Colossi During the Late Eighteenth and Early Nineteenth Centuries." *Gazette des Beaux Arts,* 6th Ser., 87 (April 1976), 113-26.

Taine, Hippolyte. *Essais de critique et d'histoire.* 14th ed. Paris: Hachette, 1923.

———. *Histoire de la littérature anglaise.* 18th ed. 5 vols. Paris: Hachette, s.d.

———. *Nouveaux essais de critique et d'histoire.* 12th ed. Paris: Hachette, 1865.

Ternois, René. "Le Stoïcisme d'Emile Zola." *Cahiers Naturalistes,* No. 23 (1963), pp. 289-98.

———. *Zola et son temps: "Lourdes"–"Rome"–"Paris."* Paris: Les Belles Lettres, 1961.

Tersen, Emile. "Sources et sens de *Germinal.*" *La Pensée,* No. 95 (Jan.-Feb. 1961), pp. 74-89.

Thérive, André. "Un vrai clerc, Emile Zola." *La Table Ronde,* No. 208 (May 1965), pp. 106-09.

Tison-Braun, Micheline. *La Crise de l'humanisme.* Paris: Nizet, 1958.

Toulmin, Stephen, and June Goodfield. *The Discovery of Time.* Chicago: The University of Chicago Press, 1965.

Toulouse, Edmond. *Enquête médico-psychologique sur les rapports de la supériorité intellectuelle avec la névropathie: Emile Zola.* Paris: Flammarion, 1896.

Tuveson, Ernest Lee. *Millenium and Utopia: A Study in the Background of the Idea of Progress.* Berkeley: University of California Press, 1949.

Van Tieghem, Philippe. *Introduction à l'étude d'Emile Zola: "Germinal" (Documents inédits de la Bibliothèque Nationale).* Paris: Centre de Documentation Universitaire, 1954.

Vinson, Elie-Honoré-Julien. *Les Religions actuelles: Leurs doctrines, leur évolution, leur histoire.* Paris: Delahaye et Lecrosnier, 1888.

Vogüé, Eugène-Melchior de. "Après M. Renan." *Revue des Deux Mondes,* Nov. 15, 1892, pp. 445-62.

Walker, Philip. "*L'Assommoir* et la pensée religieuse de Zola." *Cahiers Naturalistes,* No. 52 (1978), pp. 68-79.

_____. "The *Ebauche* of *Germinal.*" *PMLA,* 80 (Dec. 1965), 571-83.

_____. *Emile Zola.* London: Routledge & Kegan Paul, 1968.

_____. "The Mirror, the Window, and the Eye in Zola's Fiction." *Yale French Studies,* No. 42 (1969), pp. 52-67.

_____. "Prophetic Myths in Zola." *PMLA,* 74 (Sept. 1959), 444-52.

_____. "Remarques sur l'image du serpent dans *Germinal.*" *Cahiers Naturalistes,* No. 31 (1966), pp. 83-85.

_____. "The Survival of Romantic Pantheism in Zola's Religious Thought." *Symposium,* 23 (Fall-Winter 1969), 354-65.

_____. "Zola et la lutte avec l'Ange." *Cahiers Naturalistes,* No. 42 (1971), pp. 70-92.

_____. "Zola: Poet of an Age of Transition." *L'Esprit Créateur,* 11 (Winter 1971), 3-10.

_____. "Zola's Art of Characterization in *Germinal*: A Note for Further Research." *L'Esprit Créateur,* 4 (Summer 1964), 60-67.

_____. "Zola's Hellenism." In *The Persistent Voice: Essays on Hellenism in French Literature since the Eighteenth Century in Honor of Professor Henri M. Peyre.* Ed. Walter G. Langlois. New York: New York University Press, 1971.

Wellek, René. *The Late Nineteenth Century.* Vol. IV of *A History of Modern Criticism, 1750-1950.* New Haven: Yale University Press, 1961.

Woolen, Geoff. "Le Darwinisme de Zola: Réflexe ou réflexion?" *Cahiers de L'U. E. R. Froissart: Recherches en Lettres et Sciences Humaines,* No. 5 (Fall 1980), pp. 27-36.

Wurmser, André, preface. *Germinal.* By Emile Zola. Ed. Henri Mitterand. Paris: Gallimard, 1978, pp. 9-46.

Zakarian, Richard H. *Zola's "Germinal": A Critical Study of Its Primary Sources.* Geneva: Droz, 1972.

Index

Absolutes, Zola's rejection of, 77
Ackermann, Louise, 52, 116 n. 8
Adam, 25, 74
Aesthetics, Zola's: and his cult of life, 34
Agape. See Charity
Agassiz, Louis, 117 n. 12
Alexis, Paul, 97 n. 2, 115 n. 4, 120 n. 12, 131 n. 33
Ambiguity: of *Germinal,* 21, 68, 90, 94-95, 95-96, 113 n. 67, 114 n. 73, 114-15 n. 75, 127-28 n. 11, 130 n. 31, 130-31 n. 32; how achieved in Zola's fiction, 129-30 n. 29; in the thought of Zola's time, 90-94; in Zola's philosophical and religious thought, 67-68, 94, 104 n. 17
Anarchism, 114 n. 73, 127 n. 6
Animals: objects of a special kind of love, 35; rough outlines of higher forms, 29, 51; share the same life with man, 29, 39; and Zola's geological vision of reality, 49, 50, 51, 59; and Zola's monism and unanimism, 29, 33, 39-40, 44-45
Animation of so-called inanimate objects, 30-31
Anthropocentrism, 64; rejection of, 49, 50, 52, 54, 59, 63, 94, 125-26 n. 3
Apocalypticism, 57, 64-68, 74-75, 76, 79, 119 n. 6, 120 nn. 9-11, 127 n. 7. *See also* Catastrophism
Appetite, 5, 6, 40, 103 n. 9
Archetypes, 75, 76, 77, 78, 123 n. 12
Arène, Paul, 65
Art: equals life, 34; manifestation of human genius, 122 n. 10
Atoms, lovemaking of, 35
Aubigné, Agrippa, 69

Auerbach, Erich, 45, 46
Avebury, John Lubbock, 54

Baguley, David, 19, 20, 108 n. 18, 128 n. 11
Baille, Baptistin, 32
Bakunin, Mikhail Aleksandrovich, 4, 114 n. 73
Balzac, Honoré de, 3, 98 n. 3
Barbusse, Henri, 127 n. 11
Bataille's death, 13
Beauty, 4, 77, 81, 119 n. 2; is life or the force of life, 34, 122 n. 10
Beginning of *Germinal,* 13, 84
Bénichou, Paul, 118 n. 1
Bernard, Claude, 28, 88, 97 n. 1, 99 n. 12, 124 n. 1, 125 n. 2
Berthelot, Marcelin, 69
Bertrand-Jennings, Chantal, 114 n. 72
Bible, the, 10, 25, 49, 53, 61, 65, 117 n. 11
Body, the, 28, 113-14 n. 69, 125 n. 3
Boëns-Boissau, Dr. Hubert, 4
Boileau-Despréaux, Nicolas, 46
Bourget, Paul, 93
Brady, Patrick, 122 n. 22, 128 n. 11
Brain, the, 5, 100 n. 21, 100-01 n. 26
Bruegel, 14
Buber, Martin, 25
Buckland, William, 63, 116 n. 6

Catastrophism, 127 n. 6, 128 n. 11; religious, 119 n. 6; scientific, 49, 52, 53-57 passim, 60-65 passim, 79, 109 n. 30, 114 n. 73, 115-17 passim; *See also* Apocalypticism

In the PURDUE UNIVERSITY MONOGRAPHS IN ROMANCE LANGUAGES
series the following monographs have been published thus far:

1. John R. Beverley: *Aspects of Góngora's "Soledades."*
   Amsterdam, 1980. xiv, 139 pp. Bound.

2. Robert Francis Cook: *"Chanson d'Antioche," chanson de geste: Le Cycle de la Croisade est-il épique?*
   Amsterdam, 1980. viii, 107 pp. Bound.

3. Sandy Petrey: *History in the Text: "Quatrevingt-Treize" and the French Revolution.*
   Amsterdam, 1980. viii, 129 pp. Bound.

4. Walter Kasell: *Marcel Proust and the Strategy of Reading.*
   Amsterdam, 1980. x, 125 pp. Bound.

5. Inés Azar: *Discurso retórico y mundo pastoral en la "Egloga segunda" de Garcilaso.*
   Amsterdam, 1981. x, 171 pp. Bound.

6. Roy Armes: *The Films of Alain Robbe-Grillet.*
   Amsterdam, 1981. x, 216 pp. Bound.

7. *Le "Galien" de Cheltenham,* edited by David M. Dougherty and Eugene B. Barnes.
   Amsterdam, 1981. xxxvi, 203 pp. Bound.

8. Ana Hernández del Castillo: *Keats, Poe, and the Shaping of Cortázar's Mythopoesis.*
   Amsterdam, 1981. xii, 135 pp. Bound.

9. Carlos Albarracín-Sarmiento: *Estructura del "Martín Fierro."*
   Amsterdam, 1981. xx, 336 pp. Bound.

10. C. George Peale et al. (eds.): *Antigüedad y actualidad de Luis Vélez de Guevara: Estudios críticos.*
    Amsterdam, 1983. xii, 298 pp. Bound.

11. David Jonathan Hildner: *Reason and the Passions in the "Comedias" of Calderón.*
    Amsterdam, 1982. xii, 119 pp. Bound.

12. Floyd Merrell: *Pararealities: The Nature of Our Fictions and How We Know Them.*
    Amsterdam, 1983. xii, 170 pp. Bound.

13. Richard E. Goodkin: *The Symbolist Home and the Tragic Home: Mallarmé and Oedipus.*
    Amsterdam, 1983. xvi, 203 pp. Bound.

14. Philip Walker: *"Germinal" and Zola's Philosophical and Religious Thought.*
    Amsterdam, 1983. ca. 185 pp. Bound.

15. Claire-Lise Tondeur: *Gustave Flaubert, critique: Thèmes et structures.*
    Amsterdam, 1983. ca. 130 pp. Bound.